STUDIES
IN
ECCLESIASTES

John G. Reisinger

Books By
John G. Reisinger

Abraham's Four Seeds
The Believer's Sabbath
But I Say Unto You
Chosen in Eternity
Christ, Lord and Lawgiver Over the Church
Grace
In Defense of Jesus, the New Lawgiver
John Bunyan on the Sabbath
Limited Atonement
The New Birth
Our Sovereign God
Perseverance of the Saints
Tablets of Stone
The Sovereignty of God and Prayer
The Sovereignty of God in Providence
Total Depravity
What is the Christian Faith?
When Should a Christian Leave a Church?

STUDIES
IN
ECCLESIASTES

John G. Reisinger

5317 Wye Creek Dr, Frederick, MD 21703-6938
Website: newcovenantmedia.com
Email: info@newcovenantmedia.com
Phone: 301-473-8781 or 800-376-4146
Fax: 240-206-0373

Studies in Ecclesiastes

Published by: New Covenant Media
5317 Wye Creek Drive
Frederick, Maryland 21703-6938

Orders: www.newcovenantmedia.com

Printed in the United States of America

ISBN 13: 978-1-928965-28-2

Dedication

To Carrie Bates

Carrie does most of the editing of the material that *Sound of Grace* publishes. She is careful, thorough and capable. She corrects the grammar, Scripture references, and quotations and maintains general consistency. Carrie also raises 'red flags' at arguments that may be less than convincing. My books and articles are much more accurate and easier to read because of her efforts. Carrie's contributions to chapter two in this book are invaluable.

John G. Reisinger

October, 2008

Table of Contents

Table of Contents 1

Foreword 3

Preface 9

Chapter One: Verses: 1:1–7
The Treadmill Existence 13

Chapter Two
Some Definitions 41

Chapter Three: Verses 1:8–18
Secular Conceit's Balloon Punctured 63

Chapter Four: Verses 1:13–2:11
The Sure Fruits of Idolatry 85

Chapter Five: Verses 2:12–18
Looking in the Wrong Places 105

Chapter Six: Verses 3:1–8
Timing Is Everything 119

Chapter Seven: Verses: 3:9–15 #1
Relax, It's All Under Control 137

Chapter Eight: Verses 3:9–15 #2
My Times Are in Thy Hands 153

Chapter Nine: Verses 3:16 – 4:6
Wickedness in High Places 167

Chapter Ten: Verses 4:7 – 5:1
Some Advantages of Companionship 185

Chapter Eleven: Verses: 5:1–6
   Be Careful What You Vow 201

Chapter Twelve: Verses 5:7–20
   Wealth Can Be a Curse 213

Chapter Thirteen: Verses 6:1–12
   Some Great Saints Died In Poverty... 227

Chapter Fourteen: Verses 7:1–29
   Adversity Can Be Profitable 239

Chapter Fifteen: Verses 8:1–8
   Godly Wisdom Is Profitable 257

Chapter Sixteen: Verses 8:9–9:10
   Are Men No Better Than Animals? 273

Chapter Seventeen: Verses 9:12–10:20
   Living Life Skillfully 287

Chapter Eighteen: Verses 11:1-10
   Be Bold! Be Joyful! Be Godly! 303

Chapter Nineteen: Verses 12:1–10
   When the Pieces Wear Out 319

Chapter Twenty: Verses 12:10–14
   The Conclusion to the Matter 333

FOREWORD

It is now over 20 years ago since I first had the privilege of hearing the book of Ecclesiastes expounded by my pastor and friend, John Reisinger. At that time I was a student pursuing an undergraduate degree in science in upper state New York, and for three years I had the pleasure of sitting under the ministry of John as he faithfully preached and taught the whole counsel of God. I can still recall many of his expositions of Scripture, but it was probably his preaching through the often-neglected book of Ecclesiastes which I remember the best. What struck me then and what continues to strike me to this very day is how relevant God's Word is to our contemporary situation. This should not surprise us given the fact that "all Scripture is God-breathed" (2 Tim 3:16) and that there is, in the famous words of Ecclesiastes, "nothing new under the sun" (1:9), but it often does. Too much, I am afraid, we have imbibed the foolish attitude of our generation—if it is more than 10 years old, it is not important and thus out of date. Not only is this not true of the study of history, it is certainly false when it comes to Scripture. Even though the Bible was written thousands of years ago, including the book of Ecclesiastes, given that it is Scripture, namely God's infallible and inerrant Word written, it addresses our time and our generation with crystal clarity, and it demands that it must be heard and obeyed by us today afresh.

Ecclesiastes as a book is classified under the heading of "wisdom literature." Similar to books of this literary form, it lays out before us two ways to life: the way of the unrighteous who live "under the sun" and who refuse to love, serve, and trust their Creator but instead love, worship, and adore creaturely things; and the way of the righteous who live "over the sun" in constant faith and dependence upon their Creator and sovereign God. In addition, as a book, what is so memorable about Ecclesiastes is how brutally honest the author, King Solomon, is about these two ways to live because he himself lived them. As John makes clear in his exposition of the book, Solomon is no armchair philosopher, rather he, as the king both had it all and personally experienced everything life "under the sun" had to offer. Unlike many of us, Solomon was not limited in his resources, time, opportunities, and mental abilities to live life and experience it to the full. He could not say what so many of us say, "If only I had more money.... more time... more opportunities.... then I would be happy, or I would understand the meaning of life...." Rather, he knew from personal experience what it was like to live life "under the sun" and his conclusions on these matters, especially as they are given to us by inspiration of the Holy Spirit, are completely accurate, reliable, and true. Apart from the God of the Bible, our Creator and Lord; apart from living as a creature in constant trust, confidence, and fidelity to him, life is indeed meaningless. And even more than this: apart from life lived for our great Triune God, we will not only experience this life as meaningless and vanity, but we will stand before God in the end and give an account before the Judge of all the earth. I cannot think of a more relevant message to our generation than this: there are two ways to live—the way of faith and confidence in the Lord, righteousness, and true life, and the way of unbelief, rebellion, unrighteousness, and death. Choose this day which life you will live!

One of the buzzwords that describes our time and generation is that of "postmodernism." In contrast to "modernism," which is epitomized by the Enlightenment spirit, postmoderns are skeptical about whether there is a basis to know that objective truth exists and can be known by us with any kind of certainty, whether that be in the realm of knowledge, morality, or ultimate things such as religion. In being more honest than the Enlightenment era which sought to ground truth in finite human subjects apart from the God of Scripture—and fallen human beings at that—postmodernism willingly and rightly admits that without a "God's eye viewpoint," namely divine revelation, objective truth, especially truth that answers the ultimate questions of life is not attainable. This is one of the reasons why "pluralism" is rampant in our day. "Pluralism" as a philosophical or religious viewpoint basically accepts the mindset of postmodernism by arguing that no one philosophical or religious viewpoint is better or truer than any other. In the area of religion and theology, we are repeatedly told that all religious views, even though we may not personally agree with them, must be viewed as equals and simply expressions of another perspective which vies for the attention of the 21st century consumer.

For the Christian, it is important to stress that the mindset of both postmodernism and pluralism is antithetical to the gospel. Scripture will not allow us to accept such a view given the fact—to use the memorable words of Francis Schaeffer—the God of the Bible not only is there but he is also not silent! The sovereign-personal God of all-truth has

not left us to ourselves but he has graciously chosen to reveal himself to us, in creation, in history, in Word, and supremely in his Son. But in saying this, Scripture, and especially Ecclesiastes, would not disagree with the conclusion
of our generation if one lives and breathes as if "under the
sun" living is all there is. In fact, it would echo the conclusion of our generation even more forcefully and conclude
that not only is the pursuit of knowledge vanity, but all life,
relationships, work, play, leisure, and so on, is meaningless
if pursued apart from the Triune God of Scripture. In the
end, it leaves us with an all or nothing situation—either live
life apart from God and perish in this life as well as the one
to come, or know God now, enjoy life now living under his
sovereign grace, and this life as well as the life to come is not
only meaningful, it is also blessed as it fulfills the very purpose of our existence and that which brings glory to our
great Creator and Redeemer God.

It is this message which John drives home with precision
and power in this book; it is this message which Christians
must deeply think about and proclaim to our generation. If
you want to be challenged by this important book of Scripture with the goal of not only knowing God better in your
own personal life, but more than that, being able to reach
our generation with the glorious gospel of our Lord Jesus
Christ, then this book is for you. Read it with Scripture
open; mediate upon the book of Ecclesiastes afresh as you
follow John's exposition of it; and be challenged to bring all
of your life and thought captive to the obedience of Christ.
We desperately need Christians who not only understand
their times profoundly, but who are willing to proclaim
boldly the gospel as the only truth which can save now and

forevermore. May this book encourage Christians to glorify God and to enjoy him now and for all-eternity, as well as to herald faithfully the whole counsel of God to a lost and dying generation who needs to be turned from living "under the sun" to the Triune God who is "over the sun."

Stephen J. Wellum
Professor of Christian Theology
The Southern Baptist Theological Seminary
Louisville, KY 40280

PREFACE

Previously we published a series of twenty articles on the Book of Ecclesiastes in *Sound of Grace,* a monthly Bible study magazine that I edit. That series was one of the most warmly received of any we have written. Many have requested that the material be printed in book form. This is the result.

Every time I have studied and preached through a particular book in the Bible I felt like "This is the book that directly speaks to our society today." The total and clear relevance of the whole Word of God never ceases to amaze me.

Ecclesiastes is a clear and definitive confirmation that life, apart from the self-revelation of God, is meaningless. Solomon was the man best equipped to prove this painful but real conclusion. We always make an excuse for our not being thoroughly satisfied. "If we would have just had more time." Solomon could devote every waking hour to his pursuit of meaning and happiness and could find neither meaning nor purpose. "If we would only have had a bit more money to spend." Solomon had the wealth to buy anything he could wish for and still found nothing to satisfy his heart. "If only I would not have been so distracted." In Solomon's day there were no wars but total peace. There were no catastrophes to take care of. He was free to give his whole attention to his pursuit of satisfaction. He came up empty at every turn. If such a man could not find the answers to the ultimate purpose and meaning of life then no one can.

Solomon had the brains, the time, the wealth, the energy, the dedication and the opportunity to do the whole scene without a single inhibition hindering him from his pursuit. And what did he find?

> *I denied myself nothing my eyes desired; I refused my heart no pleasure. My heart took delight in all my work, and this was the reward for all my labor. Yet when I surveyed all that my hands had done and what I had toiled to achieve, everything was meaningless, a chasing after the wind; nothing was gained under the sun* (Eccl 2:10–11).

This man had it all and discovered he had nothing. He had experienced all that was possible and all he received for his efforts was a terrible headache and an aching heart. This man's conclusion will be duplicated by every sincere person who looks at reality without confidence in the Bible and the God of the Bible.

If the God of grace and power opens your mind and heart to be honest with reality, you will not escape tears and sorrow, but the tears will flow down a smiling face and the sorrow will not be the sorrow of despair but will be accompanied with the sure hope of the Gospel.

I assure you that if the cup you are drinking from is only bitter, you are drinking from the wrong cup. It will take more than false eye lashes and finger nails, a tummy tuck and face lift, a new car and new house, a change of scenery, a different mate or a total shedding of all your inhibitions to satisfy your thirst. God does not change the reality; He changes us and our world and life view of reality as seen from the point of view of eternity.

If you want a hope that will be sustained through the worst of times, follow the writer of Ecclesiastes' advice. On the one hand, see and believe that everything, apart from the grace of God, is meaningless vanity, and at the same time, fear God and keep his commandments (cf. Eccl 12:13).

John G. Reisinger

CHAPTER ONE: VERSES: 1:1–7

THE TREADMILL EXISTENCE

Back in the sixties, a good friend of mine was a leader in a hippie commune. Upon conversion, he read Ecclesiastes and said, "The guy who wrote that is my kind of guy. He really has it all together." Later, he radically changed his opinion about the content of the book. Ecclesiastes is the favorite book of skeptics, scoffers, and many of the cults. Any group that denies life after death, especially if it involves eternal punishment, will quote from Ecclesiastes to prove "the Bible agrees with me on the subject of no life after death." The Jehovah Witnesses especially like this book for this reason. The pleasure-seeking hedonist uses Ecclesiastes to justify his "eat, drink, and be merry because tomorrow you die" philosophy. The secular humanist has a field day with Ecclesiastes and the counter-culture faddists find a true soul mate in Solomon. The evolutionist will claim that Ecclesiastes teaches evolution, since we "all die like animals."

There is little disagreement among true Evangelicals concerning the identity of the author. It seems that the first verse of the opening chapter must describe Solomon. The writer calls himself *Qoheleth,* which means "one who gathers or assembles people." Many commentaries call him the "Preacher" or the "Teacher," and one writer calls him the "Seeker." I think that last term is an excellent way to describe the writer of Ecclesiastes. He was a sincere Seeker who never was able to find what he earnestly sought. He had neither inhibitions nor hindrances to prevent him in any way from doing exactly what he wanted to do. The Seeker narrates the record of his life-long search, but we do not have to wait until we reach the end of his account to learn what he discovered. He states his conclusion immediately after he introduces himself, "Meaningless, meaningless, all is meaningless" (1:2); this is the verdict from a man who 'did the whole scene,' tried 'anything and everything,' and still came away empty.

There is much discussion as to when Solomon wrote the Book of Ecclesiastes. He started his reign as a godly man but, as we know, departed in his heart from God, and this is a record of that departure. It seems that Solomon wrote the book from the perspective of old age. As an old man, he looks back and recounts his bitter experience of utter folly, in the hope that others may be delivered from the same "meaninglessness and vanity."

One of the first things to realize as we approach the Book of Ecclesiastes is that we cannot take every statement in it at face value. The author is not presenting his readers with the true wisdom of God; rather he is providing a true examination of the limits of man's wisdom. He describes the utter folly of seeking truth and searching for reality while ignoring God's self-revelation. For instance, Ecclesiastes certainly, on the surface, appears to teach that men are no better than beasts (3:18–22; 9:5). If the only information humanity has on the subject of death and what follows it is what can be observed *under the sun*, then the writer of Ecclesiastes is correct. In the Seeker's *under the sun* philosophy, there is no hope beyond the grave, and his cry of absolute frustration, "Meaningless, meaningless, all is meaningless," is more than justified. However, if God has been pleased to open our eyes to see and believe the truth of his self-revelation in his Word, then those words cannot express our standpoint. No child of God will ever stand on the shores of eternity, look back, and then say, "It was all meaningless. It was all vanity." The biblical truths of the existence and character of God, his purpose in Creation, and the resurrection of believers assure us that neither our life nor our labor is in vain (2 Tim 2:13; Col 1:15–20; 1 Cor 15: 35–58).

The key phrase in the book is *under the sun*. Ecclesiastes records the fruit of a lifetime spent in a serious and sincere search for meaning and truth. It faithfully recounts the sum total of man's best efforts to discern the meaning of the visible world without considering the revelation that God has given of himself in his Word. Like the secular humanist of our day, the Seeker never considers the revelation that comes from beyond man's power of observation. *Under the sun* describes a way of looking at all things from the ground level of time instead of eternity, of self instead of God, and of sight alone instead of faith.

Ecclesiastes is not a dry book about old and worn-out philosophies. It is relevant to the reports in this morning's paper, to the stories on last night's television news, to the tearful displays on the daily soap operas, and to the arrogant pronouncements of politicians and political pundits on both the left and right. The Seeker is talking about your life and my life today. He forces us to look at reality.

One of the earliest 'reality' television programs from some years ago was "This is Your Life." The host would gather people that had an impact on the guest's life in the past and present them, one by one, to the guest. The guest did not know in advance who would come out from behind the curtain, and the cameras captured his live, unscripted reaction for the television and studio audience. It was an interesting program, even though it was not very true to life. The producers were very selective in the people they brought to appear on the program.

The sweet English teacher in high school who gave you a break and always encouraged you to keep working was there, but never the math teacher. He was the one who flunked you, despite the fact you answered every question correctly, simply because you wrote your name on the wrong side of the final exam page. He was the teacher who called you a nerd and constantly told you that you would never make it.

The aunt and uncle who always sent Christmas presents were there, but never the relatives who were sure that you could not be part of their family. They insisted the babies got mixed up in the hospital.

The neighbor who gave you twenty-five dollars when you went to college and always asked about you was there, but never the neighbor who shot your dog when he crawled through the fence and kept your football when it accidentally bounced into his yard.

Actually, the television show really was not a true picture of your life at all. It was a sanitized version of reality: a rose-colored edition of your true life. Biographies often do the same thing as that television program. If a friend writes your biography, he will depict a different life from that chronicled by a bitter enemy. The life described in an *autobi-*

ography is usually radically different from that in a biography, in fact, some autobiographies read like pure fiction!

Sermons at funeral services often sound like fairy tales. The old joke about the widow's perplexity could easily occur at many funerals. The widow was listening to all the nice things the preacher was saying about her dead husband and she could not believe her ears. Finally, she whispered to her son, "Go up and look in the casket and see who is in it. The preacher cannot possibly be talking about your father."

Your photo album is the same kind of a record. You are very selective, and have every right to be, about what you put in a photo album or a scrapbook. You do not wish to remember or think about some people or events from your past. Your photo album may even have blank spaces where you have removed certain pictures. Those spaces may have once contained wedding pictures that are too painful a reminder of broken promises and unfulfilled dreams.

Unlike "reality" television, biographies, and photo albums, *Ecclesiastes really is a true picture of life!* The Seeker records an honest and unvarnished look at reality, and his account is not at all pretty. He recounts some high points, but primarily, he writes of a life filled with frustration. He experiences many tragic events, but no lasting joys. The writer sums up life *under the sun* as 'Vanity of vanities, all is vanity,' or as the NIV translates, 'Meaningless, meaningless, all is meaningless.' Dale Carnegie would not like the Book of Ecclesiastes at all. Norman Vincent Peale would be appalled by the writer's conclusions.

We need to say a bit more about the phrase, *under the sun*. All people have a world and life view, whether they are aware of it or not. Each person has basic presuppositions that form a grid through which he interprets all of life. *Under the sun* is the world and life view of the Seeker and of much of our present culture as well. That is why Ecclesiastes is so important today. *Under the sun* philosophy views life as consisting only of what a person can taste, touch, feel, smell, think, etc. There is nothing beyond, or over, the sun. There is no one "out there." We are alone in a universe we cannot control or understand. To put it in computer terminology, we live in a WYSIWYG society. When computers first came out, users could change the style and size of the typeface when they were typing. However, they could not see what the change actually looked like until the computer printed their composition on paper. All the type displayed on the monitor was identical to the typeface on a typewriter; it was all the same style and size. Soon, computer technology developed computers with monitors that immediately displayed the exact changes in size and type style. It was a great advancement. What the user saw on the monitor was exactly what was going to come out of the printer. This was called a WYSIWYG monitor, or "What You See Is What You Get." The Seeker is saying the same thing about life and reality. What you can see, taste, touch, etc. is all you get. There is nothing more *under the sun*. Yes, Peggy Lee, this really is a WYSIWYG world. What you see is all there is! There is neither God nor future beyond the here and now. *Under the sun* is the sum total of all reality.

Under-the-sun adherents view all of life without any thought of, or reference to, God. Unless one wears rose-colored glasses or uses mind-altering drugs, such a view of reality not only is not very pretty, but also is very tragic. If people with this worldview never feel the agony of the Seeker, it is because they refuse to face reality. They may employ all kinds of diversionary methods to keep them from serious thinking. The Seeker honestly faced the stark ugliness of *under the sun* reality and then proceeded to describe its dreary and depressing consequences. Secular humanists often accuse Christians of living in a fantasy world and of not facing reality. Actually, it is the exact opposite. Christians, like the Seeker, face the real issues of life, but they come to different conclusions. The worldview for the Christian is shaped by the revelation of one who lives *over the sun*. Christians face the truth; they see the consequences of sin; its corruption of creation, degradation of life, and the ultimate reality and finality of death, and in spite of all this, they dare to say there is still hope because there is a God who gives grace. The man who lives in a fantasy world is the one who will not face the truth; he is a lost man. Any person who never considers and prepares for death and eternity is the real fool. Is anything more certain and real than death?

I remember when a neighbor died and my wife was looking for a sympathy card. All of sudden she said, "John, did you notice there are no humorous funeral cards?" I looked and sure enough, she was right. You can choose a funny card for anything but death and a funeral. If someone graduated from school or flunked, went on a trip and got seasick, went to the hospital, got arrested for speeding, lost a job or got a new one, or whatever, card writers can make a joke out of it. However, no one can make a joke out of death. I am thinking about writing a gospel tract about death and calling it "It's Not Funny Magee!" The closer you get to reality,

the uglier it becomes; the world is upside down because of
sin. You are never closer to reality than when you attend a
funeral and look into the casket. The Seeker understood that
fact.

> Better to go to the house of mourning than to go to the house of
> feasting, for that is the end of all men; and the living will take it to
> heart. Sorrow is better than laughter, for by a sad countenance the
> heart is made better. The heart of the wise is in the house of mourn-
> ing, but the heart of fools is in the house of mirth. (Eccl 7:2–4 NKJV)

What does the Seeker find after his serious, sincere and
exhaustive search of the entire world for reality and truth?
What does his _under the sun_ philosophy teach him? He discovers at every turn the same conclusion: life is 'meaningless, all is vanity.' Here is the man's motto:

> "Vanity of vanities," says the Preacher; "Vanity of vanities, all is
> vanity." (Eccl 1:2 NKJV)

Martyn Lloyd-Jones suggests that Paul, in 1 Corinthians
2:9–11, is teaching the same truth. Paul is showing that natural means of gaining knowledge cannot acquire knowledge
of God or of any spiritual truth.

> But as it is written: "Eye has not seen, nor ear heard, nor have en-
> tered into the heart of man the things which God has prepared for
> those who love Him."
>
> But God has revealed them to us through His Spirit. For the Spirit
> searches all things, yes, the deep things of God.
>
> For what man knows the things of a man except the spirit of the
> man which is in him? Even so no one knows the things of God except
> the Spirit of God.
>
> Now we have received, not the spirit of the world, but the Spirit
> who is from God, that we might know the things that have been freely
> given to us by God. 1 Cor 2:9–12 (NKJV)

In verse 9, Paul describes the three basic methods men
use to gain understanding. He first lists the **Scientific** me-

thod of obtaining knowledge. The scientist observes by the 'eye' and records what he observes. He compares his data with all known observed data of like kind. The data enables the scientist to postulate a theory, which then may be proved or disproved. If all is correct, then the theory from the data first observed with the eye becomes an established law. We do not 'make' laws in science, we merely 'discover' them. The 'eye and observation method' of scientific discovery of facts will never find God in a test tube, under a microscope, or through a giant telescope. Only the Holy Spirit can reveal the person and power of God to a lost soul.

The phrase *ear hath not heard* is the historical method of acquiring knowledge. We 'hear' what the great minds of the past have understood and recorded for us. We gather and compare the combined wisdom of the philosophers and historians of all past ages, but often the result is confusion and contradiction. Not all of the wisdom of the ages put together can find God.

"Nor has entered into the heart of man" refers to the sensitive artist. If 'the heart of man' means the mind, the thinking process, then this is a reference to philosophy. If 'the heart of man' refers to his emotions, then it applies to the arts. If the phrase means 'the totality of man's innermost being', then it pertains to both the thinking process and the feeling process. Philosophers are supposed to be able to think far past 'non-enlightened' minds, and artists are supposed to be able to 'experience emotionally' depths of feeling to a degree and in a way that ordinary folks cannot. Paul, however, insists that neither the mind (brains), nor the heart (emotions), nor both put together can find ultimate truth apart from God's self-revelation. We, as Christians, can know for sure the difference between reality and fantasy, only because we know God himself in a way of saving faith. We have been given the mind of Christ. God has sovereignly revealed to us what the world cannot understand.

Philosophy is the history of one philosopher demonstrating the folly of another philosopher's effort at finding ultimate truth. Usually, one of the master's own students is the one who disproves his teacher. Art, whether music, painting, sculpting, drama, etc. veers back and forth from realism to abstract expressionism, from beauty to ugliness, and from rationalism to romanticism. Many interpretations of 'reality' leave behind an ugly feeling with the walls ever closing in and the options for escape running out.

Try listening to ten minutes of Mozart and then ten minutes of MTV. Are both of these true art forms? That depends on how you define art. The dictionary defines art as "the use of skill and imagination in the production of things of beauty or the works so produced" (Merriam-Webster, 1997). If beauty is defined subjectively, as only 'in the eye of the beholder,' then some people can believe that art is a repetition of loud and disconnected sounds, grotesque shapes and weird movements mixed together under flaming and pulsating colored lights. To others, this depicts utter confusion and a feeling of futility.

In a postmodern culture, some artists believe that they have the right to define both art and truth since artists "see more deeply" into reality. I read about a famous artist who sent a letter to the National Museum of Art and said, "I am donating a piece of my work to your gallery." Several months went by and nothing came. The director of the Museum wrote to the artist and mentioned that no artwork had been received. Several days later, the Museum director received a carbon copy of the original letter. The man was an artist. What he did was art. He produced the letter, which became a piece of art simply because he, an artist, produced it. I do not know if the director was enlightened enough to display the 'piece of art' or not.

The postmodern artist believes that he defines truth and conveys that truth through his work. The postmodern viewer of art believes that he defines truth, and perceives it through his emotions. Paul, by inspiration, is telling us that neither the artist, nor the viewer, nor the historian, nor the scientist, nor all of them together, can lead us to truth. Ecclesiastes is the record of the man best equipped to find truth, who searched in every place, using every method, and who came up completely empty. It is glorious that God has revealed to us, by his word and Spirit, the truth that has eluded all the *under-the-sun* scientists, historians, artists, and the Seeker that ever lived.

Immediately after stating his philosophy of the vanity of all of life, the Seeker expressed the obvious and certain conclusion to such an ideology. If everything is meaningless, then why even try to attain any goal? It is a waste of time and effort.

What profit has a man from all his labor in which he toils under the sun? (Eccl 1:2, 3 NKJV)

This is the grievous but certain consequence for the man who adopts this *under the sun* view of life. The word *profit* means "that which is left over." What is left over after we attain a given goal? After we have sucked all the juice out of any given pleasure or experience, what is left to cheer the heart and feed the soul tomorrow? Can a gold trophy sitting on the shelf give us the same thrill it did that moment we heard our name called as the winner? What about next year when we hear another name called? After the first flush of attainment, what remains that will sustain and fill that hunger for lasting satisfaction? This is surely the right question and the Seeker has no answer. All he can say is that he has found neither the bread of life nor the water of life. Every piece of bread, no matter how expensive or tasty, has become moldy and cannot satisfy the Seeker's hunger, and all the water he ever drank has become bitter in his mouth and only mocked him as he tried to quench his thirst. The hymn writer said it better than I ever could.

> O Christ, in Thee my soul hath found, and found in Thee alone
> The peace, the joy I sought so long, The bliss till now unknown.
>
> I sighed for rest and happiness, I yearned for them, not Thee;
> But while I passed my Saviour by, His love laid hold of me.
>
> I tried the broken cisterns, Lord, but ah! the waters failed!
> E'en as I stooped to drink they'd fled, And mocked me as I wailed.
>
> The pleasures lost I sadly mourned, But never wept for Thee,
> Till grace the sightless eyes received Thy loveliness to see.
>
> Now none but Christ can satisfy, None other name for me
> There's love, and life, and lasting joy Lord Jesus found in Thee.

In Ecclesiastes 1:4–7, the Seeker will compare man with nature. Humanity is transient, but nature is permanent. We are "here today and gone tomorrow," but the earth endures forever. Nature not only yields no answers, it is part of the problem. The implication of the Seeker's observations as he looks at nature in the light of his *under the sun* philosophy is that it seems to make no sense at all. We can neither (1) get rid of nature, nor (2) find any way of controlling the earthly realm that embodies the problem. It is just as the song said, "The music goes round and round, and where it stops, nobody knows."

> *One generation passes away, and another generation comes; but the earth abides forever.* (Eccl 1:4 NKJV)

We have a 'term limit' on our earthly existence and we pass on when our term is up, but not so with nature. Humans have a 'time to be born and a time to die' (Eccl 3:2) but the sun, wind, rain and mountains have no 'term limits' or 'times.' They never grow old and they never change or die. Nature is radically different from humanity, yet at the same time, the endless cycles of nature mirror the same endless and meaningless cycles of our life. The Seeker uses three examples to prove his point.

First he looks at the sun.

> *The sun also rises, and the sun goes down, and hastens to the place where it arose.* (Eccl 1:5 NKJV)

The sun comes up in the east and dispels the darkness. It appears to move across the sky and disappear in the west. While we were sleeping, the sun apparently went under the earth and came up in the east just as it did yesterday. The sun has been coming up at the same place every day since time began. Its timing is precise and predictable down to the second. There is no internal change or deviation, nor can we effect any lasting change on it. The sun comes up at the same place with split-second precision (we can tell the exact minute of sunrise on Christmas Day ten thousand years from now). It travels precisely the same course without deviating an inch and it goes down every day just as precisely on schedule as to time and place.

Tomorrow, a new day finds the sun coming up exactly as it did yesterday and every other day that has passed. You might expect something different with such a great beginning, but it doubles back, the same as the day before, to the same place. Tomorrow it will start all over again in the identical routine. The sun comes up so it can go down, so it can come up, so it can go down, so it can come up, *ad infinitum.*

This brings to mind the old song about the bear going over the mountain only to see another mountain. You can see the bear chugging up the mountain in eager enthusiasm and reaching the top, totally out of breath, only to discover another mountain. He goes down the other side and again chugs up the next mountain, only to discover still another mountain. Each time his excitement and expectations are disappointed when he reaches the top. "Oh, not another mountain" will soon do away with any enthusiasm for climbing any mountain. The same seems to be true of life. We exert every effort and expend every resource to reach a cherished goal, only to discover there is a bigger and what appears to be a better goal waiting. Verse 3 keeps ringing in our ears. *What profit has a man from all his labor in which he toils under the sun?* Was it really worth all that effort only to discover there is yet another mountain?

In verse 6, the Teacher looks at the wind. What is freer than the wind? John 3:8 tells us that it blows where it pleases. We often say, "He is as free as the wind." In reality, the wind is just as controlled as the sun.

> *The wind goes toward the south, and turns round to the north; the wind whirls about continually, and comes again according on its circuit.* (NKJV)

The wind whirls in every direction, but it is not as random as it appears. It always follows a prescribed circuit. If you could follow its course, you would see that it is just as locked in as the sun. If you could somehow tag a leaf and keep it intact, you would discover that some day, the leaf would blow back to the very spot from which it started.

In verse 7, the Teacher looks at rain and water.

All the rivers run into the sea; yet the sea is not full; to the place from which the rivers come, there they return again.

Look at the mighty Niagara Falls. Where does all that water go? You would think the lakes and the oceans would keep filling up until the world was completely under water. Yet, that is not what happens. The water all goes back to the same clouds from which it came. One day in the future, every drop of water will flow again over Niagara Falls. It will follow its course to a great body of water, evaporate back into the clouds and fall upon earth and ultimately, the same water again will flow over Niagara Falls. Label a drop of water like you did the leaf, and someday you will see it pass over the same waterfalls. That amazing and mysterious process of evaporation from the sun, union with the clouds, and transportation by the wind evens it all out so that the lakes and the oceans will always maintain their ordained level.

The perpetual propagation of humanity seems to be the same as the cycles of the sun, wind and rain. It is the same old circle that makes no sense. Generations come and go—so what? Years and years come and go—so what? Days pass, events occur, life leads to death—so what? Who cares? What difference does it make? *Meaningless, meaningless, all is meaningless.* I get up, I go to work, I come home and go to bed so

I can get up to go to work so I can come home and go to bed
so I can get up and go to work. . . I live and die and—so
what! The "Treadmill Existence" is the way one writer describes verses 5–7. Hammerstein and Kern said it well:

> Ol' man river, that ol' man river
> He don't say nothin', but he must know somethin'
> He just keeps rollin', he keeps on rollin' along
> He don't plant taters, he don't plant cotton
> And them plants em, are soon forgotten,
> But ol' man river, just keeps rollin' along.

Something is terribly wrong here. Something is back-
wards. Man, not nature, is the highest of all God's creative
order. Man should be permanent and nature transient. God
gave man dominion over the very creation that now, in
some sense, lords it over him. Man feels this fact keenly.
Why should nature go on so consistently, while we bury
friends and loved ones? How does the river just keep rolling
along unaltered, while we grow old, wither and die? Why is
it that constant change frustrates our dreams and deep hunger for satisfaction, but "ol' man river just keeps rollin'
along," unminding and unchanging? Ecclesiastes presses
these kinds of realities and questions on us while insisting
there are no answers. Such is the plight of the man who tries
to understand life apart from any consideration of God.

Christians know the answers to these questions. We express them in our great hymns, such as "Great Is Thy Faithfulness." The first verse extols God's unchanging faithfulness.

> "Great is Thy faithfulness," O God my Father,
> There is no shadow of turning with thee;

Thou changest not, thy compassions, they fail not;
As thou hast been thou forever will be.

In verse two, the author uses nature to prove the point of God's unchanging faithfulness.

Summer and winter, and spring-time and harvest,
Sun, moon, and stars in their course above,
Join with all nature in manifold witness
To thy great faithfulness, mercy and love.

(Thomas O. Chisholm, b.1866)

Solomon, in Ecclesiastes 1:4, states what both Isaiah and Peter also saw clearly. Humanity, like creation, is insignificant in itself. However, as the products of God's sovereign purpose and creation, human beings find purpose, meaning, and significance in the one who made and redeemed them. The Seeker is correct in reminding us that, *"One generation passeth away, and another generation cometh: but the earth abideth for ever"* (Eccl 1:4). That truth must, and will, lead to either worship or despair according to one's world and life view. Adherents to the philosophy of *under the sun* will see Ecclesiastes 1:4 as proof of the meaningless and insignificance of human life, but believers in him who dwells *over the sun* will see the same thing as proof of the faithfulness of God.

The New Covenant Scriptures, quoting Isaiah 40:6–8, drive home this stark similarity between man's transient insignificance and that of grass and flowers.

... having been born again, not of corruptible seed but incorruptible, through the word of God which lives and abides forever, because "All flesh is as grass, and all the glory of man as the flower of the grass. The grass withers, and its flower falls away, but the word of the LORD endures forever." Now this is the word which by the gospel was preached to you. (1 Pet 1:23–25 NKJV)

Notice how Peter contrasts the eternality and unchangeableness of God's Word to our "here today and gone tomorrow" experience. Our only hope is that everything that the eternal Word begets also is eternal! Just as everything begotten by a corruptible seed must perish, so everything begotten by an *incorruptible* seed must endure for eternity. Christians have been born of God, by an incorruptible seed, the Word of God. One cannot acquire that kind of knowledge and hope from philosophers, psychologists, sociologists, historians, hedonists, or any other place, except from the revelation of him who dwells *above the sun*.

We need to learn some lessons from this discussion. First, if we look for ultimate meaning or satisfaction from created things, we find they become insignificant and meaningless. Only as those things lead us to HIM who is *over the sun*, are they meaningful and evidence of great mercy. However, without HIM and HIS blessing, those same particulars are like soap bubbles. We must see every blessing as a gift from God, designed to reflect his glory by increasing our delight and trust in him. We must not accept the blessings and then forget the one who sovereignly gave them.

We might be tempted to trust or even worship nature, since it is so permanent and we are so transient. The problem is that, apart from God's revelation of himself as sovereign over nature, it gives us very mixed signals. A young couple may fall in love at the beach and decide to build their dream home on the very spot they first met. For five happy years, they watch the sun set, the moon bounce off the waves and feel the cool breeze on their faces. They may be tempted to worship "God's beautiful handiwork." One day a hurricane comes and the couple watches in horror as the same ocean and wind they almost worshipped destroys their home and all their possessions. Without an understanding of the sovereignty and the goodness of God, who would want to worship or trust the God who sends *that kind* of nature?

We must be careful not to deify nature. There is no such being as "Mother Nature" any more than there is a "Father Time." Nature is not my mother and surely, time is not my father. When humanistic environmentalists consider nature to be "our fair sister," they are parroting the heresy of Deism. Nature, all of it, and at all times, is totally under the control of a sovereign God. It is God's sun and rain, and he makes his sun to shine and his rain to fall where, when, and upon whom he pleases. It is also his hurricane and volcano to do with as he chooses. He not only creates and controls every aspect of nature, but, as we shall see in chapter three, he also controls everything else.

Man studies the laws of nature, but he neither creates them nor in any way changes them. Launching a spaceship does not defy the laws of nature; rather it uses and obeys those laws. Chuck Swindoll asked an astronaut in his congregation how it felt to be ready to blast off in a spaceship. The astronaut replied, "How would you feel getting ready to blast off in a piece of equipment with over three-million parts and each one made by the lowest bidder?" Imagine the ingenuity it took to design and built three-million pieces of equipment and integrate them all into one single working unit so we could send a man to the moon. That is an astounding feat, but it is child's play when compared to creating the human being capable of performing the amazing feat.

I remember watching the first man set his foot on the moon. The television pundits were calling this a giant step for man and implying that it was step back for those who believed in God. I was asked what I thought about that event. I answered, "I rejoice in every great scientific endeavor. I had tears in my eyes as I watched that first moon walk unfold. I thought, 'if man is capable of using God's ordained and minutely fixed laws to pull off such a stunt, what must the God who created the man and fixed the laws be like?'" That event enlarged both my conception of God himself and his creative powers.

Man studies "how" God made things, but he can never know "why" unless God reveals it. An elderly woman boils a pot of water on an electric stove. Her son, home from college, asks her if she knows why the water is boiling. He then proceeds to explain to her how electricity works. When he finishes, she replies, "Well, what do you know! I thought the water was boiling because I was planning on making a cup of tea." Both the boy and his mother are correct. However, if we understand the "how" perfectly and miss the "why" as revealed in Scripture, we are doomed to conclude that all is "meaningless, meaningless." This fact irks the *under the sun* philosopher (3:11). I confess I am not sure exactly *how* God made the heavens and the earth, but, because God has revealed his reasons in his Word, I can tell you *why* he did it (Col 1:15–20). I think the mother's 'why' answer is far more important in the eternal sense than the young man's 'how' answer. The Seeker could answer nearly all of the 'how" questions, but none of the 'why' questions. With all his genius and effort, man, under the sun, cannot know fully and finally the true and ultimate meaning of *one single thing,* and as I said earlier, this really vexes him.

Let me mention a few details that we must keep in mind as we study this book together.

One: The Seeker considers every conceivable goal that a man could possibly imagine; every reason a person could have for living; and he says, "Go ahead, and go for it. Give it all you have and I sincerely hope you make it. However, if you succeed, you will discover it was a waste of time. It was all a bubble."

I remember visiting some friends who had a three-year old daughter and a six-year old son. The boy was blowing soap bubbles as big as watermelons. The little girl would chase the bubbles in glee and grasp them in excitement, and of course, the moment she touched one it immediately burst. Finally, in exasperation she said, "Bubba, make me a bubble that don't break." Yes, Bubba, let us see you make one that does not break! That is the message of Ecclesiastes. Everything that is in any way attached to time or to this world is only a bubble that can give no lasting satisfaction. There may be great joy in the pursuit and a refreshing satisfaction upon successfully creating the watermelon bubble, but it will vanish the moment you grab it. There is nothing in this world that can furnish lasting meaning and purpose. Every trophy will tarnish and catch dust. The message of "Meaningless, meaningless, all is meaningless" is the message echoed by our Lord when he said, "Whoever drinks of this water will thirst again."

If a sinner, living in rebellion to God's revelation of himself, can find lasting joy, satisfaction and true meaning in this world without a saving knowledge of Christ, then that person has defeated God, and thwarted his purposes, and beaten God at his own game!

Two: We must constantly remind ourselves that the Seeker is speaking from personal experience. He is not an arm-chair philosopher. He has "done the whole scene" from top to bottom and from front to back. You name it and he has tried it. You describe it and he has been there. He has ran-sacked the entire world trying to understand reality and find meaning and purpose in life. The Seeker seems to take man's most hidden, radical thoughts and carefully pursues each one to its fullest potential in real life. He pushes down every wall, erases every boundary, and goes to every possi-ble extreme to know and experience real and lasting satisfac-tion. Here is his conclusion: All is vanity. Every attempt fails to satisfy truly and leaves him with empty hands and a bur-dened heart. Each time the emptiness grows deeper and the frustration becomes more acute.

The Seeker was not engaged in weekend pursuits. He gave all of his energy and thought to try to find ultimate truth. It was the consuming passion of every hour in every day. Nothing was out of bounds in his quest.

> And **I set my heart** to seek and search out by wisdom concerning all that is done under heaven; this burdensome task God has given to the sons of man, by which they may be exercised. (Eccl 1:13 NKJV)

> So I was great, and increased more than all that were before me in Jerusalem: also my wisdom remained with me. And **whatsoever mine eyes desired, I kept not from them. I withheld not my heart from any joy;** for my heart rejoiced in all my labor: and this was my portion of all my labor. (Eccl 2:9, 10 KJV)

Three: The Seeker was in no way limited or restrained in his efforts. He had the resources, the time, the opportunity, and the mental and physical ability without any restraints. The message is that *if this man cannot make it, no one can!* This man is not an ivory tower sociologist or liberal political theorist. He speaks from personal experience. And what is the conclusion to all his efforts?

> *Then I looked on all the works that my hands had wrought, and on the labor that I had labored to do: and, behold, all was vanity and vexation of spirit, and there was no profit under the sun.* (Eccl 2:11 KJV)

> *Therefore I hated life; because the work that is wrought under the sun is grievous unto me: for all is vanity and vexation of spirit. Yea, I hated all my labor which I had taken under the sun: because I should leave it unto the man that shall be after me.* (Eccl 2:17–18 KJV)

One of the constant undertones of this book is the utter frustration on every hand of being forced to admit that *I am not ultimately in control of anything and I hate that fact.* If ever a book exploded the myth of free will, it is the Book of Ecclesiastes.

Four: One of the problems is that, on the surface, the Seeker seems to give mixed signals. At times, we are not sure if he is serious or if he is speaking with tongue in cheek; if he is being intentionally satirical; or even if he is deliberately making fun of his readers. On the one hand, he seems to encourage us in the excellence of work and to strive to reach the top. He encourages hard work, but in the next breath, he says, "But if you reach your goal, and I sincerely hope you do, you will be bitterly disappointed every single time." He encourages education, but quickly adds that it is a waste of time if you think that it holds the answers to the ultimate questions of life and reality.

It would be easy to dismiss his message as "sour grapes" and label him a burnt-out cynic who was mad at the world. But the man is too realistic, too "right on," too honest, for us to say, "Well, he had a bad trip and needs a good night's sleep." Besides, he keeps urging us to enjoy life.

> *There is nothing better for a man, than that he should eat and drink, and that he should make his soul enjoy good in his labor. This also I saw, that it was from the hand of God.* (Eccl 2:24 KJV)

It would be easy also to imagine that this writer was a grey-headed hippie at a pot party or a hard rock concert. However, he does not speak of his emotions as those raised by loud sounds and flashing lights. He is a clear thinker and always in control of his mind and his emotions.

> *I sought in mine heart to give myself unto wine, yet acquainting mine heart with wisdom; and to lay hold on folly, till I might see what was that good for the sons of men* ...(Eccl 2:3 KJV)

He used wine as a stimulant to sharpen his senses, but he was not in any sense a drunkard. This man is a realist; in fact, it is his stark realism that is so aggravating. His world is our world—work, family, pain, misery, and death. He paints a clear and vivid picture of your life and my life. This truly is our real life!

Perhaps it would be a good idea to try to describe the Seeker's counterpart today. Let me try to picture what the Seeker would be like if he were living in your town today. We will call him Mr. N for Nice. What would this man, Mr. N, be like today?

By far, he would be the richest man in your town and probably in the entire state. He would own the largest ranch and have a stable full of thoroughbred horses. He would have the finest herd of Herefords and the milking cows from his herd of registered Holsteins would always take the blue ribbons at the State Farm Show.

Mr. N would be a past president of every civic organization there is in your town and state. He would have been voted Man of the Year and his picture would have appeared on the cover of both *Time* (three times) and *Newsweek*. He is a scratch golfer and chairman of the Greens Committee at the most elite Country Club. He is also an elder in his church and is faithful in his attendance.

He has the best box seats for every sporting event and the opera. Mr. N is extremely down to earth and can make anyone feel comfortable. He can converse on any subject. He knows the elevators boy's first name and always asks about his aging and ailing mother. He even sent flowers when she was in the hospital. Mr. N is a wonderful father, a loving husband, a kind and considerate employer, and a sincere and faithful friend.

In short, Mr. N is a man's man, a woman's dream and an enemy's nightmare.

Imagine that Mr. N has written a book about his life and appears for a televised interview on a special Sunday morning talk show. Barbara Walters, Dan Rather, Rush Limbaugh, and Larry King take turns asking Mr. N questions. The interview would go something like this:

Barbara Walters is obviously nervous and just a bit out of breath. She says, "Mr. N, I simply cannot imagine what it must feel like to have experienced and accomplished all of the things that you have." Mr. N interrupts: "Barbara, what in the world are you talking about?" Barbara is rather shocked and says, "I mean the fact that you are the only man who was ever on the cover of *Time* magazine three times. You are the only person who was ever voted as . . ." Again Mr. N interrupts: "Barbara, you did not read my book very carefully. I said over and over that all of those things are meaningless." Barbara says, "But, but . . ." as she rattles off six more of Mr. N's accomplishments. Mr. N gives her a look of pity and says again, "Totally meaningless, meaningless, every bit of it was all meaningless." Barbara has nothing more to say and nods to Dan Rather.

Dan Rather, in a very serious voice says, "Mr. N, you seem to be the most pessimistic person in the whole world. Do you enjoy anything at all in life?" Mr. N, with obvious disdain in his voice, says, "Dan, I see that you, like Barbara, did not read my book or else you do not understand what you read. I enjoy every meaningless thing I do simply because there is not anything else to do. True, it has no ultimate meaning or lasting joy, but it is the only game in town." Dan, too, is silent, and yields the floor to Rush Limbaugh.

Rush Limbaugh seems just a bit unsure of what he wants to say. "I don't mean to be rude or impertinent, but you seem to contradict yourself. I have trouble following your book. One moment you are praising hard work and education and urging us to "go for it" and then the next minute you are trashing both." Mr. N. "Well, I see you at least did read my book. It is too bad you did not understand what I was saying. Read it again and apply a bit more of that supposed talent you have on loan from God." All, including Rush, laugh.

Larry King smiles and says, "Mr. N. I have five friends who are psychiatrists. No more than two of them have ever agreed on one single thing in over twenty years and yet all five said exactly the same thing about you after reading your book. They said you had a Richard Corey complex. I assume you know what that is." Mr. N not only knows what the Richard Corey complex is, he can quote the entire famous poem from which the phrase originated. The poem goes like this:

> Whenever Richard Corey went down town,
> We people on the pavement looked at him:
> He was a gentleman from sole to crown,
> Clean favored, and imperially slim.
>
> And he was always quietly arrayed,
> And he was always human when he talked;
> But still he fluttered pulses when he said,
> "Good morning," and he glittered when he walked.
>
> And he was rich—yes, richer than a king,
> And admirably schooled in every grace:
> In fine, we thought that he was everything
> To make us wish that we were in his place.
>
> So on we worked, and waited for the light,
> And went without the meat, and cursed the bread;
> And Richard Corey, one calm summer night,
> Went home and put a bullet through his head.
>
> (Edwin Arlington Robinson, 1869–)

That ended the interview. The Seeker, our Mr. N, is not a walking time bomb. He is not going to go home and put a bullet through his head. He will live a long life. He may appear to be a mental case to those who cannot pigeon hole him into their philosophy, but that is their problem, not his.

In the next chapter, we will start at verse 8 of the first chapter and describe the sure results of following the *under the sun* philosophy. The results are the same as those produced by the secular humanism of our day. It is amazing that the Book of Ecclesiastes was written thousands of years ago, but still describes in accurate detail the problems we face today.

CHAPTER TWO

SOME DEFINITIONS

In chapter one, we introduced the theme of the Book of Ecclesiastes and covered Ecclesiastes chapter 1, verses 1–7. The key phrase in the book is *under the sun*. Ecclesiastes records the fruit of a lifetime spent in a serious and sincere search for meaning and truth. It faithfully recounts the sum total of man's best efforts to discern the meaning of the visible world without considering the revelation that God has given of himself in his Word. We saw that the writer's thesis was "meaningless, meaningless, all is meaningless." Such a message must lead to the utter futility expressed in verse 3, *"What profit has a man from all his labor in which he toils under the sun?"* If everything is without meaning or purpose, then why bother with anything?

For clarity, we will define some words that we will be using. Definitions are essential to true knowledge. Until we can define something clearly, it is questionable if we really understand it. Definitions and presuppositions go hand in hand. Our basic presuppositions determine everything else that we believe. If our basic presuppositions are wrong, *then everything built on those presuppositions is wrong.* If our belief that the Bible is the trustworthy Word of God is false, then we are fools and the unbeliever is right. Of course, the reverse also is true! This is precisely Paul's point in 1 Corinthians 15:12–20. Heaven and hell hang on the right presuppositions.

The terms we will define appear constantly on television newscasts as well as in newspapers and magazines. It is necessary to understand these terms if we are to understand the world in which we live. These words do not occur in the Book of Ecclesiastes, but the philosophy and world and life-view behind them is precisely that which the writer of Ecclesiastes addressed. You may be tempted to say, "I am not interested in philosophic words and terms," but believe me; you face the reality of these terms every time you go to the grocery store, watch television, read a book or newspaper, and even when you go to church. We need to know what these words mean in order to understand what the news media reports, what politicians express, and above all, what the Word of God communicates in the Book of Ecclesiastes. The Book of Ecclesiastes, as no other book in the Bible, lays out in living color, the philosophic arrogance and blindness of our present society. If we understand Ecclesiastes, we will:

- understand why our society is like it is today;
- why it is certain to get worse tomorrow, unless God sends revival; and
- why we ourselves often succumb to feelings of despair and act the way we do.

Solomon's words in Ecclesiastes could be those of a twentieth-century secularist. His method of searching for truth and reality, and the conclusions he reached are identical to those found in the never-ending list of self-help books on the best-seller list. Listening to the Seeker in Ecclesiastes is like watching the top ten popular music videos on MTV. The outlook and utter frustration of Ecclesiastes is the same philosophy of despair expressed in the literature and art of twentieth-century secularism and existentialism, as well as that of twenty-first-century postmodernism. "I'm OK and you're OK" may appear to mean we are both all right, but in reality it implies that neither of us, nor anyone else, is really okay, simply because there is no such state as okay. What is all right for you is not necessarily satisfactory or acceptable for me.

We must understand the biblical perspective behind the Book of Ecclesiastes as well as the world and life-view of the society in which we live. Understanding presuppositional thinking enables us to foresee the probable results of actions that spring from various ideologies.

R.L. Dabney was a presuppositional thinker who wrote an article at the time of the women's suffrage movement. Dabney was not against the movement or voting rights for women, but he was opposed to the basic arguments used to promote the movement. He predicted ten specific things that were sure to follow if the thinkers of his day left the basic presuppositions of the argument unchallenged and did not show them to be dangerous. All ten of his predictions proved true, even though others scorned him and accused him of fear mongering. Dabney was no prophet with a crystal ball, he merely recognized that if you choose 'A', then it is inevitable that 'B' must follow.

I was a pastor in Canada when the United Church of Canada declared that homosexuality was an acceptable lifestyle. Twenty years later, that denomination was dismayed when an avowed homosexual wanted them to ordain him. The Methodist and Episcopal Churches in the United States face the same situation today. The issue of homosexual pastors was settled when the church consented to homosexuality as an approved lifestyle. It was only a matter of time before our culture developed practices in keeping with the logical conclusions of permissible homosexuality. As our society works out more and more of the logical conclusions of that position, they deny more and more biblical truths.

The attitude of utter despair experienced by the Seeker in Ecclesiastes was inevitable the moment he adopted his *under the sun* world and life-view. We must understand that drugs, alcohol and loose sexuality did not produce our present perverse society. Our society needed those things to fill the pain of an empty and meaningless life. Everything the world offers by way of diversion is like a giant aspirin tablet. Aspirin does not cure what causes a headache; it merely dulls the pain. Our society's philosophy has produced the same kind of a "vanity, vanity, all is vanity" Hollywood-fantasy world in which the Seeker wandered for most of his life. That philosophy also gave our society the giant head and heartache it tries in vain to cure apart from a return to the true and living God.

The first word we need to understand is the word *secular.* It is the consistent and thorough application of practical atheism to all areas of life. Secular is the opposite of *sacred* or religious. It is a total nonreligious approach to life. Since there is no God, there is nothing sacred. A true secularist cannot be content until he has removed every reality and symbol of God and religion from public life. The only reality that exists is what you can touch, taste, see, hear, and smell. It is to life what WYSIWYG (What You See Is What You Get) is to a computer monitor.

Secularism is a conscious attempt to understand and explain life without any thought of or reference to God. It is the life *under the sun* perspective of the Seeker in Ecclesiastes. It is the Russian experiment of deliberate atheism for over forty years. It is the present *official religion* (and it is a religion) of both the government and society in the United States today. This explains our present society's attitude to former President Clinton's "mistakes." You cannot charge a person with sin if there is no such thing as sin. Our society was only being consistent with its convictions that there are no moral absolutes. It is why ninety percent of American women believe abortion is wrong *for them*, but become outraged when anyone says that it is wrong for someone else. When news commentators refer to the secularization of our society, they mean this attitude and mindset.

The word *secular* denotes that which is worldly or opposite of sacred. As early as 1846, it described the doctrine that bases morality solely with regard to the well-being of humankind in this present life, to the exclusion of belief in God or an afterlife (*The Oxford Universal Dictionary*). Today, it has come to be associated with an anti-sacred mentality wherein religion has no rightful or appropriate place in modern society and culture. Actually, the secularist views religion as the cause of all our modern ills.

The second word we must define is *humanism.* Humanism is the worship of man for his own sake. It is similar in some ways to secularism. Humanism is concerned with merely human interests: loving our neighbor, helping the human race, etc. *Humanism*, as a philosophy of life, and being *humane* in your attitude and treatment of other people are two different things. Christians ought to be humane;

their behavior and disposition towards others ought to befit a human created in the image of God—kind, courteous, and civil. They ought not to be humanists. The humanist believes that individual human beings are the fundamental source of all value, and human beings have the ability to under-stand—and perhaps even to control—the natural world by careful application of their own rational faculties. Human-ism is committed to the belief that man is good. It denies the depravity of man and therefore fails miserably at every turn.

The third term is *secular humanism*. This brand of human-ism is currently in vogue. It differs from the earlier classical humanism of Dante, Erasmus and others. The modern secu-lar brand of humanism is a naturalistic, and hence anti-super-naturalistic, rationalistic and atheistic approach to life, truth, faith and meaning. Apparently, the only absolute truth in secular humanism is that there is no absolute truth.

I was preaching in a college town when a young man walked angrily out of the church service. He waited outside after the service and was almost angry enough to fight. He insisted that I had no right to say dogmatically that Christ was **The** way, **The** truth, and **The** life. The young man had no objection to Christ being "A" way or "A" truth. He in-sisted that we could not be dogmatic about anything, since everything is an open question. He kept insisting that there is no absolute truth. I said, "Are you telling me that I cannot be absolutely sure about even one thing?" Without hesita-tion he replied, "That is correct." I then asked him, "Are you sure about that?" He replied, "I am positive." That is pre-cisely the position of the modern secular humanist; he is positive that you cannot be positive about anything.

If the secular humanists are right and there is no God, then we indeed live in a closed universe where self and sin reign and death ends all. If *under the sun* is all there is, then the secularist is right when he says, "He who dies with the most toys wins." The entire story has been written and there can be nothing new added. No new birth; No answer to prayer; No life after death; No real or lasting change; No Holy Spirit; No forgiveness. **Therefore, there is NO HOPE.** We will come back to this point. Realities for the believer are childish daydreams to the secular humanist.

The fourth term is *deism*. This is a belief in the existence of a god, with rejection of the idea of revelation beyond the natural world. A deist would be a religious secularist if those were not contradictory terms. He will use what Francis Schaeffer calls "God words." Those are words used to produce an effect, but that have no concrete meaning. These God words are meant to arouse certain feelings, but never to convey objective facts. The Environmental Movement that seeks to save God's Creation does not mean by that terminology that they really believe that God literally created the earth. When they use the word *god*, they do not necessarily mean the creator God of the Bible. When a movie star, or politician, says, "God bless you all," they could mean anything. The phrase may refer to nothing more real than Santa Claus!

The deist bases his belief in a god entirely on reason, without any reference to faith, revelation, or institutional religion. During the seventeenth and eighteenth centuries, advances in the natural sciences often fostered confidence that the regularity of nature reflected the benevolence of a divine providence. This confidence, together with a widespread distrust of the church, made deism a popular view in England and on the continent. It made it possible to say you believed in God, when in reality you had disrobed God of every vestige of deity.

The deist believes that God (some kind of power or whatever) created the world and left it to run under the control of natural law. This is the "big clock" view. The deist denies God's personal and sovereign control over the world and its events. There can be nothing new inserted into the universe (See Ecclesiastes 1:8–11). There is no new birth, no answers to prayer, and no divine intervention of any kind. The world of reality is a closed system whose only hope or help is man himself. A deist is really a religious atheist in practice. The key words in defining deism are *impersonal God* and *natural law*.

Three things characterize secularism, humanism and deism: (1) An impersonal God, if there is one at all; (2) the total rule of natural law without any super-natural intervention; and (3) the universe as a closed system. What we see *under the sun* is all there is! We are locked in—there is no outside help. There is nobody "out there."

The fifth term is *nihilism*. Nihilism is defined as negative doctrines in religion and morals. The root word *nihil* means a thing of no value or worth. This differs from humanism, which posits a value on human life, even though that value may have been arbitrarily assigned, and from deism, which values the natural world as sufficient to explain our existence. Where secularism believes that morality should be based on the well-being of humankind in this present life, nihilism believes that there is no morality and the well-being of humanity is irrelevant. A nihilist rejects all religious beliefs and moral principles and believes that nothing can be known or communicated. This philosophy is becoming increasingly prevalent in our society.

Ecclesiastes 1:9–11 gives us a good description of the fruit of nihilism. "That which has been is what will be, that which is done is what will be done, and there is nothing new under the sun. Is there anything of which it may be said, 'See, this is new?' It has already been in ancient times before us. There is no remembrance of former things, nor will there be any remembrance of things that are to come by those who will come after." (NKJV)

- No new circumstances – "What has been..."
- No new human endeavor – "What has been done..."
- No hope of significantly changing anything – "There is no remembrance of either former or future things..." only the eternal "now."

Verse 11 describes the fruits of nihilism coming home to roost. "There is no remembrance of former things, nor will there be any remembrance of things that are to come by those who will come after."

Nihilism can be understood in several different ways. Political Nihilism works itself out in an attempt to destroy existing political, social, and religious order in order to achieve future improvement. Conditions in the social order are so bad as to make total destruction of everything and everybody desirable for its own sake, independent of any plausible reconstructive program. George Bush, Senior was defeated (for better or worse) when the Democrats persuaded the country to turn to nihilism. "Anything is better than what we now have. We cannot stand four more years of this." Ethical Nihilism or moral nihilism "rejects the possibility of absolute moral or ethical values. Instead, good and evil are nebulous, and values addressing such are the product of nothing more than social and emotive pressures" (Alan Pratt, The Internet Encyclopedia of Philosophy, http://www.iep.utm.edu/n/nihilism.htm). It fosters the belief that there is no objective truth or any real ground for hope of any kind. All I know for sure is how I feel, and I feel utterly hopeless.

"*Existential nihilism* is the notion that life has no intrinsic meaning or value, and it is, no doubt, the most commonly used and understood sense of the word today" (Pratt, *Internet Encyclopedia*). Life has no meaning. Nothing has meaning. The ends justify the means because there is no legitimate basis for any moral principle. One is free to indulge in whatever behavior one desires regardless of the consequences, because it is all meaningless.

According to nihilism, life is completely amoral, a conclusion that works itself out historically in such monstrosities as the Nazi reign of terror, various other genocides, and suicide terrorist attacks. Nihilism is the philosophy that drives irrational riots where people destroy their own neighborhood. Life in the Ghetto becomes so unbearable that "anything is better than this." Blow it up! Regardless of how the pieces fall, the situation cannot possibly be worse than it is now. Light the fuse, we have nothing to lose.

Terrorists base their philosophy on the hopeless despair of nihilism. They have no concrete plan to change conditions for the better. They have nothing that others need, so they have no capital with which to negotiate or trade. The very most they can offer is to bypass you in their bombing and other terror attacks. Those who resort to terrorism often feel trapped and hopeless because they have nothing, and the enemy has everything. A terrorist does not care whom he kills or what he destroys. Regardless of what happens to him, he cannot possibly be any worse off than he is at the moment.

Nihilism breeds the philosophy of suicide since there is absolutely nothing to lose. For the terrorist suicide bomber there is absolutely nothing to lose. What ever is past death, it is impossible to be worse than the present. This attitude is fueled into a flame if you can convince the individual that a heaven with many virgins await him upon his martyrdom by suicide attack upon "the ungodly infidels" even if they are young school children or sick people in a hospital.

Nihilism is not saying that men forget, meaning that men do not learn from history. Rather, there is no valid history from which to learn anything. *There is nothing to learn that can change the present situation.* There is no enduring truth whether past, present or future in nihilism. All you have is now and how you *feel* about it. Look around! This is all there is or all that ever can be! It may make you feel utterly hopeless, but that is irrelevant, because nothing matters anyway.

As I mentioned, verses 9–11 list some of the fruits of nihilism. The past can teach you nothing. It will repeat itself again and there is no way we can change it. In the words of the NIV, *"What has been will be again, what has been done will be done again; there is nothing new under the sun."* Nothing new or different will come tomorrow. *"Is there anything of which one can say, 'Look! This is something new'? It was here already, long ago; it was here before our time."* Verse 11 reads, *"There is no remembrance of men of old, and even those who are yet to come will not be remembered by those who follow."* You may rewrite history but you cannot change it. Hitler was right when asked "What will history say of you" and he replied, "If we win the war we will write the history."

Secularism leads to nihilism, which in turns leads to existentialism. Ecclesiastes 12:1 would be utter nonsense to any of these systems. "Remember now your Creator in the days of your youth, before the difficult days come, and the years draw near when you say, 'I have no pleasure in them' ..." There is no Creator to remember! There is nothing to remember! Is not this deliberate ignorance of reality and history the very thing that God addresses in Psalm 90:12, "So teach us to number our days, that we may apply our hearts unto wisdom."

Existentialism is the doctrine that man forms his own essence in the course of the life he chooses to lead. It emphasizes man's responsibility for making his own nature as well as the importance of personal freedom, personal decision, and personal commitment (From the *Random House Dictionary of the English Language*.) It is a philosophy that leads to despair and affects our society from top to bottom. Up until this century, all philosophies had two things in common. (1) They all believed there was such a thing as absolute truth. Every philosopher set out to find that one absolute truth that would explain reality and integrate all knowledge into an intelligent and clearly defined system. (2) They not only believed there was such a thing as absolute truth, they believed it was worth seeking and finding. They believed they could understand reality and make a significant change by applying the ultimate truth they discovered to all of life.

The philosophy of existentialism changed all of that. Existentialism said, "There is no ultimate truth. All we know for sure is that we exist in the now. Life is like a giant box that has no doors or windows. We have no way of being sure about where we came from, what we are doing here, or where we go when we leave here. All we know is the existential now in which we exist. There is no real past or future, but only now. All you can really know for sure is what you yourself can personally experience. All else is guessing and your guess is as good as mine."

In the eyes of an existentialist, the truly intelligent person is the person who knows how to ask the right questions while fully realizing that there are no answers to those questions. In other words, once you realize there is no place to go then the smart thing to do is to relax and enjoy the ride to nowhere. The philosophy of existentialism is another facet of the *life under the sun* philosophy of Ecclesiastes. The Seeker could have been Jean Paul Sartre's grandfather! A clear understanding of Ecclesiastes leads to a clear understanding of twentieth century life and philosophy.

The real problem with existentialism is that man cannot continue to live in the awful despair of facing an unknowable reality. Suicide begins to look tempting. Sartre recognized this and told his students the first day of class that suicide may not be the ultimate answer. Francis Schaeffer saw this same fact. After taking students through both an honest evaluation of reality and the biblical view of truth, Schaeffer would give them a razor blade and a Bible and say, "These are really the only two real options." Man does not like either of those options. His love of self and his pride refuse to let him bow and worship God, and his fear of death keeps him from suicide. He tries every means to escape reality, but all of his efforts are useless. Both Ecclesiastes and the modern history of man are a record of how futile those attempts are. They prove to be vain and meaningless. Man is trapped in a real but unknowable reality, and he hates every minute of it. He hears his chains rattle even as he boasts about being a free spirit. It is important that we see that this awful despair is inevitable because God designed it that way. You cannot live and play in his ballpark successfully while totally ignoring HIM. If a sinner could find genuine meaning and contentment in this life while living in deliberate and open rebellion to God, then that sinner has beaten God at his own game!

Every *under the sun* philosophical approach to problem solving has failed and will continue to do so. Newscasters and politicians can be very provoking. They keep saying in sanctimonious tones, "We must find a way to be sure this never happens again" when they know there is no way to stop it from happening again. We are locked into one of two options. We either return to God and his truth or we continue the march to more and worse chaos. The strange part is that secular man would rather be in total chaos as long as he is the center of attention than he would fall down and admit he is a sinful creature who needs help from God!

The alternative to *under the sun* philosophies is an *over the sun* philosophy. This approach to interpreting the events of the world around us is best exemplified by the biblical doctrine nicknamed *Calvinism*. *Calvinism* is another term that needs definition.

A Calvinistic Christian believes in a God who sovereignly controls all things. God is holy, loving, gracious, faithful, and personally involved in all things. Key words for a Calvinist are "personality of God" and "sovereign control by God." Calvinistic Christians are often charged with believing that "what will be, will be, whether it is supposed to be or not." This is not at all what we believe. Some have wrongly responded to this caricature and said, "What will be, will be, *only because it was supposed to be.*" However, that still does not correctly state what we believe. We believe that **"Everything that has been, is now, or ever will be, was, is, and will be, only because God sovereignly ordained it and brought it to pass."** No one can either hinder or hasten one single thing that God has ordained. As we will see in chapter three of Ecclesiastes, everything, without a single exception, has a specific time and purpose. The believer sees both good and evil as coming from God's hand. They both serve a purpose (Romans 8:28). This awesome fact is a source of *hope* and assurance for the child of God and a cause of utter frustration and enmity to the lost man.

There are three things that characterize Calvinistic theology: (1) A personal God; (2) who is Creator of all things; (3) and who sovereignly controls all things, people, and events so they all move toward the end he has ordained for his own glory (Rom. 11:36).

If a deist (big-clock person), a secularist (nothing sacred fellow), a humanist, and a nihilist had a debate with a Christian and only empirical evidence (what you can see, taste, touch) were allowed, the Christian would lose every time. Why? Read the Book of Ecclesiastes! If "Vanity of Vanity" is the true interpretation of life as we observe it from ground level, or *under the sun*, and the data derived from that observation is all the evidence we can use, *we will lose every time!* We will be forced to agree with the Seeker, "All is Meaningless!" We might as well drink or drug our way into oblivion or descend into nihilistic anarchy or apathy.

The Apostle Paul understood the futility of living life on an under the sun plane. "If in this life only we have hope in Christ, we are of all men the most pitiable" (1 Cor 15:19 NKJV).

Think through what Paul has written. If the premise: "In this life only ..." is true, then the only conclusion is, "We are of all men most miserable." What is the premise of the Seeker in Ecclesiastes? This life is all there is. The only hope we have is what we can see, taste, and touch. What is the certain and honest conclusion to that premise? We must conclude with the Seeker, "Vanity of Vanities—Meaningless, Meaningless."

Paul mentions a great word that we need to define. Notice the word *hope* in the Corinthians text. Because *Christ is indeed risen*, we, as believers, have HOPE! That hope is rooted in a factual and trustworthy history from which we may learn unchanging truth. The resurrection of our Lord is a *historical fact and not a myth*. The truth of that fact, when believed today, gives absolute assurance and hope for tomorrow. We are not talking about wishing, but about hope. Hope is not the same as wishing. A person misuses the word when he says, "I hope it does not rain tomorrow." He

is wishing, not hoping. Hope is different from faith in that
(1) faith looks back to the promise of God for its foundation
and (2) hope looks forward in joyful anticipation to the fulfillment of the promise. Hope embodies not only the assurance that the thing promised will happen; it includes also
the desire of having it happen.

Suppose a father warns his son that if he misbehaves and
hassles his mother, he will receive a spanking when the father gets home from work. The son misbehaves and his
mother says, "That's it, I'm telling your father and you are
going to be spanked." The boy has explicit faith that his father will fulfill his "promise." He knows punishment is coming; however, he does not keep looking out the window,
hoping his father will come up the walk. He is not joyfully
looking forward to what he knows for sure is coming next.
This helps us to understand the text concerning the promise
of Christ's second coming. *"And every man that hath this hope
in him purifieth himself, even as he is pure"* (1 John 3:3 KJV). A
true faith in the second coming will produce a purifying effect in a believer's life. A believer can lose his hope, but he
cannot lose his faith.

Now think carefully! If there is no real history from which
we can learn anything, and if there is no possible way of
knowing anything in the future, is there any possible basis
for having a valid hope of anything? NO! If in *this life only*
we *place all our hope,* we are indeed in a meaningless and futile situation. We can feel the futility that the Seeker in Ecclesiastes describes so vividly.

An *under the sun* philosophy does not provide any expectation of justice. Most of us realize that most wrongs will not be made right in this life.

> *Then I returned, and considered all the oppression that is done under the sun: and look! The tears of the oppressed, but they have no comforter – on the side of their oppressors there is power, but they have no comforter. Therefore I praised the dead who were already dead, more than the living who are still alive. Yet, better than both is he who has never existed, who has not seen the evil work that is done under the sun.* (Eccl 4:1–3 NKJV)

That is one-hundred percent correct **IF** there is no heaven or hell. Paul does not leave us to wonder if we have been the victims of some cosmic joke. He begins verse 20 of 1 Corinthians 15 with the word *BUT*. Thank God for his **BUTS**. *"But now is Christ risen from the dead, and become the firstfruits of them that slept."* That is real history! It really happened! It is not a myth or fairy tale. The firstfruits guarantee a full harvest. There surely is more to follow in the future. Count on it! The logic of faith gives us an attitude exactly opposite of the logic of the *under the sun* despair in Ecclesiastes.

Paul continues with assurance that life and belief are not in vain.

> *"And as we have borne the image of the earthy, we shall also bear the image of the heavenly. Now this I say, brethren, that flesh and blood cannot inherit the kingdom of God; neither doth corruption inherit incorruption. Behold, I shew you a mystery; We shall not all sleep, but we shall all be changed, In a moment, in the twinkling of an eye, at the last trump: for the trumpet shall sound, and the dead shall be raised incorruptible, and we shall be changed. For this corruptible must put on incorruption, and this mortal must put on immortality. So when this corruptible shall have put on incorruption, and this mortal shall have put on immortality, then shall be brought to pass the saying that is written, Death is swallowed up in victory. O death, where is thy sting? O grave, where is thy victory? The sting*

of death is sin; and the strength of sin is the law. But thanks be to God, which giveth us the victory through our Lord Jesus Christ. Therefore, my beloved brethren, be ye steadfast, unmovable, always abounding in the work of the Lord, forasmuch as ye know that your labour is not in vain in the Lord" (1 Cor 15:49–58 KJV).

I remember preaching on this passage in a church where a woman in a wheelchair was sitting in the front row. She had a nerve disease that caused her shake when she got excited. Her hands started to shake and she put one on top of the other to try to keep them still. Her feet started to jump up and down and she tried to put one on top of the other one. Finaly she just gave up and started stomping her feet and waving her arms shouting, "Glory to God, it is true!"

The secularist, the humanist, the deist and the nihilist all mock every word in those verses in 1 Corinthians 15. None of them can taste a single drop of hope from these verses. These glorious truths are beyond their abilities to either perceive or enjoy. Their whole life is here and now, under the sun. They will cry out, "Away with your pie in the sky! I believe in the here and now!" They openly and loudly will mock the gospel in many circumstances. Did you ever notice that they do not mock either the gospel or the sovereignty of God at a funeral or in the emergency room at the hospital? I have never heard anyone standing by a grave and mocking the gospel about a risen Savior.

It is impossible to reject truth and still have valid hope. You can use any number of means to escape to a more palatable reality, but eventually, inevitably, you must come back to the real world. You can get spaced out! **But you must come back to reality!** You can stick your head in the sand! **But you must come up for air!** You can get on the fast lane. **But there are no exits!** You can have a real blast to-night, **but you have to wake in the morning.** If life *under the sun* is all there is, then the secularist, the humanist, the nihil-ist and the existentialist are right and Christians are the big-gest fools that ever lived. However, we Christians feel we have a right to ask some obvious questions. If we are so wrong and the Christ-rejecters are so correct, why do they need so many pills, thrills, frills, constant changes of every-thing (including marriage, and live-in mates, face-lifts, im-plants, etc.)? Why does nothing bring them any lasting peace or joy?

What am I talking about? I am not just talking about the Seeker in Ecclesiastes, I am also talking about twenty first century existentialism. I am talking about the philosophy of despair; the total death of hope. I am talking about the same thing that is being written, sung, painted, pictured on TV and in movies almost twenty four hours a day.

This is the age of despair! People feel like they live in a plastic society. "I feel unfulfilled in a meaningless life. I need to find myself and get in touch with the real me." The next time anyone gives you that "I need to find myself" diatribe to justify walking out of their responsibilities, smile and say, "With all my heart I hope you really find the real you. Then you will know what a really selfish and stupid nerd you re-ally are!"

We must constantly remember that *under the sun* is the life we see, experience, and try to make sense of without any reference to God. It is life seen from the point of ground lev-el only. This will teach us some essential lessons. First, no matter what we do or seek, if we make that our goal or our

God, it is meaningless and soon becomes vanity. You can hang Ecclesiastes 1:3 over every goal in life. At the end of every self-constructed tunnel, there will be a brick wall with a sign on it that says, "Dead end! You went the wrong way!"

Second, we must remind ourselves who this Seeker is, what his pursuit was, and how zealous and exhaustive his pursuit was. The Seeker was, next to our Lord, one of the wisest men who ever lived, one of the wealthiest man who ever lived, and one of the most powerful men who ever lived. His conscious goal was to find truth and reality regardless of the cost or effort. He was liberated, and without a single inhabitation.

In 1:13, the Seeker set his heart to experience anything he desired. "And I gave my heart to seek and search out by wisdom concerning all things that are done under heaven: this sore travail hath God given to the sons of man to be exercised therewith."

In 2:10, he withheld nothing his heart wanted. "And whatsoever mine eyes desired I kept not from them, I withheld not my heart from any joy; for my heart rejoiced in all my labour: and this was my portion of all my labour."

You and I may gloss over every failure to be satisfied with some excuse. We always have a "Yes, but" or an "If only":

- We did not have enough money. "If only we could have had another $100, then..." The Seeker had unlimited funds.

- We needed more time. "If only we could have had two more days, then..." The Seeker had no restraints on his time. He had no obligations that forced him to cut his quest short.

- We were not allowed to do what we wanted. "If only we could have been allowed to..." The Seeker was not restricted in any way. He did anything and everything his heart desired. Not a single thing was out of bounds.

- We were forced to deal with some situations that greatly hindered us. "If only we could not have been forced to..." The Seeker had no wars to fight since it was a time of peace. There were no problems with which he had to deal, nor were there any obligations clamoring for his attention.

The Seeker had every resource, spent it all and still found nothing. He experienced everything the human heart can imagine and had only an empty heart to show for all his effort. There were no excuses for his failure except that what he so diligently sought did not exist where he chose to look. The Holy Spirit recorded this man's futile efforts in order to show that if this man, with every possible advantage, could not find truth and reality in this world apart from God's revelation of himself, then no one can. That is the message of Ecclesiastes. Remember these facts about the Seeker as we travel with him on his wasted trips down one blind alley after another.

Third, we must keep reminding ourselves that there is someone *over the sun*. We do not live in a closed universe; we are not alone and without hope. Our God reigns!

CHAPTER THREE: VERSES 1:8–18

SECULAR CONCEIT'S BALLOON PUNCTURED

In our last chapter, we defined some philosophical terms that are currently prevalent in our society, especially as used by the news media. It is important to understand these terms on three counts: 1) They will continue to be part of our cultural vocabulary. 2) They will enable us to understand the Seeker's anguish in his dismal failure of not "living life successfully." 3) They help us to see why our society is going down the same road with the same disastrous result. An *under the sun* philosophy must and will lead to the secular humanistic philosophy of existentialism that rules our society today. The *under the sun* philosophy expressed by the Seeker in 1:2 inevitably leads to the sad lament of 1:3.

In verses 8–11 of chapter one, the Seeker finds more evidence for his thesis that all of life is vain and without meaning. There is an incurable sense of futility and restlessness in the human heart, simply because nothing apart from God himself can give real and permanent satisfaction. Augustine was right when he said that man was made by and for God and restless he will be until he rests in God. Life seems useless and without any real or ultimate meaning, simply because God designed it that way. Nothing at all finally satisfies, because God has deliberately made himself indispensable.

All things are wearisome,
more than one can say.
The eye never has enough of seeing,
nor the ear its fill of hearing.

What has been will be again,
what has been done will be done again;
there is nothing new under the sun.

Is there anything of which one can say,
"Look! This is something new"?
It was here already, long ago;
it was here before our time.

There is no remembrance of men of old,
and even those who are yet to come
will not be remembered
by those who follow.

(Eccl 1:8–11, NIV)

In verse 8, the Seeker states that it is not possible to describe fully the restlessness and meaninglessness he experienced. He gives two reasons for man's inability to find meaning and fulfillment. First, our human desires are never fully satisfied, and second (v. 9), the more and wider our experiences, the more we realize there is nothing new or lasting. It is the same old thing with a different label, packaged in a different box. We always want more and we want to it be the latest and the best, but the more we get, the more dissatisfied we become. "The eye is never satisfied" because God established it that way. Modern man may think himself superior to his predecessors, but like the ancient Seeker, he is never satisfied. The more truly 'modern' man becomes, the more dissatisfied and restless he becomes. On the one hand, it seems that there is so much to see and experience; on the other hand, the more we actually do see and experience, the more keenly we realize there is "nothing new under the sun" after all. Ours is an age controlled by the advertising experts. Their appealing promotions are designed to make sure we want the best and the latest of everything.

Too often, our latest purchase is outdated before we get home with it.

All our acquisitions and experiences are ultimately useless and without any real meaning. Nothing is worthwhile, simply because nothing at all finally or fully satisfies. This is true on both the personal and the philosophic level. Verse 8 describes humanity's never-ending search for that special something that will lead to true contentment. Our experience is that one bubble after another bursts. With all our genius and effort, we cannot know fully and finally *one single thing.*

In verse eight, the Seeker again emphasizes the total dissatisfaction of life *under the sun.* We never quench the insatiable desire for more of the latest and the best. The Seeker mentions two areas where this constant disappointment is manifest. First, *"the eye is never satisfied."* In his day, *Qoheleth* devoted himself to study and to acquisition of wealth. He observed all the things that were done under the sun, and concluded that all of them were meaningless. In our day, we do not have to go far to see our hearts' delights. Madison Avenue constantly bombards our eyes with advertising designed to make us feel we simply must have the latest product, and easy credit removes the obstacles that would prevent us from acquiring them.

In 1986, I bought my first computer. The computer and printer cost $3,500. I could store nearly one-hundred pages of print, or 512 K, on one floppy diskette! Five-hundred twelve K is half a megabyte of space. I had to take out one diskette and put in another and wait for it to load, but that was a small inconvenience in exchange for being able to store all that material on one 5¼ inch diskette.

Very shortly thereafter, the industry developed the first computer with a hard drive. It held ten megabytes (10,485,760 bytes) of information; over two-thousand pages of typed material. Best of all, I did not have to change any floppy diskettes. We thought we were in a writer's heaven. Then, the forty-megabyte hard drive came along with a "stacker program" that could double the storage capacity. Several months later, I bought an eighty-megabyte hard drive that could be stacked into one-hundred sixty mega-bytes. It was fantastic! The salesperson tried to talk me into a brand new two-hundred fifty-meg hard drive that could store an eight-thousand-volume library, and I laughed and said, "Who would ever need that kind of space?" A year lat-er, I bought a four-hundred twenty megabyte hard drive. Now standard hard drives are available up to seven-hundred fifty gigabytes. That is approximately 805,306,368,000 bytes.

I paid $3,500 for a machine in 1986, and today I can get one several times more powerful for less than $1,000. My wife refuses to allow me even to look at a computer maga-zine, let alone visit Circuit City or Staples. I really think I simply must have one of those new flat screens. Wow! It does not matter how many upgrades I buy, or how much new equipment I purchase, there will always be something newer and better tomorrow. The eye never has enough of seeing.

The Seeker then mentions the second area, *"the ear* [is never satisfied] *with hearing."* Camera buffs and pure-sound buffs amaze me with their passion for the latest piece of equipment. Just when I began to learn how to program a VHS recorder, the CD industry came out with digital sound equipment that made my equipment ancient. I am told my VHS player will soon be as obsolete as the old eight track cassettes. This passion is not limited to just equipment. I know people who own a thousand CDs and still buy new ones every week. They cannot possibly listen to more than one or two percent of all they already have. Please do not misunderstand the point. In no sense is the Seeker condemning new things, including the very latest thing; rather he is showing how shallow and insecure life is when we live only for those things.

In verses 9–11, the Seeker shows not only that man is never satisfied, but also that he has a short memory. He revels in the good old days that were, as I remember, not all that good. I remember the days before we had an inside toilet. We went about a hundred feet back of the house to a little wooden shed called the outhouse. Sometimes we had to shovel a foot of snow away before we could open the door. We sat on a very cold wooden board with a hole cut in it. The only toilet paper available was a Sears and Roebuck Catalogue. So much for the good old days! My grandmother used to say, "I would love to go back to the good old days, as long as I could take the refrigerator, the air conditioner, and the TV with me."

The Seeker's conclusions are set in a different era than the one in which we live. The ingenuity of man has produced many modern inventions, but people, dreams, hopes, sins, and conquests, the things that make up real life, remain the same under every era. As someone has said, the more things change, the more they stay the same. Some people mock the Bible by asking how a book written by men who lived in times and cultures so far removed from our own can have any relevance for us today. We will ignore the obvious twenty-first century arrogance in the question and reply accordingly.

What has really changed since Bible times? Back then, a husband and a wife had a fight at breakfast. The husband stomped out of the tent and pulled the tent flap shut so hard he made a twenty-four inch tear in it. He jumped on his camel and kicked it so hard that he broke four of the camel's ribs, and rode off in a cloud of dust. That was way back then in the dark ages before we had advanced into a modern educated and cultured society. But what has really changed? Today husbands and wives fight at breakfast over the same issues they fought over then. Husbands still stomp out of the house, slam a $400 storm door, and break the glass. They jump in a car with a four-hundred fifty-horsepower engine, floor the gas pedal, and speed off in cloud of smoke, leaving ten dollars worth of rubber on the driveway. Like the Virginia Slims ad used to say, "You've come a long way baby." What has really changed that could give modern man a basis for boasting? How is the twenty-first century world fundamentally different or better than the ancient world?

Pleasure-seeking man's short-term memory is deliberate. No matter how disillusioned he is with his latest toy, he will still go after the next one with a zeal and confidence that has no basis in reality. He never really admits that all is vanity, and therefore, he keeps going in the same meaningless circles. There really is nothing new. This reality kills twenty-first century man's egotism. If he is elated at breakfast with his latest acquisition, he is deflated by lunch when he learns something new and better has come along. When the Seeker writes that there is nothing new, he does not mean that cave dwellers had computers and aboriginals had automobiles. There are many new particulars, but there is a sense in which the things that make up life, the essentials, never change. Inventions may become obsolete while still on the drawing board, but man's sinful nature and attitudes have not changed at all.

Many of our amazing technological discoveries were already operating in nature. We merely copied what we observed. We learned a lot from the bees, even though we still do not know how they can fly. I understand it is aerodynamically impossible for a bee to fly. Happily, the bee does not know that.

Style and fashion change like the weather. It is amusing to see young girls wear clothing and shoes that are almost identical to those worn by their grandmothers. Old ways as well as old sins take on new names with new definitions. Living together without marriage used to be called shacking up, and was considered a sin, but it now is called a committed relationship without any real legal commitment. Our culture insists that we no longer view homosexuality as sinful, but as a different and socially acceptable alternative lifestyle or sexual orientation.

The Seeker is not downgrading either inventions or knowledge. He is showing how futile and empty life is without a knowledge of the Creator. At best, *under the sun*, we get a glimpse of how, but never why.

Verse 11 is the bitterest pill of all for the arrogant unbeliever.

> *There is no remembrance of former things; neither shall there be any remembrance of things that are to come with those that shall come after.* (KJV)

Rich and powerful men do everything possible to make themselves memorable. They give huge sums of money to have buildings built with the understanding that the building bears their name. They write autobiographies or pay others to write about them. However, the past is soon forgotten, along with those who made the past all that it was. The cry is, "What have you done for me today?" Remember that today is all there is in the secular existential society. The Apostle Peter, quoting the prophet Isaiah, echoes the same truth as the Seeker.

> *For all flesh is as grass, and all the glory of man as the flower of grass. The grass withereth, and the flower thereof falleth away: But the word of the Lord endureth forever.* (1 Peter 1:24–25a, KJV)

Yesterday I was a little boy, today I am a great grandfather, and tomorrow I will be gone and no one will know I was here. We are indeed like the flower. A seed is planted, a stem comes up, a flower appears, and the next day it withers and blows away. That is not true with the Word of God. That word is eternal and everything that it begets, including believers, is eternal. It is true that both our deeds and we will soon be forgotten. We will all share the fate of Joseph in Egypt. "A generation arose that knew not Joseph," and so a generation will arise that does not know us. Our peers will die, those who knew us personally will pass, and soon there will be no one who remembers us—even if our names are on the front of a five-million dollar college gymnasium. I wonder how many readers of this article know their grandfather's middle name or their grandmother's maiden name.

We need to look at the context of the Old Testament verses that Peter quoted. Some critics believe that two different writers wrote the Book of Isaiah. "First" Isaiah wrote chapters 1—39 and "second" Isaiah wrote chapters 40—66. One of the primary reasons for this idea is the radical difference in the content in these two sections. Isaiah 1—39 is concerned with judgment, and Isaiah 40—66 addresses the hope of the coming Messiah, embodied in the gospel promises. Isaiah assures the people that even though all men will forget, the everlasting God will never forget his promises. His Word is unchanging and his promises are secure.

> *The voice said, Cry. And he said, What shall I cry? All flesh is grass, and all the goodliness thereof is as the flower of the field: The grass withereth, the flower fadeth: because the spirit of the LORD bloweth upon it: surely the people is grass. The grass withereth, the flower fadeth: but the word of our God shall stand forever.* (Isa. 40:6–8, KJV)

The key word in the Isaiah passage above is the word *but* in verse 8. Everything in creation will wither and fade, **but** the Word of the Creator of all creation will abide forever. There is someone *over the sun*! Notice the radical difference between the hope expressed by Isaiah and the utter despair of the Seeker in Ecclesiastes. Isaiah is talking about a genuine hope that leads to godly comfort and security.

> *Comfort ye, comfort ye my people, saith your God. Speak ye comfortably to Jerusalem, and cry unto her, that her warfare is accomplished, that her iniquity is pardoned: for she hath received of the LORD's hand double for all her sins. The voice of him that crieth in the wilderness, Prepare ye the way of the LORD, make straight in the desert a highway for our God. Every valley shall be exalted, and every mountain and hill shall be made low: and the crooked shall be made*

*straight, and the rough places plain: And the glory of the LORD shall
be revealed, and all flesh shall see it together: for the mouth of the
LORD hath spoken it.* (Isa. 40:1–5, KJV)

The message of Isaiah 40:6–8 does not seem to speak comfort; instead, it is dismal and negative. It is not "I'm okay
and you're okay." It is not "think positively, everything is
lovely." Things are indeed bad, **but** a great change is coming! There is still hope!

Isaiah 40:9–11 expands on the comfort spoken to Jerusalem; it introduces the gospel as the means of her comfort.

*O Zion, that bringest good tidings, get thee up into the high
mountain; O Jerusalem, that bringest good tidings, lift up thy voice
with strength; lift it up, be not afraid; say unto the cities of Judah,
Behold your God! Behold, the LORD GOD will come with strong
hand, and his arm shall rule for him: behold, his reward is with him,
and his work before him. He shall feed his flock like a shepherd: he
shall gather the lambs with his arm, and carry them in his bosom,
and shall gently lead those that are with young.* (KJV)

That message of comfort is rooted in God's unchanging
covenant character. Those words spring from God's unchanging purpose of grace for his elect people. Isaiah's message of comfort is Paul's word of encouragement in Romans
8:28: *"And we know that all things work together for good to them
that love God, to them who are the called according to his purpose."* Do you acknowledge the truth of Paul's words, or is
Isaiah 40:27 your complaint? *"Why sayest thou, O Jacob, and
speakest, O Israel, My way is hid from the LORD, and my judgment is passed over from my God?"* Do you feel that nobody
really loves you; that no one really understands or cares;
that life is both futile and a heavy burden? Read the first
chapter of Isaiah!

Compare the writer of Ecclesiastes, "Who can show me anything certain and real? Who can direct me to a sure foundation where I can rest and feel secure?" with Isaiah 40:28, "*Hast thou not known? Hast thou not heard, that the everlasting God, the LORD, the Creator of the ends of the earth, fainteth not, neither is weary? There is no searching of his understanding,*" An *over the sun* philosophy recognizes that there is a God and he is not subject to the same limitations as humanity. He is the Creator that establishes the meaning of life; his self-revelation is the only means by which we can understand that meaning. Compare Ecclesiastes 2:24–26 with Isaiah 40:29–31.

Eccl 2:24–26: *There is nothing better for a man, than that he should eat and drink, and that he should make his soul enjoy good in his labor. This also I saw, that it was from the hand of God. For who can eat, or who else can hasten hereunto, more than I? For God giveth to a man that is good in his sight wisdom, and knowledge, and joy: but to the sinner he giveth travail, to gather and to heap up, that he may give to him that is good before God. This also is vanity and vexation of spirit.*

Isa. 40:29–31: *He giveth power to the faint; and to them that have no might he increaseth strength. Even the youths shall faint and be weary, and the young men shall utterly fall: But they that wait upon the LORD shall renew their strength; they shall mount up with wings as eagles; they shall run, and not be weary; and they shall walk, and not faint.*

The *under the sun* philosophy of the Seeker simply is not enough. Man's soul is vexed by what he observes and by what he concludes from those observations. There must be more, and thank God, **there is more!** True, creation has a clear witness (Romans 1:18–20), but it is a limited witness. It is more than sufficient to condemn all men, but not enough to save one man. Our spiritual blindness makes even this witness to be unclear. We need God himself to speak from his throne in the heavens and reveal himself to us.

Because of our self-will and sin, all we can see is a closed system. *Under the sun* is the sum total of the knowledge and experience of the unbeliever. A comparison of Jude 19 and John 14:16 and17 will help clarify this point.

> *These be they who separate themselves, sensual, having not the Spirit.* (Jude 19, KJV)

The word *sensual* here does not mean sexually immoral. Jude contrasts the spiritual and the physical realm; living by sight and living by faith in God's revelation. The sensual person bases his life and worldview on what his senses of touch, taste, smell, sight, etc. can teach him. He cannot discern spiritual things, simply because he is spiritually dead (1 Cor 2:14). The lost man lives completely in the flesh, that is, in the realm characterized by physical sensation alone. The Christian, because he is born of the Spirit, lives in the spiritual realm as well as the physical realm. The lost man lives in a closed universe. He can only experience what is *under the sun*. He can discern nothing by faith; neither can he understand God's self-revelation. A person without the Spirit is locked into what his senses can teach him. Jude 19 is the best verse in all of Scripture to describe a lost person. He is "sensual, having not the Spirit." The sum total of all that he can know or experience is that which he can filter through his senses. Unless he can smell it, touch it, taste it, hear it, see it, etc., it is beyond his capacity to comprehend. Since God is not known through our physical faculties, but only through the Holy Spirit's opening of our minds and hearts and his gift of faith, the lost man is locked into his self-imposed closed universe. He can live only on an *under the sun* level. John elaborates on this truth.

And I will pray the Father, and he shall give you another Comforter, that he may abide with you for ever; Even the Spirit of truth; whom the world cannot receive, because it seeth him not, neither knoweth him: but ye know him; for he dwelleth with you, and shall be in you. (John 14:16–17, KJV)

The lost man cannot know or receive the things imparted by the Holy Spirit, the Spirit of truth, simply because he cannot see the Holy Spirit. The *under the sun* view of life cannot know anything about a spiritual world. The physical senses cannot discover and experience spiritual life. Until the Holy Spirit gives spiritual life, the world of reality is a closed system, with no hope of help. Only special revelation plus the quickening of the Holy Spirit can take us past the sun. Explaining spiritual truth and reality to a man who is lost is like trying to explain what a rainbow looks like to a man who is blind. It is beyond his capacity to experience the reality that you see and are trying to explain.

Everything under the sun, including man, has been subjected, by God's sovereign decree, to vanity and futility by God (Romans 8:20–21). Sovereign grace is humanity's only hope.

The major theme in Ecclesiastes 1:3–11 is the utter futility of life when it is lived without meaning and purpose. Our greatest joys will become our deepest sorrows and our greatest exploits will turn to meaningless victories. We put our very best into attaining what appears to be a worthwhile goal, only to see its value vanish the moment we reach out to pick it up.

The story is told of a king who desired to reward a faithful servant who had been responsible for saving his life. The king told the man, "I will establish a starting point and will give you as much land as you are able to cover in eight hours. The only condition is that you must return to the exact point from which you started before eight hours are over."

The man was given two months to train and to explore the land. He carefully mapped out the places where he must turn in order to cover the most ground and to be able to return to the starting point in eight hours. He developed a clear, exact plan. The night before he was to run, he made sure he got a good night's sleep. He ate a good breakfast the morning of his run. The king placed a large rock at the beginning point and the man put his hand on the rock. When the clock began to strike twelve, the man took off. He knew exactly where to turn and he paced himself with confidence. The news quickly spread that the man was covering an amazing amount of ground. After seven hours and forty-five minutes, the crowd saw the man re-approaching the starting point. He was panting for breath and wiping the sweat from his face with his arm. The clock began to strike eight and with a last lunge, the man reached out and touched the stone just in time. The crown roared and the king smiled with pleasure.

As the crowd cheered, **"He made it! He made it!"** the man's wife went over to the stone, only to discover her husband, clutching the stone, was dead from exhaustion. People shook their heads and said, "The poor joker, all his valiant efforts were for nothing!"

That is the story of Ecclesiastes; this is the story of our lives!

Before we start to follow the Seeker on his futile search, let me say just a bit more about getting a feel for this book. We may compare the Old Testament Scriptures to an opera that utilizes a wide range of notes of music and movements of the body. It appeals to all of our senses in order to arouse us to a response. God designed Scripture to elicit worship with emotions as well as intellect. It appeals to the whole person. We have the impassioned preaching of prophets; the cool reflective logic and wisdom of clear thinkers; poetry; law; psalms; story-telling; and visions almost beyond description. There is no book quite like Ecclesiastes in the rest of Scripture. At its core, however, we find the same message as the rest of Scripture, even though at times that message is a bit hard to find. The Seeker's final word confirms his agreement with the rest of God's Word.

Let us hear the conclusion of the whole matter:
Fear God and keep His commandments,
For this is man's all.

For God will bring every work into judgment,
Including every secret thing,
Whether good or evil.

(Eccl 12:13, 14, NKJV)

Proverbs 9:10 is surely a page out of the same book of truth.

The fear of the LORD is the beginning of wisdom, and the know-ledge of the Holy One is understanding.

To fear God means to take God seriously, and to be wise means to live life skillfully. In other words, taking God seriously is the only way to live successfully in the eyes of

God. You cannot be successful at something you really do not take seriously. This message resonates throughout the entire Bible. This fear of God enables one to live and die successfully, regardless of the circumstances of life. A believer takes God seriously, but a lost man ignores God. The believer sees past time and *under the sun* to eternity with God *over the sun*, but the unbeliever experiences only what he can touch, taste, smell and see *under the sun*. It is impossible to live successfully as God meant life to be lived without taking God and his revealed truth seriously. In the end, the unbeliever's greatest successes will be his greatest defeats, because God defines success as moral uprightness or rectitude.

Given his basic presupposition, the Seeker's conclusions are no surprise. If one looks for truth while consciously rejecting God's revelation of himself, then the sad lament of 1:3 is inevitable. What is surprising, however, is the way the Seeker arrives at his conclusion of "Meaningless, meaningless, all is meaningless," as well as the way he states that dismal conclusion. He does not speak as a stern prophet with a sword, demanding law and order; he is not a monk suggesting withdrawal to a mountain monastery and renunciation of good food, refreshing drink, fun and laughter. He does not try to enlist recruits in a revolutionary cause, nor does he use a politician's approach of promising everything to everybody. Most of all, he is not a dreamer who speaks and writes of an unreal world of fantasy. He is a realist who accurately pictures life *under the sun*, lived without any reference to God.

We have established the Seeker's presuppositions and his conclusions. Let us look next at how he organizes and presents his information. Here is a short outline of the early chapters of Ecclesiastes.

Chapter 1:1–3. Introduction of author, theme, and tenor: We see the **man,** Solomon, son of David (v.1), his **message,** "Meaningless, meaningless, all is meaningless" (v.2), and his **mood** of despair (v.3).

Chapter 1:4–7. Argument from nature: The author describes the ever constant and but never-deviating monotony of nature. He compares its permanence to human transience.

Chapter 1:8–11. Argument from human endeavor: There is no true and lasting meaning or satisfaction in anything.

Chapter 1:12–18. Argument from human wisdom: Wisdom is both a joke and a burden. The best that wisdom can do is to clarify how bad things really are without being able to change anything. There is a sense in which ignorance is bliss.

Chapter 2:1–3. Argument from human pleasure: Mirth and laughter are hollow and empty, and only highlight the misery of life.

Chapter 2:4–11. Argument from human wealth and work: The attainment of even the greatest of accomplishments offers no true enjoyment. The result rarely compares to the initial dream, and the process of working toward the goal drains the finished product of all its satisfaction.

Chapter 2:12–23. Argument from certainty of death: Ultimately, the wisest man seems to be no better off than the fool is. Both die and leave everything behind. There are no U-Hauls behind the hearse as it heads for the graveyard.

Are you ready to quit? Are you about to ask, "John, why did you ever pick such a depressing book, especially in view

of the particular society in which we live? Why don't you
write about Romans 8 and give some hope instead of nothing but despair?" If we truly understand both Ecclesiastes
and Romans 8, we will know they both have the same basic
message. They merely arrived at the same place by different
routes. Ecclesiastes 2:24–26 is, in one sense, the heart of the
book. Consider these verses.

> *Nothing is better for a man than that he should eat and drink, and
> that his soul should enjoy good in his labor. This also, I saw, was
> from the hand of God. For who can eat, or who can have enjoyment,
> more than I? For God gives wisdom and knowledge and joy to a man
> who is good in His sight; but to the sinner He gives the work of ga-
> thering and collecting, that he may give to him who is good before
> God. This also is vanity and grasping for the wind.* (Eccl 2:24–26,
> NKJV)

On the surface, verse 24 sounds like the motto of the sixties, "Strike up the band, bury every inhibition and let it all
hang out." It echoes the philosophy of hedonism, "Let us
eat, drink and be merry. Let us enjoy ourselves and forget
everything and everybody and 'do our own thing.'" However, we must look at the rest of the verse. The author's conclusion pushes him to acknowledge the existence of God.
"This also, I saw, was from the hand of God." Solomon's attitude
at this point reflects a deistic viewpoint. He acknowledges
that there is a God who has established a certain order in the
affairs of men. Yet, that God is not connected intimately to
his creatures; he is not involved personally in the lives of
those he has created. This kind of a God does not inspire
meaning in life any more than no God at all does. Up to this
point, the Seeker has been looking at all of life as man-
centered. It is *life under the sun* without thought of any special revelation from God. Remember that *under the sun* sees

everything in the light of what man wants, what he thinks he needs, how he feels, how he reacts to reality. Everything so far (apart from a brief mention of God in 1:13) has started and ended with man. Now, the Seeker recognizes that God orders life's experiences, but, apart from revelation, God seems distant and uncaring. What is the sure result of the world and life-views of both atheism and deism? A life without God personally connected to humanity at its center and its foundation cannot possibly have true and lasting meaning, but only will lead to ultimate despair.

The child of God has a God-centered world and life-view. Everything begins with God and reflects his glory. Everything, including the bumps in the road and the tough hills to climb, are seen as a gift from God. One of the gifts from God includes the ability to see and believe that all things come from God! In the age of the New Covenant, a God-centered worldview will focus on Jesus Christ as God's ultimate and final revelation of himself to humanity. Knowing and loving God as he has revealed himself in Christ provides meaning and fulfillment in all of life.

No child of God, no matter how difficult his life may be, will ever stand on the shores of eternity, look back over his life, and lament with the Seeker, "Meaningless, meaningless, all is meaninglessness."

We must remember that everything said by the Seeker is the product of his *under the sun* philosophy. He will make statements as they appear to his human wisdom, but in reality are not true. The situation is similar to the words of Job's friends. The Holy Spirit has faithfully recorded exactly what they said, but some of what they said was false; it did not reflect reality. So too, the Book of Ecclesiastes records the conclusions of the Seeker's reasoning, although his reasoning often is wrong in the light of God's revealed Word. The Seeker, in several places, insists that men are no different from animals because both die. Likewise, a wise man is no better off than a fool, since both die. Ecclesiastes contains many statements that appear to solely human reasoning to be true, but are seen as false by any student of Scripture. We must remember that what is true of the man in 1 Corinthians 2:14 (a man without the Spirit of God is unable to discern the things that come from the Spirit of God) is true of the Seeker.

What view of God do we find in Ecclesiastes? Even though the Seeker writes out of his *under the sun* philosophy, he is a man who once knew and walked with God, and who later was restored to fellowship with God. This fact is never very far from the surface.

The first mention of God is in 1:13 and sets an undertone for the book.

> *And I gave my heart to seek and search out by wisdom concerning all things that are done under heaven: this sore travail hath God given to the sons of man to be exercised therewith.* (KJV)

God is sovereign in all the affairs of man! The only word for God used in Ecclesiastes is *Elohim;* used thirty times. *Elohim* is a name that denotes the absolute sovereignty of God. The writer never uses the word *Yahweh,* translated LORD, which is the covenant name for God.

In spite of his *under the sun* philosophy, the Seeker has three distinct views of God that come through in the book. God is (1) *the Creator, (2) the Lawgiver, and (3) the Judge.* He designs, controls, and judges all of life. If life were a play,

God would be the writer, the director, the producer and the stage manager. If life were a ballgame, God would own the ballpark, make the rules for the game, and enforce them as the umpire. He is the sovereign Creator who controls everything. He chooses the times, the seasons, the places, and the events; he ordains them all and his absolute sovereignty brings each one to pass in his time, and each thing is beautiful in his time (Eccl 3:11). The *under the sun* philosophy finds this perplexing and frustrating, because God is, in this philosophy, impersonal and unknowable.

For those with an *over the sun* philosophy, the message is, "Relax!" "Trust him!" Just say "Great" and keep on going. The sovereign creator, lawgiver and judge is the father who loves his children and works all things together for their good. He is not distant and uncaring, but loves his people so much that he came to earth to become one of them. He identifies with their limitations and temptations, and is not ashamed to call them brothers. Such a sovereign and loving God is one whom we can trust and love in return.

THE SURE FRUITS OF IDOLATRY

In this chapter, we will examine the teacher's argument from human wisdom.

As he posits his thesis of the meaninglessness of life, Solomon frames part of his argument in the form of questions. The first question is in 1:3.

> *What does man gain from all his labor at which he toils under the sun?* (NIV)

The Seeker raises the right question. "Does life really make any sense? Does my life have any real purpose? Are there any enduring and lasting joys or is my life just like nature's endless and meaningless cycles?" In verses 4–7, the writer describes those endless cycles in what we might call a treadmill existence.

> *Generations come and go, but the earth remains forever. The sun rises and the sun sets, and hurries back to where it rises. The wind blows to the south and turns to the north; round and round it goes, ever returning on its course. All streams flow into the sea, yet the sea is never full. To the place the streams come from, there they return again.* (NIV)

The second question is in 1:10.

> *Is there anything of which one can say, "Look! This is something new"?* (NIV)

Here, the Seeker asks if there is any light at the end of the tunnel. Is there any legitimate ground on which to expect a change for the better in the future? His conclusion is that there is no real hope of change for the better in the future; rather, things will get worse. We already know the entire story; we are locked into a closed system. This is the certain conclusion to an honest application of the *under the sun* philosophy.

In his book, *Ecclesiastes, An Introduction and Commentary*, Michael Eaton provides an excellent outline of chapters one and two. It will be helpful to use this as a road map in our travels through Ecclesiastes.

"The Failure of Wisdom to Satisfy Secular Life" (1:12–18)

> After the pessimism of 1:2–11, the following section shuts off all escape routes. Will a man seek refuge in wisdom? It will only frustrate its secular devotees (1:12–18). Will he then hide from life's problems by squeezing the juice out of its pleasures? The juice turns sour (2:1–11). Does he live in a man-centered world devoid of absolutes? There is one undeniable absolute: death (2:12–23). Elsewhere, the Teacher portrays wisdom as one of life's blessings, but in 1:12–18 the argument is different. Wisdom has value, but it will fail to solve the problems of life. (Michael A. Eaton, *Ecclesiastes, An Introduction and Commentary* [Leicester, England: IVP, 1983], 61.)

In 1:12, the Seeker identifies and describes himself as a king over Israel in Jerusalem. As king of Israel, he belonged to the only nation that had received special, personal revelation from God that included the one true gospel. Unhappily, he ignored that revelation during the time-period described in Ecclesiastes. When the Seeker had become king of Israel, he had prayed to God for wisdom because he knew that was one of the greatest gifts that God could give (1 Kings 3:5–9). God heard and answered that prayer positively (1 Kings 3:10–12). Solomon was a man who knew from personal experience the snares of sin and devices of Satan. The proverbs that he wrote verify this. This man had tasted the love of

God and recorded it in a poetic analogy in the Song of Solomon. However, he also was the man who forsook the beloved for the world, the flesh, and idols. He left the bread of heaven for the tasteless husks of this world.

Most important of all, the Seeker was a man loved and chosen by God before he was even born. This is why God rescued him from his journey into existential meaninglessness and brought him back to the joy of forgiveness and fellowship. With his father David, he could say from personal experience, "He restores my soul."

These facts, when considered soberly, warn us against playing with fire. If a person like the Seeker, who had known God as well as his other writings indicate, could be so careless and backslide so far, then what about us? If ever there was a legitimate warning and a beacon, it is the Seeker. His behavior teaches us to stay close to the Savior.

In verse 13, we have an indication of the intensity of the Seeker's search. He gave his heart (the NIV reads, "I devoted myself") to finding truth and reality. His was not a weekend pursuit, but a complete preoccupation with one all-consuming goal. This is the story of a true believer who temporarily lost sight of God's objective revelation (the Bible) and forgot him who is *over the sun*. The Seeker is not the only true believer who experienced this problem. The author of Psalm 73 traces identical steps away from and back to God.

Ecclesiastes 1:13 through 2:11 presents a perfect picture of you and me when we turn our eyes and hearts away from the truth. We do not have to fashion a golden calf in order to turn away from God and commit idolatry. Worship of false gods can take place at a very subtle level. The books we read, the television we watch, the art we view, and the music we hear affect us, both emotionally and spiritually. Artists are promoters of their view of truth and reality. They peddle religion, and not just entertainment. This is why many Christians feel uncomfortable in the presence of abstract art. The more meaningless a piece of abstract art is, the more successful the artist has been in his work. The abstract artist sees no rhyme or reason to life, but only chaos, confusion and despair. If ten people look at a piece of abstract art and each person interprets it differently, the artist would be elated. If most of the ten people saw the same thing, the artist would feel he had utterly failed. There is no single correct interpretation, because there is no fixed meaning. Utter confusion and meaninglessness is the abstract artist's goal. A biblical worldview is opposed to this philosophy and its proponents would respond to such an artist, "Your unbelieving heart has misrepresented both my Father and his world."

You, your children, and the rest of society, will feel an emotional response to an artist's message, whether presented on canvas, music or dress style. If you, or your children, immerse your minds and emotions in the counterculture's art forms, you may find yourselves overcome by the negative feelings produced by those stimuli. You cannot put pork into the top of a meat grinder and expect beef to come out the other end. Likewise, you cannot immerse your mind and heart in the Word of God and not experience something of a joy unspeakable.

Both MTV and Mozart express their *feelings* about reality with the same vehement intensity as does the Seeker in Ec-

clesiastes. They express what they think about God, his creation, and themselves. Different ideas about God produce
radically different feelings and lifestyles. Respective feelings
and attitudes must follow various theologies. Actions do not
exist in a void; they spring from beliefs. Ideas have consequences. Your ideas about God precede and lead to your
lifestyle. I cannot emphasize too strongly that human beings, living as apostates from God's revealed truth, ultimately must become cynical and frustrated about life and reality.
God fixed it that way. Do not be surprised when it happens
and be fully prepared for it to get worse! People often ask,
"How can Mr. X feel the way he does with all he has?" I
usually reply, "How can he NOT feel that way, given his belief and lifestyle?"

The Seeker, in chapter one and verse thirteen, speaks of
life as a "sore trial' or "heavy burden."

*I devoted myself to study and to explore by wisdom all that is
done under heaven. What a heavy burden God has laid on men!*
(NIV)

The "sore trial" or "heavy burden" of this verse is the en-
forced journey through life with no compass or map that
leads to one blind alley after another. It is the treadmill existence described in chapter one. The Seeker echoes Allen
Ginsburg's Theorem, "You can't win, you can't break even,
and you can't even quit the race." At this point, the Seeker is
not expressing repentance for his folly. He is merely being
honest as he expresses pain and despair in his failure to find
truth and meaning in life.

Notice the two sections of verse 13. The first sentence introduces three facets of the search for meaning. (1) Approach: The search is intense. The Seeker informs us that he

"devoted himself" in his search. (2) Method: The search is careful. He did not discard his brains and follow his emotions. He did not seek in a hit or miss fashion, but rather, he used wisdom. (3) Scope: The search is thorough. The Seeker did not take a "random sampling" but explored "all things" done under the sun. The second sentence comprises part two of the verse. After Solomon considers all the things he has explored, he heaves a deep sigh of despair. The more thorough the search that results in the acquisition of more true wisdom, the deeper will be that sigh of despair. In verses 17 and 18, the Seeker develops the idea that here he only mentions; namely, that wisdom, true wisdom, is a plague and not a cure for the problem that he faces. This is an amazing, but correct, conclusion.

In verse 14, the Seeker reviews his position. He reminds himself of what he has seen and how he has evaluated all of the things that he has done. His conclusion is still the same, "all of them are meaningless."

> *I have seen all the things that are done under the sun; all of them are meaningless, a chasing after the wind.* (NIV)

Here, the Seeker adds a new descriptive phrase. He compares the meaninglessness of life to chasing after the wind. The KJV translates verse 14 this way:

> *I have seen all the works that are done under the sun; and, behold, all is vanity and vexation of spirit.*

I find the NIV "chasing after the wind" far more descriptive than "vexation of spirit." The word *chasing* in the phrase means, "to tend a flock, to graze, to feed upon." All the things done under the sun are meaningless and are like *feeding upon wind*. Trying to find meaning and permanent satisfaction out of anything *under the sun* is like trying to eat the wind to satisfy your hunger. Imagine a starving man trying to pick up and swallow a spoonful of wind. That is exactly what a person, made in the image of God, does when he tries to find meaning and purpose in life, in an empty and fleeting world.

Imagine a table full of food: a steaming T-bone steak, a baked potato with butter and sour cream, green salad, and apple pie with ice cream. Beside it is an empty table. Now imagine a starving man who has been hypnotized and told that the first table was empty, and the second table had a full-course steak dinner. The man puts on a napkin that does not exist and smiles as he eats an imaginary feast. When he is finished, he may even burp. He gladly pays a waiter $50.00 and walks away, rubbing his stomach. When he is brought out of the state of hypnosis, he has stomach cramps from his intense hunger. He asks, "How can I possibly be so hungry after all I ate?"

That is precisely what the lost man does every day of his life! He chases the wind and keeps gulping down imaginary food that cannot satisfy his soul. The ultimate and eternal vexation of spirit will be the moment in eternity when he realizes that while he was "chasing the wind," he was wasting and rejecting every moment and every good gift given by God. He spurned the real steak for imaginary meat. He will see one opportunity after another forever lost, and all for a mouthful of wind!

Grey-headed secularists are hard to counsel. They have seen all that the eye can see, and they have concluded that it all is meaningless. Grey-headed saints do not need counsel;

they are more than qualified to give it. They have tasted and seen that the Lord is good.

Verse 15 reminds us that all ideas have consequences. Basic presuppositions have certain results that are not always desirable, but are inescapable. Verse 15 is one of the sure conclusions that secular humanism cannot escape.

> *That which is crooked cannot be made straight: and that which is wanting cannot be numbered.* (KJV)

As we mentioned earlier, *under the sun* offers no hope of real change from anything or anyone. There is no new birth, no answer to prayer, no grace to either forgive or change. There are no answers to life's real problems apart from special revelation.

The existing state of affairs is fixed and unchangeable. Crooked things are twisted beyond repair, because *under the sun*, there is no power greater than man's own will, and that is what caused the problem in the first place. The heart of man is deceitful and cannot cure itself, let alone affect a cure for others. A leper can infect a healthy man, but he cannot cure either himself or another leper. The sinner cannot restore anything, but he is too proud to seek God and his grace for help. The secularist will watch his world crumble and know in his heart that there is not an ounce of hope of real change and still refuse to admit he is merely a poor creature, totally dependent on a sovereign God.

My mother lived next door to a doctor who tested drug treatment programs for the government. She told us she had never tested a program that had over a three or four percent success record. She somehow became involved in testing Teen Challenge, a Christian group. The cure rate was so high that she deliberately padded the figures as low as she could. If anyone slipped one time in the three-year testing period, she did not count that as a success. She then made this amazing admission, "Next week I go to Washington and give my report. When I give the statistics that prove a cure rate of over sixty percent, ten different government agencies will whip out their checkbooks and ask 'To whom should we write the check?' They will ask, 'How did they do it?' The moment I mention the Bible, every single person will close his checkbook and walk away." Secular humanists are so opposed to the Bible and the grace of God that they would rather have a person stay on drugs than have him cured by faith in Christ! The ACLU, and those who share their secular humanistic philosophy, would cite separation of church and state and sue any government agency that used religion to cure people on drugs, no matter how successful the program was. The gospel of God's sovereign grace has no place in the secular humanists' ideology; they must deny it as an option for effective cure, even if the result is that addicts stay on drugs.

By *that which is wanting*, the Seeker means the things that are the real essentials for a full, meaningful, and contented life. The fruit of the Spirit—love, joy, peace and all those other good conditions for which the human hearts yearns—cannot be produced by the philosophy of secular humanism or any other philosophy based on human wisdom. Only the Holy Spirit can produce those blessed things through the gospel.

This fact is true physically. Our Lord taught in Matthew 6:27 that no one, by worry or self-effort, is able to add a single hour to his life, change his height or the color of his eyes, or alter many physical deformities. Man cannot change his basic temperament, and surely, he cannot change his wicked heart! By sheer willpower, he may suppress some of the worst sins, but usually not for any great length of time.

This fact is true **intellectually.** There is a limit to every person's basic IQ and nothing can change it. A child with Down's syndrome cannot, by an act of free will, a magic pill or an operation, turn into an Einstein.

This fact is true **socially.** Man's wisdom cannot identify the real problems in life, let alone find the correct answers. Rule by reason, conscience, and truth very quickly turns into rule by guns and terror when the God of the Bible is ignored. Evolution claims we have climbed our way up from our animal ancestors in the jungle, but when we look around, it appears that animal instinct and the lust of the flesh still rules in our modern jungle. "Might makes right" is not only the rule of the jungle; it is the rule among nations.

God's providential rule of the universe may include painful incidents that we cannot avoid, and some things that cannot in any way be changed or shared. If we could see beyond today, it would probably destroy us! We would think only of the bad things. The awful realization that I could do absolutely nothing to effect lasting change would be an intolerable reality.

Imagine that you were a genius who truly understood history. You grasp the truth of humanity's sinfulness. You clearly see what is inevitable, and yet you can do absolutely nothing to change or stop it. What would you do without Romans 8:28 as a pillow on which to lay your head? You would share the vexation of spirit the Seeker experienced.

One of the most amazing anomalies recorded in Ecclesiastes is that the more true wisdom the Seeker gained, the keener he felt his frustration and hopelessness. Wisdom is not the answer; but is actually part of the problem. The best and the brightest in every field of endeavor, whether science, history, art, poetry, dress, psychology, travel, friends, etc., will testify that it is impossible to find reality, meaning, purpose or enduring satisfaction in anything *under the sun.*

In verse 16, the Seeker reflects on his acquisition of wisdom.

> *I thought to myself, "Look, I have grown and increased in wisdom more than anyone who has ruled over Jerusalem before me; I have experienced much of wisdom and knowledge."* (NIV)

He evaluates his progress. He has indeed seen and experienced whatever his heart desired. He has exceeded everyone before him in his wisdom and knowledge. In verse 17, he tells us that he stopped and carefully analyzed all he had learned. Exactly what did he learn from all his wisdom and knowledge, including his experiences with madness and folly? He again comes to the same conclusion; it was a "chasing after the wind;" it was all meaningless.

> *Then I applied myself to the understanding of wisdom, and also of madness and folly, but I learned that this, too, is a chasing after the wind. (NIV)*

In verse 18, we find a very surprising statement.

> *For with much wisdom comes much sorrow; the more knowledge, the more grief.* (NIV)

This is the conclusion to the discussion that began in 1:13. If the Seeker were writing in our day, he could have decided to try the intellectual route. "I need to go to college and get a few degrees. The university is the place where true know-

ledge is gained." That is a popular, but very misguided notion today. An individual spends a few years to research,
explore, synthesize, analyze, deduce and induce and graduates with an A+. When he is finished, he looks at the dip-
loma and realizes how stupid he still is! A freshman in college knows everything. By the time he is a senior, he has far
more questions than answers.

Learning, education, as an end in itself is like an addiction. It is easy to become a "professional student." Scripture
speaks of those who are "ever learning, but never coming to
the knowledge of the truth." People can love the pursuit of
truth even while denying that there is such a thing. "True
Truth," a phrase coined by Francis Schaeffer, is really the
last thing they want. They are looking for intellectual reasons to reject the clear truth that God has revealed about
himself. Romans, chapter one, makes this abundantly clear.

Malcolm Muggeridge was the favorite guru and idol of
the intellectual radicals in England during the twentieth century. Through the influence of C.S. Lewis, Muggeridge converted to Christianity. He said this about education:

> Education, the great mumbo jumbo and fraud of the ages,
> purports to equip us to live, and is prescribed as a universal
> remedy for everything from juvenile delinquency to premature
> senility. For the most part, education only serves to enlarge
> stupidity, inflate conceit, enhance credulity and put those sub-
> jected to it at the mercy of the brainwashers with printing
> presses, radio, and television at their disposal.

It is essential to see that the Seeker does not disparage
education. To the contrary, he encourages you to get all of it
that you possibly can. What he is saying is that the meaning
of life and eternity cannot be found in all of the classrooms,

science labs, and libraries in the world. Reality and truth can only be found in a right relationship with God our Creator. If you enter college as a spiritual idiot, and God does not enlighten you, you will graduate as an *educated* spiritual idiot. The only difference will be that you are now a hundred times more conceited and arrogant in your spiritual ignorance!

If education, in and of itself, made life meaningful, then a university campus should be a place of peace and contentment. It is the exact opposite. During the turbulent sixties, the average college campus was the scene of constant unrest and uprisings. In our day of postmodernism, the university is the breeding ground of existentialism and apathy. The official attitude of the administration may be multi-cultural tolerance, but it too often results in intellectual pride and intolerance towards those who disagree. Many movements that have started on university campuses have resulted in rebellious attitudes and riots. How many new vices have begun among the educated? Drugs, alcohol, and unbridled sex are the hallmarks of the average college fraternity. Education, like everything else, is meaningless apart from God.

Remember, the Seeker is not saying, "Do not think." He is saying, "Do not think independently of God. Think God's revealed thoughts after Him."

Verse 17 and 18 are a summary statement.

Then I applied myself to the understanding of wisdom, and also of madness and folly, but I learned that this, too, is a chasing after the wind. For with much wisdom comes much sorrow; the more knowledge, the more grief. (NIV)

Is the saying, "Ignorance is bliss" true after all? We have all heard people say, "What you don't know won't hurt you," implying that the hurt comes in the knowledge of the truth. In 1:13, the Seeker asserted that wisdom is not good, but a plague; verses 17 and 18 are his support. In order to understand the point, we must follow the logic of the Seeker's argument.

First, earthly things are all vanity—meaningless. This point has been established many times over.

Second, the more deeply we search for the truth, the more distinctly we see the utter vanity of all things. The closer we get to reality, the uglier it becomes. This is because of man's sin and selfishness.

Third, in this way, *wisdom utterly destroys illusions and makes things appear in their true light.* In other words, wisdom destroys daydreams. Wisdom forces us to face and acknowledge reality.

Fourth, the possession of wisdom, therefore, can only highlight how futile and vain things really are, and this realization in turn can only cause pain and distress. The wiser, and more truly honest with reality a man is, the deeper his despair apart from hope in the grace of God. Man is indeed boxed in, but the box, or prison, is of his own making.

Fifth, if the world is nothing but vanity, and the Seeker has proven that it is, then the more you recognize how vain it all is, the worse off you really are. This is the statement in verse 18, *"For with much wisdom comes much sorrow; the more knowledge, the more grief."*

It is vital to remember that the Seeker is talking about man's wisdom apart from God. This is the viewpoint of the person who put all his hope in this world and what it has to offer. All of his vaunted wisdom is, in reality, a lie. The more such a person comes to terms with reality, the more he realizes the hopelessness of the situation.

Some years ago, my wife started to listen to Ted Koppel on *Night Line*. Then she subscribed to a few conservative magazines and papers, and she started listening to Rush Limbaugh. I watched my wife change from a quiet, unassuming woman to an outspoken militant conservative. My son phoned me one day and said, "Did you hear your wife on the radio today?" Then came Crossfire and next, the Capitol Gang. Sometimes, my wife would be listening to a liberal news program and come into my office saying, "John, they are lying through their teeth and they know it!" At times, I felt like going into the living room to see if she had smashed the television with a brick.

It really is frustrating watching people spin the truth into a lie and vice versa. It is hard to see how one-sided the liberal media is, and at the same time know there is not a single thing you can do about it. But dare we just give up and quit trying? Dare we allow wrong to stand unchallenged? Do we believe that the election of conservatives can fundamentally change our society? No! Do we really believe we will win the fight and turn this planet into another Garden of Eden? No! Are we therefore going to stop trying to defeat error? No, no, a thousand times no! Maybe God will send revival in spite of politicians. Regardless, we will work and pray for the truth, as we understand it, to be heard and believed. We have no illusions; it is impossible to win the struggle unless God himself bares his arm and speaks with power. Wisdom clearly reveals that we can expect things to get worse and worse, but by God's grace, we want our Lord to say of us what he said of the woman in Mark 14:8, "she did what she could."

The failure of wisdom in 1:12–18 does not downplay true wisdom nor does it discourage the search for it. Rather, it rubs the secularist's nose in his own philosophy. It says, "So you were too intelligent to follow God's wisdom and went on your own. How did you make out? How well are you sleeping at night? How do feel as you face a new day, fully understanding the utter hopelessness of reality?"

The problem is not with the concept of wisdom, but rather with the origin of wisdom. Whose wisdom will we follow? James presents the other side of the coin on the subject of wisdom.

> *Who is wise and understanding among you? Let him show it by his good life, by deeds done in the humility that comes from wisdom. But if you harbor bitter envy and selfish ambition in your hearts, do not boast about it or deny the truth. Such "wisdom" does not come down from heaven but is earthly, unspiritual, of the devil. For where you have envy and selfish ambition, there you find disorder and every evil practice. But the wisdom that comes from heaven is first of all pure; then peace-loving, considerate, submissive, full of mercy and good fruit, impartial and sincere. Peacemakers who sow in peace raise a harvest of righteousness.* James 3:13–18 (NIV)

What a difference the revelation of God's truth makes in every area of life!

We may compare Ecclesiastes to a wise old man who instructs youth about life. He lays it all out clearly, honestly, logically, and realistically. His listeners know that the old man understands his subject matter and that he is speaking the truth. However, each one also believes, "I am different." Without exception, they all "know better." They are convinced that they will escape the problems and errors of which the old man speaks. In order to be consistent with their belief about their personal freedom, they must trust themselves alone. The wise old man will someday hear every one of the youths lament, "meaningless, meaningless, it was all meaningless." He will say, in pity, not contempt, "See, I told you so."

Proverbs 1:20–33 is the story of every person who lives without the wisdom that comes from knowledge of God.

> *Wisdom calls aloud in the street, she raises her voice in the public squares; at the head of the noisy streets she cries out, in the gateways of the city she makes her speech: "How long will you simple ones love your simple ways? How long will mockers delight in mockery and fools hate knowledge? If you had responded to my rebuke, I would have poured out my heart to you and made my thoughts known to you. But since you rejected me when I called and no one gave heed when I stretched out my hand, since you ignored all my advice and would not accept my rebuke, I in turn will laugh at your disaster; I will mock when calamity overtakes you — when calamity overtakes you like a storm, when disaster sweeps over you like a whirlwind, when distress and trouble overwhelm you. Then they will call to me but I will not answer; they will look for me but will not find me. Since they hated knowledge and did not choose to fear the LORD, since they would not accept my advice and spurned my rebuke, they will eat the fruit of their ways and be filled with the fruit of their schemes. For the waywardness of the simple will kill them, and the complacency of fools will destroy them; but whoever listens to me will live in safety and be at ease, without fear of harm." (NIV)*

The disasters written there reflect the kind of consequences that await every person who rejects God's wisdom and goes on his own. Every person who plays God and makes his own rules will have to endure the experience of Proverbs 1:26. This portion of Scripture contains a horrible indictment of the self-will that defies God's wisdom. However, it will never be true of the person who puts his faith and hope in

Jesus Christ. That person will never be ashamed or disappointed.

As we consider the failure of *under the sun* wisdom, we must remember chapter two and verses 24–25, or we, too, will succumb to the Seeker's despair.

> *A man can do nothing better than to eat and drink and find satisfaction in his work. This too, I see, is from the hand of God, for without him, who can eat or find enjoyment?* (NIV)

On the surface, the first sentence sounds like more of the same pessimism. Is this merely the "Eat, drink and be merry, for tomorrow you die" philosophy of the Hedonist? No, it is not. When we read the next sentence, we see God very much considered. Eliminate the phrase *without him* in verse 25, and the MTV crowd is dead right! It really is an either/or situation. Either the *under the sun* philosophy is correct, and this life with its empirical experiences is all there is to our existence, or the *over the sun* approach is true and is the only ideology that will lead to ultimate satisfaction. Hollywood and *Playboy* respond appropriately **IF** the *under the sun* experience is all there is in life. It is a tragedy, but we must admit that the modern secularist is often more honest in facing the logical conclusions to his philosophy than many professing Christians are in facing the clear implications of their faith. Every Sunday, in many evangelical churches, those who call themselves God's people duplicate the essence of the following dialogue between Elijah and the people of Israel.

> *Elijah went before the people, and said, "How long will you waver between two opinions?* [A common question] *If the LORD is God, follow him; but if Baal is God, follow him."* [A common sense response] *But the people said nothing.* [A common answer] (1 Kings 18:21, NIV)

The preacher preaches the Word, the people nod in agreement or say amen, and life goes on without a single change. The great problem is not that people do not know, but that people do not care. A university student took a survey on campus attitudes. He asked this question: "Which do you think is the bigger problem on campus today, ignorance or apathy?" The first student polled responded, "I don't know and I don't care." He could have said, "Apathy rules, but who cares." It is one thing for the secularist who openly denies there is truth to be apathetic, but a child of God who openly professes faith in the grace of a sovereign God should not carry a similar attitude. Elijah's ultimatum, "If the Lord is God, then follow him" is ignored by the secularists, because there is no God in their system. Their actions are consistent with their beliefs. However, too many of God's people openly say, "Yes, the Lord is indeed God," but they do not follow him. If pressed with their inconsistency, they "answer not a word."

Seeing and consciously acknowledging that all things are of God is the only way to have comfort now and hope for the future. We will see in Ecclesiastes 3 that there is genuine hope for believers because all things are under the control of a sovereign God. God's children are not immune from the pain that results from living in a fallen and cursed world, but they can have confidence in the loving God who orders all the events of their lives to bring about their good and his glory. Without that trust, the vicissitudes of life may well lead to an attitude of despair or a retreat into apathy.

Do you feel the unbearable burden of reality? Is your personal situation ugly and painful? Are you ready to adopt the

Seeker's philosophy of meaninglessness? Then listen carefully to the words of a much greater teacher than Solomon.

> *Come unto me, all ye that labour and are heavy laden, and I will
> give you rest. Take my yoke upon you, and learn of me; for I am meek
> and lowly in heart: and ye shall find rest unto your souls. For my
> yoke is easy, and my burden is light.* (Matt. 11:28–30, KJV)

Are you ready to say, "I cannot make it! I give up!
Enough is enough. I quit! It is not worth the effort"? If you
are a child of God, let me assure you that *not only are you
going to make it,* you are going to make it with flying colors.
You are going to be *"more than* a conqueror" because the
mighty grace of God is more than sufficient to keep you.
You can, and by sovereign grace and power, you most assu-
redly will be enabled, to *"do all things through Christ who
strengthens you."*

I often tell a believer going through a difficult time, "I
read the last chapter and we win—big time!

LOOKING IN THE WRONG PLACES

In previous chapters on Ecclesiastes, we have called the author of this unique book The Seeker. In chapter one, The Seeker introduces his thesis that all is vanity. We have delineated his characterization of life as a treadmill existence, because of the way he himself describes the endless, busy, meaningless world of existence. In Chapter 2, the focus sharpens. The Seeker shows what can, and cannot, be learned from the personal experience of the one man who "has done the whole scene." The Seeker enumerates a list of the pleasures and achievements that he had experienced in life. Many of them were very pleasant and extremely enjoyable, but they were all short lived. There was not a single thing that gave the man any true and lasting satisfaction.

One of the first lessons we can learn from his narration is that **getting** things and **enjoying** them are two different matters, both of which are gifts of God.

"Thus we must conclude that even the most mundane and earthly things of life do not lie within man's grasp to donate to himself. The source of all good, contrary to the expectations of most systems of humanism and idealism, cannot be located in man. "He doesn't have it," as the old saying goes. It is all beyond him. Rather, it must come from God. Man must get accustomed to realizing that if he is to receive satisfaction from his food and drink, that satisfaction, like all satisfaction, must come from God." (*Ecclesiastes — Total Life,* by Walter C. Kaiser, Jr., Moody Press, p. 45)

The writer of Ecclesiastes was both king and teacher. He had wealth, power, freedom, knowledge, and wisdom without limitations. He was neither a rich simpleton nor a poor genius. He had all the resources and all the abilities necessary to qualify him to evaluate reality. There were no excuses if he did not find that for which he looked.

The author's choice of words in 2:12 demonstrates that he means for his experience to be definitive for all men. If he, with all his power and resources, could not find it, it does not exist for anyone to find.

> *Then I turned myself to consider wisdom and madness and folly; for what can the man do who succeeds the king? – Only what he has already done.* (Eccl 2:12, NKJV)

The Seeker is not just out on a lark looking for fun. He knows that temporary pleasure is a bubble; he is looking for lasting satisfaction. His goal is reality, truth, and the ultimate meaning of life. He wants an accurate explanation of the world around him and his place in that world. He is also looking for power in his struggle with his inner self.

At the outset, in 1:13–15, The Seeker warns us that the pursuit was in vain. We must not come to an erroneous conclusion based on the brevity of 1:13–15. These verses are brief, not because The Seeker was casual in his quest for the meaning of life, but because they are a summary of the means that he used in his pursuit. The Seeker was so thorough in his search that he uses the word *devoted* to describe how he studied and explored with every ounce of his strength as he sought to find truth. His endeavor was not like that of a person who worked forty hours a week and carefully planned his weekends. His efforts were full-time. All of his energies, resources, and waking hours were spent in studying, exploring, testing, and analyzing life. The conclusion he reached is the same one at which every honest secularist arrives, even though the secularist often will not admit it.

In 1:16—2:11, The Seeker takes us through the journey that he took. We looked at his attempt to gain insight from human wisdom in a previous chapter. In 2:12—2:26, he shares the lessons he learned from his journey—all is meaningless—life is not really worth living. The Seeker's pronouncement in 2:22–26 is both honest and frustrating.

> *What does a man get for all the toil and anxious striving with which he labors under the sun? All his days his work is pain and grief; even at night his mind does not rest. This too is meaningless. A man can do nothing better than to eat and drink and find satisfaction in his work. This too, I see, is from the hand of God, for without him, who can eat or find enjoyment? To the man who pleases him, God gives wisdom, knowledge and happiness, but to the sinner he gives the task of gathering and storing up wealth to hand it over to the one who pleases God. This too is meaningless, a chasing after the wind.*
> (NIV)

The author is not condemning any of the things that he mentions. He is telling us that when we live for them, any of them or all of them, they become our gods, and, as the Seeker so painfully discovers, they make very poor gods. Trust in gods that cannot deliver ultimately leads to disillusionment and futility.

In 2:24 and 25, the Seeker traces the problem to God. He even sees God as giving the problem of utter futility to the sons of men. Paul, in Romans 8:18—25, says much the same thing as he addresses the futility to which creation was subjected as a result of Adam's sin. This subjection was not by its own will, but by God's will.

Genesis 3:16 describes how thoroughly sin reversed the God-ordained roles for men and women established at creation. The helpmate becomes a competitor for the throne and the protector becomes a tyrant. Women use their need and right for nurture to force men to give them what they want. "If you loved me, as God tells you that you should, you would give me what I want." Men use their God-ordained responsibility to be the leader as justification to force women to be their personal slaves. "Scripture says that you must do whatever I tell you. You must submit to me." Sin destroyed everything. The creature who has lost God would now use everybody and everything for his own ends. Interpersonal relationships are subject to futility.

Genesis 3:17–19 describes how the good and perfect environment became a hostile enemy. The ground that had produced good plants now produces thorns and thistles. Labor that had been pleasant is now painful. Man, who had lived harmoniously with his environment, is now in constant competition with everything and everybody: himself, his wife, the physical environment, and even God himself. Humanity's relationship to the physical world is subject to futility.

Romans 8:18–25 refers to these results of man's apostasy. This explains the frustration in Ecclesiastes. This shows why we must look *past the sun* to find any hope. Only there will we see eternity and the great change that will be wrought by sovereign grace at the return of our Lord.

Note verses 20 and 21 in Romans 8 carefully.

> *For the creation was subjected to futility, not willingly, but because of Him who subjected it in hope; because the creation itself also*

will be delivered from the bondage of corruption into the glorious liberty of the children of God. (NKJV)

God himself has subjected all things to frustration or vanity. The frustration is part of the judicial judgment of God. If man can find true meaning and satisfaction as a rebel in a hostile environment, then rebellious man can evade justice and defeat God's purposes. Imagine for a moment, a spoiled brat who destroys great works of art, expensive furniture, and priceless jewels for fun, because of his ignorance and selfishness. That is exactly what fallen man does with God's creation. He takes the greatest gifts that God gives and destroys them while he gathers garbage and junk in the expectation of finding something tasty and satisfying.

Suppose a genius had made the greatest computer possible and you stole it. When you got home, you discovered that you could not use it. The man who built the computer made it impossible to understand and use without key passwords. Since it was impossible for you figure it out those code words, you could not use the computer. You would be frustrated because you would know what the computer was capable of doing, and yet you could make it do nothing. You would push the on button and the screen would read, "If you admit that this computer is mine because I made it, and come and ask my forgiveness for stealing it, I not only will forgive you for stealing it, I also will give you the passwords and even let you keep the computer. I even will teach you how to run it." If you remained in your rebellion and kept trying to start it on your own, you would just become even more frustrated.

Paul, in Romans 1, shows that man would rather be the *center of total chaos*, than to admit he is a dependent creature, yea, a sinful dependent creature who needs grace. God has written eternity in man's heart in such a way that he cannot totally escape God no matter how hard he tries to do so. (We will see this in Chapter 3). Man knows that he is different from the animals, despite all of his loud claims about evolution. He knows better, but will never admit it until God, in sovereign grace, opens his eyes.

The world will grow worse and worse in proportion to its deliberate and conscious attempt to be autonomous from God's authority. The more "free" from God man becomes, the more controlled by sin and self he will be. The more God gives man over to sin, the worse life on earth must become. It is a terrifying thought, but nonetheless true, that God rewards sin with sin. Although we see personal instances of redemption that radically change one person at a time, the ultimate redemption of all creation awaits the second coming of Christ. Then, but not until then, the entire order of nature as we know it will be changed. The Bible describes this as a new heaven and new earth.

In 1:12–18, we saw the utter failure of wisdom to satisfy the secularist. Can a person escape pessimism and despair by the acquisition of wisdom? Verse 18 answers a resounding no. So far, The Seeker's wholehearted search ends exactly where it started—totally empty. The irony is that the more one learns about reality, the more ugly and unbearable it becomes. That is because the world is upside down and sin rules. Reality is ugly because God rewards sin with sin. Reality is also very painful when one looks at life without a God-ward focus. Asaph attests to this in Psalm 73, where he records his struggle with bitterness when he considered the easy life of the wicked. When he viewed life from an *under the sun* perspective, his efforts at moral purity seemed futile; the wicked prospered, while the innocent and upright suffered.

Chapter 2 continues the record of The Seeker's vain attempts to find meaning and satisfaction in life. One writer has labeled this section *"The Failure of pleasure and accomplishments."* If you try to hide from life's real problems by squeezing all of the juice out of a given pleasure in life, the juice turns sour.

In Ecclesiastes 2:1–3, The Seeker turns from wisdom to mirth, from rationalism to romanticism

I said in mine heart, Go to now, I will prove thee with mirth, therefore enjoy pleasure: and, behold, this also is vanity. I said of laughter, It is mad: and of mirth, What doeth it? I sought in mine heart to give myself unto wine, yet acquainting mine heart with wisdom; and to lay hold on folly, till I might see what was that good for the sons of men, which they should do under the heaven all the days of their life. (KJV)

From 1:18 to end of chapter 2 (thirty-two verses), The Seeker uses the words, *I, me,* and *my,* over fifty times. Notice the self-centeredness in just one verse.

Whatever my eyes desired I did not keep from them. I did not withhold my heart from any pleasure, for my heart rejoiced in all my labor; and this was my reward from all my labor. (Eccl 2:10, NKJV)

The Seeker immediately tells us exactly what he got for all his self-efforts.

Then I looked on all the works that my hands had done and on the labor in which I had toiled; and indeed all was vanity and grasping for the wind. There was no profit under the sun. (Eccl 2:11, NKJV)

These statements describe the sure and certain conclusion of anyone who tries to understand life and reality without acknowledging God. Here is the sum total of the *under the sun* philosophy that trusts only its own wisdom. This describes Eve's approach when she turned from God's way and went her own way. Her action did not stem merely from a desire to have personal knowledge of good and evil, it came from a desire to be like God (Gen. 3:5, 6). The knowledge of good and evil was knowledge by personal experience, which Eve thought would enable her to be autonomous from God. She would be free to choose for herself, instead of following orders about what she could and could not do. That tree would enable her to be free to make her own decisions.

The Bible describes the person who wants to be free from God's control as the fool of the Book of Proverbs. He is the man in chapter one of Romans who deliberately turns away from God's revelation and staggers down the path of ungodly behavior to the place where his conscience no longer can tell the difference between right and wrong: the place where he does not feel the least shame in the most wicked lifestyle.

After the failure of wisdom, The Seeker tries a new direction. He rejects wisdom for its own sake and embraces folly (2:3). I sought in mine heart to give myself unto wine, yet acquainting mine heart with wisdom; and to lay hold on folly, till I might see what was that good for the sons of men, which they should do under the heaven all the days of their life (KJV).

The Seeker's idea of folly is philosophically similar to today's counterculture. Historically, a culture moves from romanticism, where people think with their hearts, to rationalism, where people reject emotions and follow reason, or brains, alone. When romanticism and rationalism fail, a culture rejects them both and seeks spiritualism. This may take the form of out of body experiences, including mystical and strange states of consciousness induced by drugs; yoga; and other practices of eastern mystical religions. When this fails, and it always does, a culture then moves into the form of Nihilism that deliberately cultivates the ugly, the obscene, the absurd, and the ridiculous. This is the sick, dark, destructive, and weird world of MTV. It manifests itself in the strange dress, outlandish hair, bizarre looks, loud music and screaming speech of today's pop culture. To people steeped in this worldview, the weird and ugly is reality, because their world has no ultimate meaning or absolute truth. Sick, destructive humor results from their inner hatred of reality and anything that confines their freedom to *"do whatever I please, whenever I please, with anyone I please."*

The Seeker's quest for folly does not mean that he is looking to have irresponsible escapades, as many with no wisdom are. The words *madness* and *folly* in Scripture do not usually indicate mental oddness, but *deliberate moral perversity*. This man's actions are thoughtful and deliberately controlled. Any resulting mad mental frustration is part of the judicial judgment of God. This exchange surfaces again as God deals with Nebuchadnezzar after Daniel interprets the king's dream of a tree. Daniel tells the king that God has decreed the events that will occur, and pleads with him to repent. Nebuchadnezzar, like modern man, responds by doing all in his power to evade any thought of God. His response was a bigger and better party as a means of getting his mind off the truth.

One of the tragic mistakes that people commit is to think that alcohol, drugs, and pornography have produced the wicked society in which we currently live. It is actually the other way around. Our society has produced those things as essential means to kill the pain of an empty and futile life. If our culture, believing as it does, did not have drugs, booze and unbridled sex as distractions, it would finally find suicide the only acceptable option. The sinful pleasures of the world are like a giant aspirin tablet that hopeless people keep taking to kill the pain of a meaningless life. Like real aspirin, the world only kills the pain; it never touches that which causes the problem. As the problem gets worse and the pain gets deeper, more and more aspirin are required to dull the pain.

When we read Romans 1, we see how a creature, designed to be a prince, deliberately chose to act like a pig. What we believe always precedes and causes the attitudes we have; attitudes produce acts and behavior. We are what we think. If we think wrongly, we will live wrongly. All ideas have consequences. Feelings do not float in the windows to become part of our emotions; they grow out of the things we believe. If we believe in our hearts that we are worthless, then we will soon start feeling worthless, and in a short time, we will start acting as if we are worthless. As Christians, we must learn to bring our minds and emotions under the control of Scripture. When we feel that there is no hope, we must ask, "Who is telling me there is no hope?" Surely God does not say, "Romans 8:28 does not apply to you." It is neither the Word of God nor the Holy Spirit that convinces us that the grace of God is not enough. We must learn to think God's thoughts after him. We must bring our thinking and our emotions under the control of the Scriptures and the Holy Spirit. A sinner's view of God must change before he can change his view of reality, which then will result in a change of lifestyle.

Look with me at The Seeker's list of accomplishments in 2:3–11. It is quite impressive.

> *I searched in my heart how to gratify my flesh with wine, while guiding my heart with wisdom, and how to lay hold on folly, till I might see what was good for the sons of men to do under heaven all the days of their lives. I made my works great, I built myself houses, and planted myself vineyards. I made myself gardens and orchards, and I planted all kinds of fruit trees in them. I made myself water pools from which to water the growing trees of the grove. I acquired male and female servants, and had servants born in my house. Yes, I had greater possessions of herds and flocks than all who were in Jerusalem before me. I also gathered for myself silver and gold and the special treasures of kings and of the provinces. I acquired male and female singers, the delights of the sons of men, and musical instruments of all kinds. So I became great and excelled more than all who were before me in Jerusalem. Also my wisdom remained with me. Whatever my eyes desired I did not keep from them. I did not withhold my heart from any pleasure, for my heart rejoiced in all my labor; and this was my reward from all my labor. Then I looked on all the works that my hands had done and on the labor in which I had toiled; and indeed all was vanity and grasping for the wind. There was no profit under the sun.* (Eccl 2:3–11, NKJV)

"Whatever my eyes desired I did not keep from them. I did not withhold my heart from any pleasure ..." In this amazing statement, The Seeker clearly presents his all-consuming goal. He is determined to find true meaning and satisfaction at any price or with any amount of effort. Can you imagine some of the parties that took place in Solomon's palace? It is hard for us to envision the possibilities contained in these sentences. When we remember who wrote this, and we con-

sider all of the assets, financial, physical, and mental, that he possessed, we barely can begin to list the possibilities. Note the frequent occurrence of the word *myself* in 2:1–8. This is the cult of self. All that counts is my needs, my feelings, my liberty, my rights, and my happiness.

Can you imagine what it would be like to be able to have anything at all, regardless of cost or inconvenience, that you wanted? **Anything** that your heart desired or your mind conceived would be yours for the asking. There would be no limitations or roadblocks of any kind put on any of your desires. This describes the Seeker's situation. He could do exactly whatever he pleased, whenever he was pleased to it. He had no boundaries and was free to indulge in whatever struck his fancy. He made all the rules.

If you could be in that position, do you think that would guarantee that you would be satisfied and truly happy? If having all you ever wanted could not satisfy your heart, and you know it could not, then what could? Be sure you realize what The Seeker is saying. He never experienced a dull moment in any day or felt frustrated by any unfilled longing or desire. Life was one constant good time of doing what ever he wanted to do.

What would the average person today describe as a good time? What would he consider a recipe for happiness? How would you describe it? Does laughter prove that you are having a good time or is it only a temporary diversion?

Samuel Johnson, the famous English writer, received the privilege of a personal tour of a very wealthy man's estate. His host showed him vast barns and herds of every kind of animal. He saw paintings, jewelry, ornate decorations, furniture, rugs, and every form of famous art from all over the world. Finally, the man, obviously very proud of his possessions, asked, "Well, Johnson, what do you think?" Johnson thought a moment and responded, "These are the things that make it hard for a man to die and leave it all behind." As I have said before, you will never see a U-Haul behind a hearse.

Shortly after the above episode, the wealthy man did indeed die. A friend inquired, "Johnson, that man was a friend of yours; do you have any idea of how much he left when he died?" Johnson replied, "All of it."

We could call 2:11 "The morning after the night before."

Yet when I surveyed all that my hands had done and what I had toiled to achieve, everything was meaningless, a chasing after the wind; nothing was gained under the sun. (NIV)

There will be a final "morning after" for every person that ever lived. Even if hell were no more than a vivid memory of the arrogant unbelief that led a person to turn away from the true and living God and look to a sin-cursed word for hope, it would still be a torment indeed.

The Seeker relentlessly confronts the secularist with the fact that in the secularist's world of "no-absolutes," there is one sure absolute that he cannot deny, and that is death. However, he does not stop there. The final blow to the ego of the self-sufficient man is the realization that he cannot control what happens to all his attainments. Not only is he unable to take his toys with him, he has no guarantee about who will play with them after he is gone.

Yea, I hated all my labor which I had taken under the sun: because I should leave it unto the man that shall be after me. And who knoweth whether he shall be a wise man or a fool? Yet shall he have rule over all my labor wherein I have labored, and wherein I have shewed myself wise under the sun. This is also vanity. (Eccl 2:18–19, KJV)

We must understand that the Seeker is not condemning wealth. We may own five cars, as long as none of them owns us. His point is that the material goods we acquire while on earth remain on earth after we die.

CHAPTER SIX: VERSES 3:1–8

TIMING IS EVERYTHING

As we venture further into the book of Ecclesiastes, we must remind ourselves of the writer's main thesis in 1:2: "Everything is meaningless; all is vanity." These could be the words of a man in despair, ready to jump off a bridge to his death. They could be the words of a man in mid-life crisis who feels insignificant and unfulfilled. They also could be the confession of a burnt-out hippie with thin gray hair, trying desperately, but without success, to retain the appearance of youth. These words could even describe a modern secular humanist who is coming to grips with the true and certain implications of his man-centered philosophy of life. Apart from an absolute confidence in God's unchanging love and sovereign power, the fatalism inherent in those words is inescapable. Never, though, will they be the pronouncement of a child of God who is walking in fellowship with his Savior. No believer will ever stand on the shores of eternity and cry out, "it was all meaningless." A sure confidence in God's promise and his power to fulfill his promises affirms the exact opposite of the words "Meaningless, meaningless, everything is meaningless." A child of God looks at the same world of reality that produced such a dismal declaration and cries in hope, "Romans 8:28 is true! God does work everything for his glory and my good. "

In Ecclesiastes 2:24–26, we encountered the beginning of a radically different world and life view from "All is meaningless." Here is a life with God at the center; here is a world and life view that sees past the sun to the eternal throne of God. This view accords with Romans 11:36 as the accurate philosophy of history.

> *O, the depth of the riches both of the wisdom and knowledge of God! how unsearchable are his judgments, and his ways past finding out! For who hath known the mind of the Lord? or who hath been his counsellor? Or who hath first given to him, and it shall be recompensed unto him again? For of him, and through him, and to him, are all things: to whom be glory for ever. Amen.* (Rom 11:33–36, KJV)

Wow! What a difference it makes when we put God into the equation! If we draw a one-inch circle with a compass and then add nine more circles, each one an inch bigger than the last one, without changing the center point, all of the ten circles will be in perfect symmetry. Now, move the center point and draw another circle of any size. Everything is askew. That last circle distorts the balance of all the ten previous circles. It is the same with life. Our view of God affects far more than our "church" life; it affects every area of our life.

My wife had a housecoat that had twenty buttons. One day, before she had her coffee, I watched her put the number one button into the number two hole. When she finished buttoning her robe, she had an extra button with no hole. Did she make one mistake or did she make nineteen mistakes? She made nineteen mistakes and she had to undo all of them and start over. If our starting point for understanding life is wrong, then our whole life is wrong. We may sail along with everything seeming to fit, as my wife did with the first nineteen buttons, but in the end, we discover that our entire life was wrong.

Ecclesiastes 3:1–8 presents the biblical world and life view. It encompasses the truth of both Romans 11:36 and Romans 8:28; all things originate in God and he uses them all for the good of his children. The phrase *there is a time for everything* is one of the best-known and most often quoted texts in the Bible.

> *There is a time for everything, and a season for every activity under heaven: a time to be born and a time to die, a time to plant and a time to uproot, a time to kill and a time to heal, a time to tear down and a time to build, a time to weep and a time to laugh, a time to mourn and a time to dance, a time to scatter stones and a time to gather them, a time to embrace and a time to refrain, a time to search and a time to give up, a time to keep and a time to throw away, a time to tear and a time to mend, a time to be silent and a time to speak, a time to love and a time to hate, a time for war and a time for peace.* (Eccl 3:1–8, NIV)

Everything depends on correct timing. The right thing at the wrong time may be worse than the wrong thing. Scripture commends those who 'understand the times' and act accordingly (see 1 Chron. 12:32). We cannot "understand the times" completely. Some things and times make little sense to us with our finite minds. We can however, learn enough to come to some understanding. *"I have seen something else under the sun: The race is not to the swift or the battle to the strong, nor does food come to the wise or wealth to the brilliant or favor to the learned; but time and chance happen to them all"* (Eccl 9:11, NIV).

In all times and seasons, under all circumstances, the children of God are to be content and joyous:

> *Go, eat your food with gladness, and drink your wine with a joyful heart, for it is now that God favors what you do. Always be clothed in white, and always anoint your head with oil. Enjoy life with your wife, whom you love, all the days of this meaningless life*

that God has given you under the sun – all your meaningless days.
For this is your lot in life and in your toilsome labor under the sun.
(Eccl 9:7–9, NIV)

This attitude is possible only if you agree with the Psalmist. *"My times* [that means **all** of them] *are in your hands;*
deliver me from my enemies and from those who pursue me" (Ps
31:15). The next verse, Psalm 31:16, is a 'felt' answer to that
prayer: *"Let your face shine on your servant; save me in your un-*
failing love" (NIV).

In Ecclesiastes 3:1, the writer announces that we are
locked into times and seasons the same way that we were
locked into nature in 1:4–7. *"There is a time for everything, and*
a season for every activity under heaven." In chapter 1, the
teacher described the monotonous sameness of nature and
our inability to change it. Chapter 3 is his presentation of the
constant but unpredictable change from one extreme to
another in nearly every area of life. Again, the changes are
beyond our control or choice in any way.

Change is pleasant. Who would want all summertime
and no fall or winter?

Change is essential. If we had all spring and no summer,
we would have an abundance of flowers, but we would
have no wheat. We would starve to death in a beautiful environment that smelled good.

Who could tolerate all planting and never a harvest?
More positively, how about a life that is all laughter and
never a tear? Before we say we agree, we had better read Ecclesiastes 7:2–4.

Better to go to the house of mourning than to go to the house of
feasting, for that is the end of all men; and the living will take it to
heart. Sorrow is better than laughter, for by a sad countenance the

*heart is made better. The heart of the wise is in the house of mourn-
ing, but the heart of fools is in the house of mirth.* (NKJ)

If we are looking for ultimate meaning, however, the back
and forth extreme swings are no better than the endless circles of meaninglessness described in chapter one.

Derek Kidner, in his excellent book on Ecclesiastes, en-
titles chapter three, "The Tyranny of Time." He says,

> Perhaps tyranny is too strong a word for the gentle ebbs
> and flows described here, which carry us all our days from one
> kind of activity to its opposite, and back again. The description
> is pleasing, with its varieties of mood and action and its hints
> of different rhythms in our affairs. Rhythm itself appeals to us,
> for who would wish for perpetual spring—'a time to plant' but
> never to pick—or envy the sleepless business we met in the last
> chapter?
>
> Yet in the context in the quest for finality, not only is a
> movement to and fro no better than the endless circling of
> chapter one, but it has disturbing implications all its own. One
> of them is that we dance to a tune, or many tunes, not of our
> own choosing; a second is that nothing we pursue has any
> permanence. We throw ourselves into some absorbing activity
> which offers us fulfillment, but how freely did we choose it?
> How soon shall we be doing the exact opposite? Perhaps our
> choices are no freer than our responses to winter and summer,
> childhood and old age, dictated by the march of time and of
> unbidden change.
>
> Looked at in this way, the repetition of 'a time...and a time'
> begins to be oppressive. Whatever may be our skill and initia-
> tive, our real masters seem to be these inexorable seasons; not
> only those of the calendar, but that tide of events which moves
> us now to one kind of action which seems fitting, now to
> another which puts it all into reverse. Obviously, we have little
> to say in the situations which move us to weep or laugh,

mourn or dance; but our deliberate acts, too, may be time-conditioned more than we suppose. 'Who would have imagined.' we sometimes say, 'that day would ever come when I would find myself doing such and such, and seeing it as my duty.' So peace-loving nations prepare for war; or the shepherd takes the knife to the creature he has earlier nursed back to health. The collector disperses his hoard; friends part in bitter conflict; the need to speak out follows the need to be silent. Nothing that we do, it seems, is free from this relativity and this pressure—almost dictation—from the outside.

(*A Time to Mourn and a Time to Dance, the Message of Ecclesiastes,* by Derek Kidner, InterVarsity Press, Downers Grove, Illinois, p. 38).

Several things from this passage are important. First, change is not bad if God is in total control of all the changes. Second, the real problem for us is not that life refuses to keep still, but that we see such a very small sliver of its movements and we cannot see the big design. If we could see God's great purpose to bless his people and to glorify himself in everything, our perspective would change. Kidner writes,

"We are like a desperately nearsighted man, inching his way along some great tapestry or fresco in an attempt to take it all in. We see enough to recognize something of its great quality, but the grand design escapes us, for we can never stand back far enough to view it as its Creator does, whole and entire, from beginning to the end" (Ibid, page 39).

In Ecclesiastes 3:2–8, the writer uses fourteen couplets to describe a wide range of human activity and experience. He starts in verse 1 with a general fact: *To every thing there is a season, and a time to every purpose under the heaven.*

The writer employs a common Hebrew couplet method. The couplets are meant to describe the two extremes, and by implication, everything in between them. Thus, when a couplet writer pens, "man and woman," he means "everybody." "Land and seas" indicates "everywhere." From the "smallest to the greatest" expresses the two extremes and all that is in between them.

Verse 2a starts with the two most momentous and sure events of every person's existence, life and death (and everything in between): *A time to be born, and a time to die.* There is a time, ordained by God, for you to be born. You were no accident. Maybe your parents did not plan your birth, but God did. There is a time, already fixed by God, for you to die. It is an ordained appointment that you will keep, and you will not be one minute late. Your very first event and your very last event, and everything in between those events, is under God's sovereign control. God picked the day of your birth and the day of your death.

The next three couplets (verses 2b, and 3) show various destructive and constructive activities: A time to plant, and a time to pluck up that which is planted; a time to kill, and a time to heal; a time to break down, and a time to build up.

First, the writer mentions planting and harvesting. He could be talking about vegetables and crops. He also could be referring to planting and destroying nations. He may be speaking of 'planting our roots' in one place and at another time 'uprooting' and moving on.

Second, there is a time to kill and time to heal. He may be thinking in medical terms, but not necessarily just medical. There is a time to amputate a leg to save the person's life and there is a time to take the risk of not amputating. There is a time to shut off the machine and a time to keep it running. The writer also may be talking about healing or destroying a good or bad relationship. Likewise, we kill a bad business venture and at other times, we hang on and hope.

Third, there is a time to break down and time to build up. There is a time to tear down false hopes and conceit, but other times call for building confidence and self-esteem. There is a time to demolish an old house and start over, but other times we should repair the old one. It also can refer to times when God tears down nations, just as there are times when he builds up nations. This happened in biblical history when God raised up even ungodly nations to use them to fulfill his purpose to punish Israel. Additionally, the writer could be talking about building up or ending a relationship.

Walter Kaiser has an interesting note on this verse:

> Having established that the terms of life are fixed for men as well as for the plant world, Solomon teaches that even those situations that seem to be in the hands of men and, therefore somewhat unpredictable–such as the condemnation of murders by the state to the penalty of death–are likewise embraced in the plan of God. There is a time for executing murders or destroying enemies in a just war (v.3). (Incidentally, such an action against murders is favored in Scripture, not because men are sovereign or because society and the bereaved are some how benefited, but because man is so vastly important to God–he is made in the image of God [Gen 9:6]. To kill another person is to kill God in effigy. Thus, the only alternative that the state, God's duly authorized agent in such a case, has is to show respect for God and for the value of the image of God in man by taking the murder's life. Such a moral reason has not been antiquated by any subsequent revelation in the gospel.

Can the character of God be offered at discount value in generations to come?) *Ecclesiastes, Total Life,* by Walter Kaiser, Moody Press, pages 63, 64.

In verse 4, the author deals with human emotions: *A time to weep, and a time to laugh; a time to mourn, and a time to dance.* Charles Bridges has some excellent comments on this text.

There is obviously a repetition with increasing emphasis. The *mourning* is the most poignant weeping. The dancing expresses not only the laughter of the lips, but exuberant excitement of the whole man. These are God's *times.* Beware of changing them. It is a fearful thing to respond with "joy and gladness" when the Lord of hosts calls for *weeping* and *mourning.*

Who has not found the *time to weep and mourn?* "Man is born to trouble as the sparks fly upward" (Job 5:7; 14:1). And yet lesson after lesson is needed to make us know the world is a vale of tears. We look around to the right or to the left to avoid this or that trouble. Is not this looking out for some byepath from the road, where we shall meet neither promises, comfort, nor guidance? Be content with thine appointed lot. The tears of the child of God have more the element of happiness than the *laughter* of the ungodly. The darkest side of the Canaan road is brighter than the light of a thousand worlds. Yet we may look for a change of seasons in God's best and fittest time. "Thou hast turned my *mourning into dancing...*" was the experience of the man of God. Into Job's bosom was poured a portion "double for all his sorrows." The mouths of the returning captives were filled with *laughter,* and their tongues with singing (Psalm 136:1, 2).

Let God's afflicted ones mark the wisdom and grace of these appointments. He giveth both these *times* in their season. Yea, he maketh the one to spring out of the other. *"Joy"* is the harvest of the seed-time of tears. "I will make them rejoice", so runs the promise, *"from their sorrow."* The sorrow may not "for the present" seem (Heb. 12:11) acceptable to us. But let it be accepted by us. As time rolls on, the special ends of the divine love in the sorrow will be displayed in beauteous arrangement. And that which in the beginning was accepted in dutiful acquiescence, will afterward become acceptable matter for adoring praise. The child of God will acknowledge, "It may be a dark dispensation. But I know it is a wise one. It brings God to me, and I am happy."

But far from us be that anomaly in religion—the gloomy religionist. Truly he is a stumbling block to the world, and a discouragement to the saint. He who lives, as if he were afraid of being happy, as if he doubted his right to be so—as if God begrudged him his happiness. With perverse ingenuity he believes the Gospel to be true for others, not for himself. 'Look up and be cheerful; honor God and his Gospel', was the wise counsel given one of this class. Take the balances of the sanctuary. Compare the moment of the night-*weeping* with the eternity of the morning joy. The vicissitudes of weeping and joy will soon be overwhelmed in one unmingled eternity of joy. This is the only world where sickness, sorrow, and death can enter. And the world of health and joy and life, without sin, without change, without tears (Rev. 21:4), is near at hand. Oh! let it be in constant view, and him with it, who, 'when he overcome the sharpness of death, opened this kingdom to all believers. (From: *Ecclesiastes*, by Charles Bridges, Banner of Truth, reprinted 1981).

Next, in verse 5a, we find *a time to cast away stones, and a time to gather stones together.* We gather stones to build a house or a wall and we cast stones out of a field so we can plow it. We gather the stones out of our yard and use them to make a walk.

Verse 5b speaks of showing and withholding affection. There is *a time to embrace, and a time to refrain from embracing.* In our culture, it is proper and fitting to dance and laugh at a wedding. The same action, even with the same people, would be improper at a funeral.

The next couplet (verse 6a) contrasts perseverance with knowing when to give up: *A time to get, and a time to lose.* If we have an incurable disease, there will come a time to stop running all over the world for a miracle cure. Some difficulties have no solutions; when faced with them, we just submit to God's sovereignty. Difficulties fall into two categories: problems, and facts of life. Many people never learn the difference between a problem and a fact of life. A problem has an answer and we do not give up until we find and apply the answer and solve the problem. A fact of life has no answer and requires we give up and submit to God's sovereign providence. To treat a problem as a fact of life is to be a coward. To treat a fact of life as a problem is to be a fool.

Verse 6b contrasts a pack rat with a wise and frugal saver. There is *a time to keep, and a time to cast away.* Yesterday's useless junk sometimes becomes tomorrow's priceless antique. Don't you wish you had saved some of Grandma's junk that you hauled off to the dump twenty years ago? In 1956, we had a public sale. We had to pay a man $5.00 to haul away two bear-claw tables and an oak poster-bed that did not even garner a $1.00 bid. They would both be worth over $500.00 today. There was also an oak chest of drawers whose worth today I cannot even guess.

My wife and I are both pack rats. We keep saying that we are going to have two garage sales. She will go away for a

weekend and I will sell all her stuff and then I will go away
for a weekend and she will sell all my stuff. In my case it
may take two weekends.

Verse 7a is a variation of verse 6: *A time to rend, and a time
to sew.* I hate new clothes. I could wear the same clothes and
keep patching them up until it was almost all different fabric
on the garment. In the culture of the Seeker, people displayed sorrow and grief by tearing their clothing. A bride,
however, would want to be married in a new dress, and
would not consider leaving her father's house without new
linens. Jacob demonstrated his special affection for Joseph
by giving his son a new coat. When Joseph's brothers re-
turned the coat to their father with a tale of Joseph's death,
Jacob tore his clothing and mourned (Gen. 37).

Verse 7b is a well-known and little-practiced truth. There
is *a time to keep silence, and a time to speak.* The classic com-
plementary text is Proverbs 26:4–5.

> *Do not answer a fool according to his folly, lest you also be like
> him. Answer a fool according to his folly, lest he be wise in his own
> eyes.* (NKJV)

The biggest difficulty in all of these couplets lies in knowing which part applies in a given situation. How do I know
when to shut up and when to speak up? When is discretion
the better part of valor? The people who advocate, "Always
speak your mind" usually reveal how small their mind is. It
is said, "Better to keep your mouth shut and have people
think you are stupid, than to open your mouth and have
them know for sure you are stupid." We agree that what is
cowardly at one time may be honorable and noble at another, but how do we know which action to take in a specific

situation? Certainly, Matthew 7:6 applies here, "... *do not throw your pearls before swine ...*"

Verse 8a disconcerts some people who misunderstand the true nature of love: *A time to love, and a time to hate.* We must not hate individuals unless God's glory is involved.

Verse 8b is a text for today. There is *"a time of war, and a time of peace."* This assumes that some wars are justifiable. It is difficult for pacifists to deal with this verse. Their only argument is, "But that is in the Old Testament." There is a time when war is legitimate and necessary, and there is a time when war is both unjust and insane. There is also a time for peace, but never a time for peace at any price. Times of war and times of peace affect our attitude and behavior. What is good at one time may be bad at another.

There are different views on appropriate approaches to chapter 3 of Ecclesiastes. One view sees the writer feeling trapped by a sequence of times or events over which he has no control. He is forced to go through each experience without understanding why. In other words, the chapter is a beautiful, poetic way of saying, "All is meaningless."

Another view is that the writer is a rigid believer in predestination. He is a fatalist who is mad because he cannot anticipate the events in this pre-arranged (without his consent) timetable. As a result, he cannot enjoy today. It is a blessing we cannot see and anticipate tomorrow. "If we could see beyond today, we often say, but God in love, a veil doth throw, across our way."

The story is told of a Primitive Baptist who fell down the stairs. He picked himself up and said, "Well, I am glad that is over." An Arminian would ask, "What did I do to deserve that?"

I believe the chapter teaches predestination, or else we would be driven to atheism and fatalism. It, however, is not saying, "What will be, will be, whether it was supposed to be or not." It is not even saying, "What will be, will be, only because it was supposed to be." The truth is, "What will be, will be, only because it is an essential piece in the great purposes of our great God." In other words, (1) "Yes, everything happens because God purposed it to happen," and (2) "Yes, it happens at the exact time that God ordained. Predestination, however, does not reflect the actions of a cruel, unfeeling tyrant, running the world as if it were an Ouija Board. No, no! The Father of our Lord Jesus Christ predestinated all things. Our wise, holy, gracious heavenly Father planned each event and every time for that particular event.

Genesis 21:1, 2 illustrates this point.

> *And the LORD visited Sarah **as he had said,** and the LORD did unto Sarah **as he had spoken.** For Sarah conceived, and bare Abraham a son in his old age, **at the set time of which God had spoken to him.*** (KJV, emphasis added)

It is really difficult to not write a chapter on this verse. What a powerful text of Scripture!

Luke 2:1–5 is another example.

> *And it came to pass in those days, that there went out a decree from Caesar Augustus, that all the world should be taxed. (And this taxing was first made when Cyrenius was governor of Syria.) And all went to be taxed, every one into his own city. And Joseph also went up from Galilee, out of the city of Nazareth, into Judaea, unto the city of David, which is called Bethlehem; (because he was of the house and lineage of David:) To be taxed with Mary his espoused wife, being great with child.* (KJV)

Why did Caesar issue that decree at that particular time? A historian, a sociologist, and a psychologist may give us three different answers and all three will be partly correct. An economist may say the queen was spending too much on clothes and the royal treasury was getting low. I will not comment on that. The ultimate reason for the tax at that time was that it was the means God chose to move a specific pregnant woman into a specific town, so the birth of her child could fulfill a specific prophecy uttered many years before. We must remember that God accomplishes his sovereign purposes in a world of sin and rebellion, without infringing on the free moral agency of any creature. He uses temporal means to reach ordained ends.

Basically, Ecclesiastes 3:1 teaches that God not only ordains all things, he also ordains the time of their happening. That is the way it is—period—whether you like it or not. The unbeliever hates the very idea of God's controlling all events and their timing. He cries, "If that is true, then I am only a robot. I am like a trapped animal!" On the other hand, the believer is glad that Jesus rules and reigns over every aspect of life. He sings, "His eye is on the sparrow, and I know he watches me." Pain is still pain, grief is still grief, but now we can see it as serving a purpose in God's plan.

Ecclesiastes chapter 3 emphasizes our non-control over both the event and the particular time that the event takes place. God ordains both the "thing itself" and the "timing" of the thing. His plan includes every detail and embraces every person. Jesus said, "Even the hairs of your head are numbered." Spurgeon has a great quote on that text:

> There is no attribute of God more comforting to His children than the doctrine of Divine Sovereignty. Under the most

adverse circumstances, in the most severe troubles, they believe that Sovereignty has ordained their afflictions, that Sovereignty overrules them, and that Sovereignty will sanctify them all. There is nothing for which the children of God ought more earnestly to contend than the dominion of their Master over all creation—the Kingship of God over all the works of his own hands—the throne of God, and His right to sit upon that throne. On the other hand, there is no doctrine more hated by worldlings, no truth of which they have made such a football, as the great, stupendous, but yet most certain doctrine of the Sovereignty of the infinite Jehovah. **Men will allow God to be everywhere except upon His throne.** They will allow Him to be in His workshop to fashion worlds and to make stars. They will allow Him to be in His almonry to dispense His alms and bestow His bounties. They will allow Him to sustain the earth and bear up the pillars thereof, or light the lamps of Heaven, or rule the waves of the ever-moving ocean; but when God ascends His throne, His creatures gnash their teeth; and when we proclaim an **enthroned God,** and His right to do as He wills with His own, to dispose of His creatures as He thinks well, without consulting them in the matter, then it is that we are hissed and reviled, and then it is that men turn a deaf ear to us, for **God on His throne is not the God they love.** They love Him anywhere better than they do when He sits with His scepter in His hand and His crown upon His head. But it is God upon the throne that we love to preach. It is God upon His throne whom we trust. It is God upon His throne of whom we have been singing this morning; and it is God upon His throne of whom we shall speak in this discourse. (From: *Divine Sovereignty,* by CH Spurgeon, New Park Street Pulpit, Vol 2, page 305).

Let me illustrate the idea of "times" and "timing" with a wedding. The bride has carefully planned every part of her wedding, and the day has finally arrived Everything is going as scheduled, until her father, walking her down the aisle, falls over with a heart attack and instantly dies. Everyone, including the father and daughter, knew he would die "someday." But why did he have to die on that particular day and at that specific hour? Everyone knew this event would happen, but no one had any way of knowing or controlling when it would happen. There was no way to prepare for that tragedy that day. How often have you said, "Why **this**? Why **me**? Why **now** of all times?" We ask this question both of the things we knew would happen "someday" and also of the things we never did expect to happen. It is easy to think that everything is against us, just because on one day, it rained on our parade. We forget all the many good days when things went right.

No one chooses a "time to weep" any more than one would choose to die at a wedding. But there is an ordained time for all to weep, and an ordained time to for all to die, even for some to die at a wedding. Remember verse 4, "There is a time to weep and a time to laugh." Weeping times are just as essential as laughing times. True, they are painful, but they are also far more spiritually beneficial than laughter.

> Better to go to the house of mourning than to go to the house of feasting, for that is the end of all men; and the living will take it to heart. Sorrow is better than laughter, for by a sad countenance the heart is made better. The heart of the wise is in the house of mourning, but the heart of fools is in the house of mirth. (Eccl 7:2-4, NKJV)

The Christian knows something that the unbeliever does not. We know that Romans 5:1–5 is true even while we often fail to apply it. Suffering produces perseverance, which in turns leads to character and character produces hope. Comfort and assurance from that verse is not automatic; we must consciously fight our emotions with truth! We must put what we know into actual practice in a given situation. When an unexpected tragedy happens, no matter what kind, we automatically go into panic mode. The Devil will paint the worst possible scenario. We must stop and say, "Wait a minute! I know that this is under God's control. I know that Romans 8:28 includes what is happening right now." I repeat; we must bring our emotions under the truth of Scripture.

If you have never wept, you have never missed Eden or felt the effects of the fall. You have never felt your sin and shame if you have never shed tears. Tears prove the reality and pain of the effects of sin; weeping makes us long for better days when all of the effects of sin will be gone. This world will be a vale of tears. Most of the time, the good guys do not win. We are engaged in a war that we know we cannot fully win in this life time, but we dare not and will not give up and quit. We know we will win eternally.

CHAPTER SEVEN: VERSES: 3:9–15 #1

RELAX, IT'S ALL UNDER CONTROL

In the last chapter, we looked at Ecclesiastes 3:1, where the writer announces that we are locked into times and seasons the same way that we were locked into nature in 1:4–7. *"There is a time for everything, and a season for every activity under heaven."* In chapter 1, the Seeker describes the monotonous sameness of nature and our inability to change it. Chapter 3 is his presentation of the constant but unpredictable change from one extreme to another in nearly every area of life. Again, the changes are beyond our control or choice in any way. The Seeker uses fourteen couplets (3:1–8) to describe a wide range of human activity and experience that cover various aspects of our lives. We concluded that this chapter in Ecclesiastes sets forth the sovereignty of God in a personal and extremely practical way. What are some of the useful lessons we can learn from Ecclesiastes 3?

First, contrary to William Henley's poem *Invictus*, it is obvious that we are neither "masters of our fate" nor "captains of our souls." Masquerading as a noble attempt to take responsibility for one's own destiny, Invictus epitomizes the rebel's cry of defiance against the truth of Ecclesiastes chapter three.

Invictus

Out of the night that covers me,
Black as the pit from pole to pole,
I thank whatever gods may be
For my unconquerable soul.

In the fell clutch of circumstance
I have not winced nor cried aloud.
Under the bludgeonings of chance
My head is bloody, but unbowed.

Beyond this place of wrath and tears
Looms but the horror of the shade,
And yet the menace of the years
Finds, and shall find me, unafraid.

It matters not how strait the gate,
How charged with punishments the scroll,
I am the master of my fate;
I am the captain of my soul.

William Ernest Henley (1849–1903)

A young lady named Dorthea Day wrote the following response to Henley.

Out of the light that dazzles me,
Bright as the sun from pole to pole.
I thank the God I know to be,
For Christ – The Conqueror of my soul.

Since His the sway of circumstance,
I would not wince or cry aloud.
Under the rule, which men call chance,
My head, with joy, is humble bowed.

Beyond this place of sin and tears,
That life with Him – and His the Aid,
That, spite the menace of the years,
Keeps, and will keep me unafraid.

I have no fear though straight the gate:
He cleared punishment from the scroll.
Christ is the Master of my fate!
Christ is the Captain of my soul.

The second thing we learn is that a person's response to the truth of God's sovereign control as set forth in this chapter will show whether they have a heart renewed by grace or a heart committed to being one's own god. The true believer will rejoice that God controls both the events in our lives as well as the timing of each event. He sings with hope and confidence, "Whatever my lot, Thou hast taught me to say, it is well, it is well, with my soul." In contrast, the rebel cries, "It matters not how straight the gate, How charged with punishments the scroll, I am the master of my fate, I am the captain of my soul."

Fallen humanity, by nature, thinks life would be wonderful if we could order every event of every day of our existence. If that were possible, do you really believe that all your days would be happy and without care? At first, you probably do, but upon reflection, you know better. You realize that you would change five things before noon the first day simply because something unforeseen happened. By mid-afternoon, you would be lamenting that you had not chosen something else at noontime.

This thing we call "happiness" is a monster that we can neither tame nor destroy. It was let loose in the Garden of Eden when man forsook pleasing God as the chief purpose in life. Man chose to go his own way and make his own rules, believing that therein lay the route to happiness. Did you ever ask yourself, "Exactly what is happiness? What would it take to make me a truly happy person?" We would love to be able to make everything and everybody that does not line up in a way that pleases us to "un-happen." I cannot be happy until everything in my life contributes to my personal well-being. Anything that does not promote my felici-

ty should "un-happen." That means I may have to destroy
your happiness and your individuality if they in any way
hinder me from getting what I need (meaning my own way)
in everything.

Your children really believe that they have both the ability and the right to choose what they are positive will make
them happy. They are convinced that the day they move out
of your house and go on their own they will experience the
first day of true personal happiness. They cannot wait to be
free to make their own choices so they can be happy. "Oh,"
you say, "but they do not know any better. They are young
and have not faced the real world." Of course, you are correct, but the question remains for you, "Have you faced the
world of reality or do you still have this fantasy about happiness?"

Would a five-year old pick spinach or a candy bar? The
candy bar, of course. Would a teenager pick doing home-
work instead of going to a movie? We all know both the answer and the reason behind the answer. We fail, however, to
see the same principle operating in our own adult spiritual
lives. Would you ever choose a trial, a disappointment, or a
sickness over ease, comfort, and health, even if you knew
beforehand the unbelievable grace that you would experience through the trial or sickness? We really are not so different from our five-year olds!

Let us look a little more closely at chapter three in detail.
Everything in life revolves around an ordained time. _To
every thing there is a season, and a time to every purpose under
the heaven_ (Eccl 3:1, KJV). Both the Old and New Testament
Scriptures see purposefulness in all of life's events. There is

no hint that fate or chance controls human destiny. The biblical message is, "it came to pass," not, "as luck would have it."

God has ordained a time for sending rain and for withholding rain. He supplies it or suppresses it right on schedule. "Then I will give you rain in due season, and the land shall yield her increase, and the trees of the field shall yield their fruit" (Lev. 26:4, KJV)

God has ordained a time for the destruction of his enemies. "To me belongeth vengeance, and recompence; their foot shall slide in due time: for the day of their calamity is at hand, and the things that shall come upon them make haste" (Deut. 32:35, KJV). Other times, God strengthens the hand of the enemies of his people when he purposes to use them as instruments of judgment (see Habakkuk).

There is an ordained time for conception and birth. In Genesis 21:1–2, we read that the LORD visited Sarah as he had said, and the LORD did unto Sarah as he had spoken. "For Sarah conceived, and bare Abraham a son in his old age, at the set time of which God had spoken to him" (KJV).

All *times* serve God's eternal unchanging purpose. We saw this in Luke 2:1–5, when God used a universal tax to get Mary to Jerusalem. We often hear preachers say, "The time was ripe. Rome had built roads and expanded communications. There were great expectations for something major to happen" and God "took advantage of these prevailing conditions." NO! God prepared all those things. He did not take advantage of the conditions; he *created* the necessary conditions to fulfill his sovereign purposes!

Chapter 3, verse 1 shows that times (events) and seasons (purposes) go together. The KJV says, "a _time_ for every _purpose_," and the NIV says "a _season_ for every _activity_." Certain seasons dictate certain activities and make other activities impossible. Spring means it is time to get the lawn mower in shape. Why? Spring means growing grass, whether I like it or not. The pessimist says, "Oh no, not already. It is so useless to cut the grass, it just grows back." The optimist says, "Great! Everything will be green and beautiful again. I love working in the fresh air and sunshine and getting the exercise." I never cease to be amazed at how a pessimist and an optimist can look at exactly the same thing and see two opposite situations. I think I mentioned this before but it is worth repeating. Someone scrawled "Apathy rules" on the outside of a university library. Someone else wrote the words, "True, but who cares." It is tough to live with either a consistent optimist or a consistent pessimist.

We swallow a bitter pill when we are forced to admit that we have no control over, nor can we change, the times, the seasons, or the things that go along with each. Sometimes, different circumstances radically change the response to the same event. For instance, we usually associate a birth with laughter and joy. Psalm 127:3–5 accompanies many baby shower gifts.

> _Lo, children are an heritage of the Lord: and the fruit of the womb is his reward. As arrows are in the hand of a mighty man; so are children of the youth. Happy is the man that hath his quiver full of them: they shall not be ashamed, but they shall speak with the enemies in the gate._ (KJV)

Suppose the child is born blind and deaf? We would be tempted to say, "Some gift!" As we think of all the hardships that child must endure and all the effort and labor its parents must expend to care for it, we would want to mourn rather than laugh. What good can ever come out of such a tragic situation? Yet, suppose that baby's name was Helen Keller. Although she was born with vision and hearing, she suffered a severe fever when she was just nineteen months old that left her blind, deaf, and mute. How many children with perfect sight and hearing have affected the world as much as Helen Keller did?

Some years ago, my wife took a nurse's aid course. The nurse who taught one of her classes was obviously an evangelical Christian. When she came to the subject of abortion, she asked the following question. "Do you think an abortion would be justified if the unborn child was the pregnant woman's sixth child, the family lived in poverty, the husband had venereal disease, and the wife supported the family by taking in laundry? One child was already born blind, another was born dead, and the doctors knew this new child was going to be born with some severe abnormalities." All but two out of nearly forty said, "Yes, under those circumstances an abortion is justified if not actually mandated." The teacher said, "You just aborted Johann Sebastian Bach."[1]

Psalm 31:15 expresses David's hope, "My times are in Thy hands." This is the practical application of the theology of sovereignty. It applies the truth of ordained times and

---

[1] All of the information in the teacher's story cannot be verified with historical data. Web-based biographical data on Johann Sebastian Bach includes no references to poverty, his father's venereal disease, or his mother as a laundress.

seasons to personal life. Think about all the times and circumstances of David's life.

- There is a time for David to be a shepherd even though he is ordained to be a king.

- There is a time for him to be misunderstood and hated, which will equip him for later work.

- There is a time for him to hide in a cave in fear for his life, which teaches him to learn confidence in God.

- There is a time for David to be anointed as king, but he will have to wait to exercise the rights of king.

- David will not use the energy of the flesh to achieve or avoid any of these things, even though he knows they ultimately must occur. He will wait for God's time.

- In the cave, he resisted the flesh and refused to kill Saul. There is never a right time to follow the flesh.

- David refused to use the sword to defend his throne against his own son. "I did not need a sword to get this throne and I will not use a sword to defend it. God gave it to me in his time and he can take it away if he so chooses."

If you had been David's mother and you had been given the power to control the events surrounding his life, how many of the very unpleasant experiences he endured would you have eliminated from his life? How many children do you know who have been ruined by sincere parents who determined that their children would not have to endure the things that they did? Were not all of David's bad experiences the very things that helped make him such a great king?

We must not view the writer of Ecclesiastes as an emotionless stoic saying, "Well, that's the way the cookie crumbles, so grin and bear it, even if does not make sense." Nor is he an Epicurean saying, "Who can trust a God like that? Eat, drink and be merry and do not think about the problems." He also is not a disappointed romantic asking, "Where is the goodie-giving God I heard about?"

Ecclesiastes chapter three is another way of presenting the truth of Romans 11:36, "Of him, and through him, and to him, are all things." Paul records the worship that follows heartfelt submission to God's sovereign ordaining of all things, "To whom be the glory forever." The Teacher echoes Job, "Though he slay me, yet will I trust in him" (Job 13:15, KJV). This worshipful attitude towards God's sovereignty finds expression in the hymn "Whate'er my God Ordains is Right."[2]

> Whate're my God ordains is right:
> Holy, His will abideth;
> I will be still what'er He doth;
> And follow where He guideth;
> He is my God; though dark my road,
> He holds me that I shall not fall:
> Wherefore to Him I leave it all.
>
> Whate'er my God ordains is right:
> He never will deceive me;
> He leads me by the proper path:

---

[2] Written in German by Samuel Rodigast (1676) and translated into English by Catherine Winkworth (1863). Rodigast wrote this poem for his friend Gastorius, who was seriously ill at the time. Gastorius recovered and wrote the tune for Rodigast's words.

I know He will not leave me.
I take, content, what He hath sent;
His hand can turn my grief's away,
And patiently I wait His day.

What e'er my God ordains is right
Though now this cup, in drinking,
May bitter seem to my faint heart,
I take it all unshrinking.
My God is true; each morn anew
Sweet comfort yet shall fill my heart,
And pain and sorrow shall depart.

Whate'er my God ordains is right:
Here shall my stand be taken;
Though sorrow, need, or death be mine,
Yet am I not forsaken.
My Father's care is round me there;
He holds me that I shall not fall:
And so to Him I leave it all.

Let me review the main lessons in this great chapter. (1) Everything happens by God's decrees. (2) Everything happens according to God's timetable (3:1), and (3) everything is beautiful in God's time (3:11). This includes death, the ugliest experience of man. Only God can say at a graveyard, "How beautiful in the sight of the Lord is the death of his saints."

The Seeker now begins to apply what he has been saying. Verses 9–15 of chapter 3 record some of the practical implications of this theology in real life.

What does the worker gain from his toil? [Good question! The ungodly answers, "No profit at all – it is meaningless. The child of God says, "Nothing is in vain. Even pain has a purpose."] *I have seen the burden God has laid on men. He has made everything beautiful in its time.* ["Everything" really does include "all things!"] *He has also set eternity in the hearts of men; yet they cannot fathom what God has done from beginning to end. I know that there is nothing better for men than to be happy and do good while they live. That everyone may eat and drink, and find satisfaction in all his toil – this is the gift of God.* [The Apostle Paul, "I have <u>learned</u> in whatsoever state I am in, therein to be content."] *I know that everything God does will endure forever; nothing can be added to it and nothing taken from it. God does it so that men will revere him. Whatever is has already been, and what will be has been before; and God will call the past to account.* (NIV)

There is an essential and certain cause/effect relationship between theology and life, between what we believe and how we feel and act. One of the most stupid statements ever made is, "It does not matter *what you believe* as long as you are *sincere."* Sincerity has absolutely nothing to do with truth. Sincerity is to truth what the gas peddle is to your car. The gas peddle determines how fast you drive your car, but it has nothing to do with the direction in which you are going. I used that illustration once when I was speaking at a youth retreat. On the way home, we became lost. One of the youngsters with me said, "Go a little faster Mr. Reisinger and then we will be sure we are going in the right direction." Everyone laughed and a girl said, "Floor the gas peddle and we will be positive we are going the right direction." I am sure everyone can see how ridiculous that is, but it is no more so than saying, "It does not matter what you believe as long as you are sincere." Your sincerity in what you believe determines how zealous you are in practicing your beliefs, but sincerity has nothing to do with whether what you believe is true or false.

One of the dangers of this idea is that the more sincere you are in what you believe, even when you are wrong, the more zealous you will be in actions that stem from that thinking. Like driving a car, the more assured you are that you are going in the right direction, the further you will go before you turn around. No one is more sincere than the typical cult member is. The terrorists of our day are the most fully convinced people there are, but they are dead wrong. A terrorist may be so sincere that he will gladly die for his beliefs, but he is still wrong in both the beliefs and the actions growing out of those beliefs. He will never change until his thinking changes.

Dr. Donald Grey Barnhouse used to say, "All of the world's real problems are theological!" He was correct. For instance, the race problem in the United States involves theology. We can never solve that problem until we all believe in the creatorship of God and that all men and women are brothers and sisters. If you want to solve the race problem, study Acts 17. Do you want to make the race problem worse? Teach people the Darwinian theory of evolution and the survival of the fittest. You cannot deny God as creator and still maintain that all human beings are "created equal in the sight of God."

Whether we like it or not, we will see everything in life from only one of two points of view. If, on the one hand, all we see is a mess of unrelated pieces without any meaning, then we will agree with the writer of Ecclesiastes and say, "Meaningless, meaningless, all is meaningless." If, on the other hand, we see the hand of God ruling all things for his own glory and for our good, then we can always, in all situations, bow and worship.

Our Lord told a parable of a wealthy farmer who hoarded his goods. He kept building bigger and bigger barns.

And he said, This will I do: I will pull down my barns, and build greater; and there will I bestow all my fruits and my goods. And I will say to my soul, Soul, thou hast much goods laid up for many years; take thine ease, eat, drink, and be merry. But God said unto him, Thou fool, this night thy soul shall be required of thee: then whose shall those things be, which thou hast provided? So is he that layeth up treasure for himself, and is not rich toward God. (KJV)

The rich fool made three mistakes: (1) He mistook his body for his soul, (2) he mistook time for eternity, and (3) he mistook himself for God. If you who read this are not converted, then you are making those same three mistakes every day of your life! Our Lord will someday say to you, *"Thou fool, this night thy soul shall be required of thee: then whose shall those things be, which thou hast provided? So is he that layeth up treasure for himself, and is not rich toward God."*

We simply must see a cause/effect in what a society, or an individual, believes and how they act. We have said it before; it is not the drugs, unbridled sex, and pills of every description that produced our present society. Our society's beliefs about the purpose and meaning of life drove it to a place where every form of diversion became necessary even to get out of bed.

If we dwell on verse 9, we could develop a defeatist attitude that leads to either apathy or cynicism. *What profit hath he that worketh in that wherein he laboureth?* If we know before we start an endeavor that even though we will succeed we will still be bitterly disappointed, then why even start?

In Verse 10, *I have seen the travail, which God hath given to the sons of men to be exercised in it,* Solomon repeats the question asked in verse 9, but now brings God into the picture. The real burden on man is that he must bear both the travail and its meaningless results without ever understanding either.

Verse 11a is one of those Halleluiah texts; *He hath made every thing beautiful in his time* . . . . When we begin to grasp its truth, we want to shout for joy. Like Romans 8:28, the "everything" here really means everything without exception. God ordains the events and the times and it all serves his purpose. All of our times are really his times for me. The message is, "Relax, brother, he's got the whole world in his hands."

My brother Ernest owned a large construction company. He employed a man who knew more about Caterpillar tractors than the Caterpillar Company. One day when I was visiting with my nephew, we happened to be on a job site when a large Caterpillar tractor broke down. They immediately radioed for the expert mechanic. When he arrived, my nephew smiled and said, "Watch this guy." When the tractor broke, it meant that four heavy dump trucks, a large scoop shovel, plus a number of workers also were idle.

The mechanic got out of his pick-up truck and walked over to the tractor. He walked around it about three times pushing and pulling wires and other things. He asked the operator some questions. Then he slowly walked back to his pick-up and got a thermos jug, poured himself a cup of coffee, and proceeded to sit down and drink it. I looked at my nephew who was grinning from ear to ear. If my brother Ernest had been there, he would have shot the man. Finally, the mechanic stood up and said, "It is one of three things. If it is 'A,' I can have it fixed in an hour. If it is 'B,' we will need such-and-such a part, so radio and get one just in case. If it is 'C,' we will have to take it back to the shop. Get a flatbed out here just in case. I will know which it is in twenty minutes." He was always right. My nephew looked me and said, "It is beautiful to watch him work."

The man was not goofing off while sitting there drinking his coffee. He was running everything through his brain and was not going to start tearing anything apart until he knew what was wrong. Sometimes, we feel that God is on a coffee break. Rather than fret and worry, we must relax, because God has it all under control. All of our times are in his hands. It really is beautiful to watch God work. He is always right.

The second part of verse 11 shows the source of the lost man's pathetic situation. *"...also he hath set the world in their heart, so that no man can find out the work that God maketh from the beginning to the end.* Humanity can neither escape God nor figure him out. God has put eternity in man's heart. In his heart of hearts, man knows that God is there, but he will do anything and everything possible to avoid any confrontation. Man brags about his freedom while his chains of self and sin drag him into one bad situation after another. We must keep reminding ourselves that sinful man would rather be the center of total chaos then he would admit he is a creature, a lost creature, desperately in need of grace.

The child of God learns to look at everything that happens as coming from the hand of a heavenly Father. How radically different is the view of time and events for a lost man and a saved man. Imagine a convicted criminal in a prison cell, unable to sleep. At six o'clock in the morning, he faces execution. He can see the stars through his cell window. He wishes the sun would never replace them. The most dreaded words he will ever hear are when the jailer comes and says, "It is time!" What horrible words. Now, imagine a bedroom where a girl is tossing and turning because she cannot sleep. She too will soon hear those same words, "It is time!" However, she cannot wait to hear them. She is eagerly waiting for her mother to knock on the door and say, "It is time." Tomorrow is her wedding day. They will be some of the sweetest words she ever hears. Does it amaze you that the same words could carry such different connotations? Imagine the lost man and the believer hearing the grim reaper say, "It is time." What will be the reaction of each to the same words?

How do we apply sovereignty theology to our lives? If you are asked, "What all are you going to do today?" just say, "I don't know for sure. My father has a bunch of appointments for me." Whatever you face, you can say, "It is time." You, however, do not say it with stoic resignation. You can also say, "Whatever it is, I am sure it will be beautiful in his time and his purpose."

There is a time for everything. There is a time to be converted and that time is now. "Today is the day of salvation." There is a time to get earnest with God and that time is right now. There is a time to return to our first love and that time is now.

CHAPTER EIGHT: VERSES 3:9–15 #2

MY TIMES ARE IN THY HANDS

The writer of Ecclesiastes keeps reminding us that life under the sun has no real meaning. Everything is meaningless to the man who views the world apart from any revelation from God. Thus far, in chapter 3 of Ecclesiastes, we have seen that God sovereignly ordains every event as well as the timing of that event. While this leads an unbeliever to question of the meaning and purpose of work, it is a great comfort to a child of God. The believer knows that everything God ordains will ultimately be for God's glory and the believer's good.

Walter Kaiser calls the section that runs from 3:1 through 5:20 "Understanding the All-Encompassing Plan of God." He suggests the following outline for the section.

1. 3:1–15: The Principle: God has a plan that embraces every man and woman and all of their actions in all times.

2. 3:16–4:16: The Facts: The anomalies and apparent contradictions in this thesis are examined and reflected upon.

3. 5:1–17: The Implications: Certain cautions and warnings must be raised lest a hasty calculation lead men and women to deny the reality and existence of God's providence and plan.

4. 5:18–20: Conclusion.

We saw how verses 2–8 show that God controls everything that happens, as to both substance and timing. His control covers the day of our birth and the time of our death. God ordained your birthday and your funeral and everything in between. Likewise, God fixed the seasons for planting and harvesting. Whether we look at man's life or the world of vegetables and fruits, we see God's sovereign control. God's reign extends even to timing. Useless stones are discarded, but the same stones may later be gathered to be used in a building. Sometimes God's providence puts us in a place where we are stirred up to anger and in other times and places we are stirred up to love.

In 3:9, the Seeker again asks the nagging question he first asked in 1:3: "What does the worker gain from his toil?" The answer is "nothing." That answer is both clear and frustrating to an unbeliever, but very reassuring to a child of God. Since every event in life has its origin and its timing from God, nothing man does can control or change the timing or circumstances of those events. Everything unfolds under God's sovereign control, right on schedule: birth/death, growth/harvest, joys/sorrows, acquiring/losing, speaking up/being silent; and war/peace.

> *What does the worker gain from his toil? I have seen the burden God has laid on men. He has made everything beautiful in its time. He has also set eternity in the hearts of men; yet they cannot fathom what God has done from beginning to end. I know that there is nothing better for men than to be happy and do good while they live. That everyone may eat and drink, and find satisfaction in all his toil – this is the gift of God. (Eccl 3:9–13, NIV)*

Verses 9 through 13 address the theme of the vanity of toil. The author begins the idea back in 2:4–26, references it from the point of view of time in 3:1–8, and then directly confronts it again in 3:9. Even though it is vanity, God has laid work on humanity (vs. 10: *burden* in the NIV, *busyness* in the ESB, and *tasks* in NKJV). What function does all this toil serve, since all things come in God's timing (the point of the preceding passage; verses 1–8)? Why bother to work for anything since it really accomplishes nothing? It is not men who make things beautiful by their effort (toil), but God, who makes everything beautiful in its time. As if the idea that work is a waste of time were not disheartening enough, God has put this idea of timelessness into the psyche of human beings. We are limited creatures stuck in a limited function called time, doing work that accomplishes nothing, and we know that there is more to life than this. We do not know what eternity is like, nor can we find out through all our efforts. The Seeker concludes that since we cannot find out what God has chosen to not reveal, the best response is to enjoy what God has given food, drink, and work—and to appreciate them as gifts that direct our attention back to God, and not as ends in themselves.

Although sin has made everything ugly, including work, God's grace will make everything "beautiful in God's time." In God's world, he has made everything fit together in a perfect whole. The old saying, "A place for everything and everything in it place" reaches it highest fulfillment in God's good work. Everything fits into its appointed time and place.

The Seeker's comments in verse 11 go past mere acknowledgment of the sovereignty of God's ordaining of each event. He adds that everything God does is beautiful in God's time. Walter Kaiser has caught the essence of verse 11.

The key word in verse 11 is "eternity": "God has put **eternity** in their heart." This quest is a deep-seated desire, a compul-
sive drive, because man is made in the image of God to appreciate the beauty of creation (on an aesthetic level); to know the
character, composition, and meaning of the world (on an academic and philosophical level); and to discern its purpose and
destiny (on a theological level). There is the majesty and the
madness of the whole thing. Man has an inborn inquisitiveness
and capacity to learn how everything in his experience can be
integrated to make a whole. He wants to know how the mundane "down under" realm of ordinary, day-to-day living fits
with the "up-stairs" realm of the hereafter; how the business of
living, eating, working, and enjoying can be made to fit with
the call to worship, serve, and love the living God; and how
one can accomplish the integration of the sciences and humani-
ties. But in all the vastness and confusion, man is frustrated by
the "vanity" of selecting any one of the many facets of God's
"good" world as that part of life to which he totally gives himself.[3]

Man must come to terms with his limitations. He must
bow to the sovereignty of God and learn why godliness with
contentment in every situation is the real goal of life. He can
only know that as God sovereignly reveals it to him. Not only is every good thing we have a gift from God, but even the
ability to receive and enjoy it as such is also a gift from God.

In 3:12, the writer uses what will later become one of
Paul's favorite expressions, "I know." The KJV and the NIV
each have a different slant on this text. The KJV says, "I
know that there is no good in them, but for a man to rejoice,

---

[3] Walter Kaiser, *Ecclesiastes, Total Life* (Chicago: Moody Press,
1979), 66–67.

and to do good in his life." The NIV says, "I know that there is nothing better for men than to be happy and do good while they live." The KJV would emphasize that there is no good in any and all work, so man must find his meaning and purpose some other place. The NIV emphasizes the best thing a man can experience is true happiness in whatever God's providence gives him. In verse 12, the writer knows the secret of life. This is the same idea that Paul expresses by "godliness with contentment is great gain" (1 Tim 6:6). Before we were Christians, we failed in all our attempts to hang on to happy relationships or joyous occasions. Now we can say, "There really is a 'joy unspeakable' and it really is lasting."

In 2:24, we encountered the beginning of a radically different worldview. Secularism had begun to give way to theism. God had come into the picture. The Seeker repeats that focus in 3:13. Here, secularism gives way to theism. Pessimism gives way to optimism. Human autonomy gives way to the humility of faith. Philosophy gives way to biblical revelation. The song now becomes, "What ever my lot, Thou hast taught me to say, it is well, it is well, with my soul."

In verse 14, the writer again says, "I know." Two of Paul's favorite phrases are "I know" and "I am persuaded." If you want a good Bible study, look up the specific things that Paul knows and of which he is persuaded. Our postmodern culture "insists that objective knowledge is neither attainable nor desirable."[4] This translates into boasting about its ignorance and its lack of assurance about anything. To be

---

[4] D. A. Carson, *Becoming Conversant With the Emerging Church* (Grand Rapids, MI: Zondervan, 2005), 97.

open-minded is to reject all absolutes and to be sure of nothing. "All truth claims are merely true for some people, even if not for all people at all times and places."[5] The problem is that when you are sure of nothing, you are ready to believe anything that comes down the pike (See Acts 17:19–21). It is no accident that our present society has produced so many weird and outlandish cultic religious organizations. The strong postmodern voice in our society is positive that you cannot be sure of anything except that you cannot be sure of anything. In their dogmatism, they do not realize how inconsistent their statement is. How can you be positive that you cannot be positive about anything? Contrast their anti-foundational stance with the words of the Seeker, *"I know that everything God does will endure forever; nothing can be added to it and nothing taken from it."* The absolute language is striking: know, everything, forever, and nothing. The Seeker uses unqualified terminology to convey his faith in the full-blown sovereignty of God.

If all that is under the sun is futile, transient, and unreliable, then security can be found only in God's sovereign unchanging grace. God's purposes are just as sure as his power in grace is sure. God's work is effective and complete. In glorification, he will conform us completely to the image of Christ. God's redemptive work, or new creation, is secure. Nothing can destroy or mar it in any way. It is not like the first work of creation. This kind of sovereignty fills a lost man with fear, but it fills a believer with joy and hope. I often tell people who are going through tough times, "I read

---

[5] Ibid., 97.

the last chapter! We win – big time." We know that "he who hath begun a good work in [us] will perform it until the day of Jesus Christ" (Phil. 1:6). Likewise, we know we are sealed with no less a seal than the Holy Spirit himself, and that sealing is "unto the day of redemption" (Eph. 4:30). That seal remains until the day of our full redemption is reached. It is the absolute guarantee that we will make it to heaven! Man cannot add to or take away one single thing from the sovereign purposes of God.

Verse 15 emphasizes the absolute unchangeableness of God's purposes and plans. The Seeker offers a poetic expression of his conclusions about toil, beauty and eternity and introduces the idea of judgment, which will occupy the next several verses. *"Whatever is has already been, and what will be has been before; and God will call the past to account."* Derek Kidner, in his commentary on Ecclesiastes, writes,

> The earthbound man, in the light of verses 14 and 15, is the prisoner of a system he cannot break or even bend; and behind it is God. There is no escape, and nowhere to jettison what encumbers and incriminates him. But the man of God hears the verse with no such misgivings. To him verse 14 describes the divine faithfulness that makes the fear of God a fruitful and filial relationship; and verse 15 assures him that with God all things are foreknown, and nothing overlooked. God has no abortive enterprises or forgotten men.[6]

Nothing is outside the scope of God's providence or care. Even our tears are remembered by God:

---

[6] Derek Kidner, A Time to Mourn and a Time to Dance, The Message of Ecclesiastes (Downers Grove: InterVarsity Press, 1976), 40.

*"Thou tellest my wanderings: put thou my tears into thy bottle:
are they not in thy book? When I cry unto thee, then shall mine enemies turn back: this I know; for God is for me. In God will I praise his
word: in the LORD will I praise his word."* (Psalm 56:8–10, KJV.
See also Ecclesiastes 4:1.)

"Whatever is has already been," means that the present is as
sure as the past, because God's decree is that trustworthy.
We know that we cannot go back and change the past because the events have already occurred—they are historical
facts. The present is just as secure, because God chooses to
bring it to pass. "Whatever will be has been before." Like the
past and the present, the future is secure because God has
determined it. Nothing can change God's decree, and nothing can escape his judgment. The past may be hidden from
us, but God will call it to account.

Verse 16 introduces the subject of the rule of injustice and
the harshness of life. At first glance, it looks like a new
theme, but it is not. The thought of set times and their power
over us is still present in verse 17. Justice may seem to be
missing, but God has set a time for that as well. As D. A.
Carson is fond of saying, "A time will come when justice
will be done, and will be seen to have been done." Chapter 4
will elaborate on this subject. It will also come up at least
five more times in the rest of the book.

The writer brings forth six facts of life as he sees and understands it that seem to contradict his thesis that God sovereignly controls all people and all events. How can God be
in total control and allow even the courts of justice to be corrupted and used against the very people those courts were
designed to protect? Are men no better than beasts? Is it true
that the fortunate position is never to have been born?

1. The halls of justice are filled with unrighteousness (3:16, 17).

And I saw something else under the sun: In the place of judgment – wickedness was there, in the place of justice – wickedness was there. I thought in my heart, "God will bring to judgment both the righteous and the wicked, for there will be a time for every activity, a time for every deed." (NIV)

2. Men, just like beasts, die (3:18–21).

I also thought, "As for men, God tests them so that they may see that they are like the animals. Man's fate is like that of the animals; the same fate awaits them both: As one dies, so dies the other. All have the same breath; man has no advantage over the animal. Everything is meaningless. All go to the same place; all come from dust, and to dust all return. Who knows if the spirit of man rises upward and if the spirit of the animal goes down into the earth?" So I saw that there is nothing better for a man than to enjoy his work, because that is his lot. For who can bring him to see what will happen after him? (NIV)

3. Man is oppressed (4:1–3).

Again I looked and saw all the oppression that was taking place under the sun: I saw the tears of the oppressed – and they have no comforter; power was on the side of their oppressors – and they have no comforter. And I declared that the dead, who had already died, are happier than the living, who are still alive. But better than both is he who has not yet been, who has not seen the evil that is done under the sun. (NIV)

4. Man is in constant rivalry (4:4–6).

And I saw that all labor and all achievement spring from man's envy of his neighbor. This too is meaningless, a chasing after the wind. The fool folds his hands and ruins himself. Better one handful with tranquillity than two handfuls with toil and chasing after the wind. (NIV)

5. Men are alone and isolated (4:7–12).

Again I saw something meaningless under the sun: There was a man all alone; he had neither son nor brother. There was no end to his toil, yet his eyes were not content with his wealth. "For whom am I toiling," he asked, "and why am I depriving myself of enjoyment?" This too is meaningless — a miserable business! Two are better than one, because they have a good return for their work: If one falls down, his friend can help him up. But pity the man who falls and has no one to help him up! Also, if two lie down together, they will keep warm. But how can one keep warm alone? Though one may be overpowered, two can defend themselves. A cord of three strands is not quickly broken. (NIV)

6. Popularity is only temporary (4:13–16).

Better a poor but wise youth than an old but foolish king who no longer knows how to take warning. The youth may have come from prison to the kingship, or he may have been born in poverty within his kingdom. I saw that all who lived and walked under the sun followed the youth, the king's successor. There was no end to all the people who were before them. But those who came later were not pleased with the successor. This too is meaningless, a chasing after the wind. (NIV)

In five of the six cases, the writer introduces his argument with "Moreover I saw" (3:16), "I indeed saw" (3:18; 4:4), or "again I saw (4:1; 4:7); only 4:13 does not use some form of this introduction. Let us look at these problems one at a time.

First, there is wickedness in the courts. This seems to contradict the concept of a good God who is in charge of things. Surely, the one place that God would assure that justice prevailed is in the courts, but the writer sees the courts as hotbeds of tyranny and wickedness. After all, was not God's purpose in setting up human tribunals for the express purpose of protecting the poor and vulnerable in society? "And I saw something else under the sun: In the place of judgment—wickedness was there, in the place of justice—wickedness was there" (v. 16).

As soon as the writer faces this troublesome fact, he imme-diately, in verse 17, proposes an answer to his distress. He knows that God has a time for everything, including the judgment of both the righteous and the wicked. "I thought in my heart, 'God will bring to judgment both the righteous and the wicked, for there will be a time for every activity, a time for every deed'" (v. 17). Wicked men may appear to prevail in their tyranny over the poor and helpless, but they will someday face the Judge of all judges, God himself. Just as the cold and bitter winter will come to an appointed end and spring shall come in all of its beauty, so the night of weeping will end and the righting of all wrongs shall take place. Kidner comments,

> ... It reinforces the purely moral conviction that God will judge (17), by the realization that for this event, as for every-thing else, He has already appointed its proper time.

> This is all very well, we may feel; but why the delay? Why is the present not the time for universal justice? To that unspo-ken question verses 18 ff. gives a typical abrasive answer, since our first need is not to teach God His business but to learn the truth about ourselves, a lesson we are very slow to accept. ... But we have to admit that quite apart from our tendencies to cruelty and squalor, which puts us in a class below the beasts, there are at least two facts about us which support the charge: the role of greed and cunning in our affairs (which is the sub-ject under discussion, verse 16), and the mortality that man shares with all earthly creatures. The first of these sad facts reappears in the next chapter; the second occupies the re-mainder of this one, and interacts with the rest of the Old Tes-tament. Verse 20, showing us man on his journey from dust to dust, as in Genesis 3:19, confronts us with the Fall, and with

the irony that we die like cattle because we fancied ourselves as gods.[7]

In 2 Kings 8:12–13, we find one of the most fearful incidents in the Old Testament Scriptures. The passage concerns a man named Hazael who would soon be king of Syria.

> *And Hazael said, Why weepeth my lord? And he answered, Because I know the evil that thou wilt do unto the children of Israel: their strong holds wilt thou set on fire, and their young men wilt thou slay with the sword, and wilt dash their children, and rip up their women with child.*
>
> *And Hazael said, But what, is thy servant a dog, that he should do this great thing? And Elisha answered, The LORD hath shewed me that thou shalt be king over Syria.* (KJV)

When the prophet told Hazael about the crimes that he foresaw Hazael would commit, Hazael was horrified. He sincerely protested, "What, is thy servant a dog, that he should do this great thing?" He could not believe that he was capable of such crimes, but Hazael became King of Syria and acted exactly as the prophet predicted. Have not we all, under certain circumstances, been amazed at some of the things that we have done, or wanted to do, to get what we wanted? If anyone had told us that we would do those things, we would have protested with Hazael that we were not capable of such things only to discover that we, creatures made in the image of God, were more than capable of acting on a level lower than animals.

Our refusal to come to grips with total depravity in ourselves demonstrates the terrifying power of sin to deceive us. We can see a specific sin in another person and yet be blind to that same sin in ourselves. When David cried out to

---

[7] Ibid., 42.

Nathan, "The man that committed that sin should die," he was not being a hypocrite. He simply did not see his own sin in Nathan's vivid and accurate description. He was just as blind as Hazael and as you and I. Of all God's creatures, only man can fall so far below his original creation. We who were created to be princes can sink to a position worse than pigs and snakes. It is this awful power of sin that makes people so very self-righteous and constantly critical of other people for the very thing of which they themselves are guilty.

In our next chapter, we will look at the other five disturbing observations of the Seeker in the rest of chapter 4.

CHAPTER NINE: VERSES 3:16 – 4:6

WICKEDNESS IN HIGH PLACES

The author of Ecclesiastes writes from the point of view of a person seeking meaning and purpose in life without reference to, or acknowledgement of, God. The conclusion he reaches at every point is that life is "meaningless, meaningless, all is meaningless." To escape meaninglessness, the Seeker must acknowledge that God exists and is in control. However, God's sovereignty presents the Seeker with multiple difficulties. If God is in control, how does the Seeker explain the terrible plight of humanity? How does he reconcile divine sovereignty with the unrighteousness that reigns in God's good creation, even in the very halls of justice? Why does God allow the oppression of the helpless? How can the triumph of the wicked over the godly in this life be part of God's plan? We, too, echo the Seeker's questions. No matter how firmly we are convinced that there is a day of reckoning in the future, we wonder if there is no hope or help for the present.

The opening phrase of 3:16, "I saw something else" (NIV, *Moreover* in the ESV and NKJV) indicates a new section, which the Seeker introduces with a lament concerning wickedness in the halls of justice. He tries to understand the problem of corruption and wickedness in high places.

And I saw something else under the sun: In the place of judgment
– wickedness was there, in the place of justice – wickedness was there.
I thought in my heart, "God will bring to judgment both the righteous and the wicked, for there will be a time for every activity, a time for every deed." (Eccl 3:16–17, NIV)

In the subsection that runs from verse 16 to verse 22, we find an observation (*I saw,* v.16), two passing comments (*I said...I said,* vv.17, 18–21), and then a conclusion (*So I saw,* v.22). The opening "I saw" indicates another observable problem (the Seeker has already compiled an impressive list of problems: pleasure, wisdom, folly, and work are all meaningless); the closing "I saw" presents the Seeker's philosophy in light of this new problem.

It is one thing to see oppression and wickedness at a personal level, but it is quite another to see them in the halls of justice. That is the worst kind of irony. God's purpose in instituting courts and tribunals was to protect the widow and the weak from the rich and the tyrant. When the very people who are appointed to uphold truth and justice use their position and power to destroy the very things they are appointed to uphold, society cannot long endure. When those sworn to uphold righteousness reject all moral values, wickedness of the worst kind must rule. When "might makes right" replaces "righteousness and truth," a society will quickly deteriorate into one ruled by animal lust and raw power. All men intuitively know that a wicked court system is the worst of evils. This acknowledgement is why the problem tears at the foundation of our faith.

The problem of corrupted justice also exists in the realm of religion and the church. When leaders of God's people no longer uphold God's truth and standards, but allow sin to flourish and their friends to make the rules, their churches will soon crumble from within. A corrupted church loses her positive influence on the broader culture. Even the world is amazed when a church leader openly sins or becomes a tyrant. They say, in amazement, "And he was a preacher."

The only thing that can sustain an honest person in a wicked and ruthless society is belief in a sovereign God who, in his own fixed time, will bring every person into a final, righteous judgment. The truth of eternity is built into every human being (3:11): the world calls belief in an eternal justice 'pie in the sky'; the Christian makes it a pillow upon which to lay his weary head. (See Psalm 73:17 and Genesis 18:25 for examples of saints who were comforted by the expectation of a future judgment.) The Seeker reasons that since there is a time for everything (his theme in 3:1–8), there will be a time for judgment as well.

Verses 18–21 seem, at first glance, to be thrown into the discussion without regard to context, but such is not the case.

> I also thought, "As for men, God tests them so that they may see that they are like the animals. Man's fate is like that of the animals; the same fate awaits them both: As one dies, so dies the other. All have the same breath; man has no advantage over the animal. Everything is meaningless. All go to the same place; all come from dust, and to dust all return. Who knows if the spirit of man rises upward and if the spirit of the animal goes down into the earth?" (Eccl 3:18–21, NIV)

The Seeker has considered delayed judgment from the perspective of God – no matter how long it takes, judgment will surely occur. Now he considers it from a human perspective. One reason God postpones judgment and permits wickedness is to allow man to reveal how depraved his heart really is. Man, in spite of education and philosophy, is still capable of living worse than animals do. When we ask, "Why does God allow men to get away with these things," the correct response is, "They really don't get away with anything." There is an eternal tomorrow. There is an ultimate accountability. There is a day of justice. All men will face God as judge; in his chamber hall, absolute righteousness will prevail. An unbeliever wrote a Christian editor of a small newspaper in the midwest and said, "I plowed one of my fields on a Sunday; I planted corn in the same field on a Sunday; I cultivated it on Sundays; I harvested it on a Sunday, and I reaped the best crop I ever had. So much for your belief in God." The editor, who believed and taught that the Sabbath was still binding, replied, "God does not settle all of His accounts in November."

The Seeker shows that, from an *under the sun* position, man is indeed not any better than an animal is. Under certain circumstances, man will turn from reason and truth and follow the law of the jungle. Might will dictate right, even in the halls of justice. Even more emphatic is the fact that humans, just like animals, wind up as worm food. It matters little whether a person is buried in a $50,000 casket or if his body is thrown on the dump. Like an animal, the human dies and returns to dust. If human beings honestly face reality, verses 18–20 will grate on their consciences. It does not matter what outstanding lives they lead, death comes to all, and human corpses are no more significant than animal remains.

Human beings are sinners who must die and face God in judgment. This fact is a caveat that follows every accolade human beings may earn. Naaman's leprosy illustrates this concept. In 2 Kings 5:1, we have a description of a remarkable man.

> *Now Naaman was commander of the army of the king of Aram. He was a great man in the sight of his master and highly regarded,*

because through him the LORD had given victory to Aram. He was a
valiant soldier, but he had leprosy. (NIV)

Notice the last phrase, *"But he had leprosy."* Naaman was a
commander – *but he was a leper;* he was a great man – *but he
was a leper;* he was highly regarded – *but he was a leper;* he
was victorious in battle – *but he was a leper;* he was a valiant
soldier – *but he was a leper.* It does not matter what you could
say about Naaman, or how true each statement was, you
would have to add, **"but he was a leper."** The same is true
of every son and daughter of Adam. No matter what honor
or title you bestow upon him, you must add, **"but he is a
sinner who will die and face God in judgment."** Neither
personal attainment nor societal value matter; all human beings are sinners who will die. They may have lived in palac-
es as privileged royalty or in cardboard boxes as homeless
bums, but they all will die and face God in judgment. Man
will die, just as animals will die. No matter how high he to-
wered over his contemporaries in wealth, power, or attainment, the angel of death will lower him to the same level as
a dog or a cow.

The Seeker is demonstrating that death is the time and
place that levels all men, without exception, to the same status. The burial practices of some of our Anabaptist forebears
illustrate this truth. A Mennonite cemetery is radically different from other graveyards. All of the gravestones are exactly the same size, color, and shape. They are rectangular,
white, and about nine inches wide and eighteen inches high.
They contain no information other than name, and date of
birth and death. A Mennonite cemetery constantly reminds
visitors that death levels all men. In our present society, men
may commit any number of crimes and oppressive actions,

and avoid punishment by bribing a corrupt judicial system, but they will not be able to buy off the angel of death or bribe the final judge. Verses 19–21 show us what verse 18 means.

> Man's fate is like that of the animals; the same fate awaits them both: As one dies, so dies the other. All have the same breath; man has no advantage over the animal. Everything is meaningless. All go to the same place; all come from dust, and to dust all return. Who knows if the spirit of man rises upward and if the spirit of the animal goes down into the earth?" (Eccl 3:19–21, NIV)

Jehovah Witnesses (and others who deny the doctrine of hell or an afterlife) misuse these verses. We must consider these verses in their context within the Book of Ecclesiastes. Remember, this conception of reality comes from a man who thinks (and records his thoughts) without any reference to God's self-revelation. This is an *under the sun* view of life and reality. Anyone who looks at life without reference to God will come to the same conclusions as the Seeker does. Those who adopt the *under the sun* explanation of life will live in the light of the Seeker's hopeless conclusion. Man cannot believe he is no different from an animal without starting to live like an animal.

On the surface, it appears that since both men and animals die, there is no real difference between them. Man has no advantage over the animal. If death ends everything, if there is no human existence after death, this conclusion is correct. Does a close reading of the text support this idea? First, the author bases his denial of intrinsic differences on the word *fate* (v. 19). He assumes that what can be observed of fate is all there is. This assumption leads to the belief that the grave is the ultimate fate of all living creatures. This conclusion does not consider any kind of afterlife, since that is not an observable phenomenon. If the only comparison you can make between men and animals is that they both die, then indeed, "all is meaningless" and man appears to be no different from the beast.

Second, "all go to the same place" (v. 20) is another way of saying "all die and go to the grave." All go back to the ground from which they were created. Everything that has the breath of life must lose it; the grave is the final stop for all. The point the Seeker drives home is that death not only levels all men, rich and poor, it levels all breathing creatures, and proves that man is, in the end, no better than any other animal.

Please note that the Seeker is not comparing believers and unbelievers. He is not talking about heaven and hell; he is comparing man with beasts. He writes, "the spirit of *man* rises upward," not "the spirit of *godly men* ..." and "the spirit of *the animal* goes down into the earth," not "the spirit of *ungodly men* ..." The spirits of all human beings, saved and lost, go upward; that means the spirits of all people return to God. Some will remain forever with the Lord and some will be sent away from the Lord into everlasting damnation. On the other hand, the animal goes into the ground and is no more. Man has immortality but the animal does not.

Verse 21 posits a question implicit with despair. We could paraphrase the verse, "In the final analysis who, if anybody, really knows what happens after death? Nobody knows for sure! Who can prove beyond question if the spirit of man rises upward and if the spirit of the animal goes down into the earth?" As I read that, I want to shout, **"I know, and I know for sure! I know because God has clearly revealed it**

in his Holy Word." However, Christians are the only people who can know with certainty, because they have talked with someone who was dead and who came back to life.

Some years ago, I spoke to the graduating nurses at our local hospital. Every year, the hospital asked a Jewish rabbi, a Catholic priest, and a Protestant clergyman each to lecture the student nurses on "How to help persons of different faiths die." I learned that two patients had recently died, and all of these nurses had attended those two people. Some of the nurses had been present at the time of the patients' deaths. I started my lecture by saying, "Before you can teach someone how to do something you must know how to do it yourself. *Do you yourself know how to die?*" The graduates were not paying close attention. I continued, "If that had been you, instead of Mr. Sweeny, in the bed in Room 204, would you have known how to die when someone pulled the sheet over your head?" Suddenly, I had their full attention. I then asked, "How would you like to talk to someone who had been dead and came back to life? I know someone who was dead but is now alive. I talk to him every morning and so can you." Only a faith in a resurrected Lord who has conquered death and the grave can make that kind of a statement.

Although the Seeker is not presenting a biblical theology of death, he indicates that he retains remnants of his faith. In Ecclesiastes 12:6–7, the Seeker is clear concerning the subject. There he writes that the spirit returns to God who gave it, a parallel to the "spirit of man rises upward" in verse 21.

> *Remember him – before the silver cord is severed, or the golden bowl is broken; before the pitcher is shattered at the spring, or the*

wheel broken at the well, and the dust returns to the ground it came from, and the spirit returns to God who gave it. (Eccl 12:6, 7, NIV)

The author concludes this section (3:22) with another reality check that leads to the same conclusion he has presented in verses 11 through 13 and verse 21: since nobody knows what happens after death, the best thing for man to do is to enjoy his work while he is alive.

So I saw that there is nothing better for a man than to enjoy his work, because that is his lot. For who can bring him to see what will happen after him?

If God really controls all events (3:1–15), has a definite purpose in allowing all things –including the worst of tyranny and injustice – (3:16–20), and commands the ultimate destiny of all creatures (21), then wisdom dictates we should gratefully pursue the earthly responsibilities God gives us and we should enjoy their fruit. Once we admit to God's sovereignty, we should begin to enjoy any and every pleasure that comes to us from the hand of God. The words *his lot*, in verse 22, remind me of one of my favorite hymns. "What ever my lot/ thou hast taught me to say/ it is well, it is well, with my soul."[8] This is true even when "sorrows like sea billows" threaten to overturn our frail vessel.

The question, "For who can bring him to see what will happen after him," does not anticipate an answer because it does not consider God's revelation. For the person who views things from *under the sun*, there is no ultimate resolution to his quest for reality. The writer is not concerned with knowing future events; his concern is with eternal destinies.

---

[8] From "It is Well with My Soul" by Horatio G. Spafford (1828 – 1888).

Eternity is hidden from the man who rejects God's revelation. However, the child of God knows not only that there is a heaven to be gained; he knows also how to gain it. As for specific events in this life, the believer does not know what tomorrow holds, but he does know who holds tomorrow. God is kind to hide the future from us. The hymn writer was correct when he wrote, "If we could see beyond today/ ... we often say/ but God in love a veil doth throw/ across our way."[9] God intends us to enjoy today. If we knew everything that was going to happen next week, we would concentrate on the bad to the extent we would not be able to enjoy the good of today.

The section from 4:1 through 10:20 continues to picture life *under the sun*. One writer has described the section this way.

> From this point it is not easy to trace a clear consecutive argument. Later on (11:1 – 12:8) a note of exhortation breaks in, moving the argument forward again. Between 4:1 – and 10:20 Ecclesiastes resembles the Book of Proverbs, with short epigrams dealing with various aspects of life. Groups of sayings, however, can be seen clustered around particular themes. Every unit between 5:8 and 6:12 deals in some way with wealth; each unit of 4:1–16 bears on the need for companionship; chs. 9:13 – 10:20 directly consider the limits of wisdom and the various manifestations of folly. The book bears evidence, therefore, of structure and arrangement, although it is at times difficult to discern. It is also conspicuous that the presuppositions in 1:2 – 3:22 continue to underlie each theme taken up. The vanity of "life under sun" comes in for heavy fire;

---

[9] From "If We Could See Beyond Today" by Norman J. Clayton (1903 – 1992).

the life of faith in a sovereign God is urged from time to time as the only remedy.

It is best, therefore, to treat the middle of Ecclesiastes as a guide to life "under the sun," presenting a series of major issues, each in turn from the viewpoint of "under the sun" limitation and from the viewpoint of faith. The Preacher faces the big issues; the hardships of life and the companionship it demands, poverty and wealth, the vexations of circumstances of life and of man himself, the authority of kings and authority misapplied, the limits of wisdom and the encroachment of folly. "Look!" he says in effect. "This is what it is really like. Can you face life in this world as it really is? There is only one way to do so." The various themes overlap considerably, so that several topics are considered more than once from different angles.[10]

In the beginning of chapter 4, the author returns to the subject of oppression.

> *Again I looked and saw all the oppression that was taking place under the sun: I saw the tears of the oppressed – and they have no comforter; power was on the side of their oppressors – and they have no comforter. And I declared that the dead, who had already died, are happier than the living, who are still alive. But better than both is he who has not yet been, who has not seen the evil that is done under the sun.* (Eccl 4:1–3, NIV)

We could all provide accounts of this kind of injustice. It is terrible to see the tears of the oppressed (usually the weak, the helpless, and the infirm). The hopeless ask, "Where can we turn for help", only to find there is no help.

God, in the Old Testament Scriptures, constantly exhorts people to show compassion for the oppressed. The identity

---

[10] Michael A. Eaton, *Ecclesiastes, An Introduction & Commentary* (Downers Grove, IL: IVP, 1983), 90.

and status of the oppressors are irrelevant: an oppressive king over his people, a master over his slaves, or the rich over the poor. God repeatedly warns the oppressor of the eternal consequences of that kind of wickedness. The problem is compounded because the power to oppress is in the hands of the very people who alone could change the situation.

It is no coincidence in the fact that the power is found on the side of the oppressor, since it is power that most quickly breeds the habit of oppression. Paradoxically it limits the possibility of reform itself, because the more control the reformed wields, the more it tends to tyranny.[11]

Likeable and easy-going individuals sometimes seem to undergo personality changes when they become leaders. When they accept authority, they become unbearable. In reality, they did not change; the new authority simply provided the first opportunity of revealing their true nature. "Power is on the side of the oppressor," therefore, there is "no one to comfort the oppressed." Even Job's religious friends were the worst of comforters. Job called them "Physicians of no value" (Job 13:4). It would be cruel indeed to tell a slave beaten without provocation, "God has a wonderful plan for your life." Religion, though well meaning, can aggravate some problems if its theological base is wrong.

After urging his readers to enjoy life, and then proceeding to tell them that oppression will probably make enjoyment impossible, the Seeker admits the case is grim. He sees it as so bad that he wishes he were dead or had never lived.

---

[11] Derek Kidner, *A Time To Mourn & A Time To Dance* (Downers Grove, IL: IVP, 1976), 44.

The following two verses are, in a sense, the saddest lines in the entire book. If we feel the Seeker is over-reacting, we may not have looked carefully enough at reality. As Christians, we have glimpsed a future that fills us with hope; that future does not excuse us from being honest with the present.

> *And I declared that the dead, who had already died, are happier than the living, who are still alive. But better than both is he who has not yet been, who has not seen the evil that is done under the sun.* (Eccl 4:2, 3, NIV)

So much for the Seeker's advice to do your best and enjoy life!

In 4:4-6, we see that human beings are in constant rivalry with each other because of envy and selfishness. Selfishness continually manifests itself as one of the root causes of man's misery.

> *And I saw that all labor and all achievement spring from man's envy of his neighbor. This too is meaningless, a chasing after the wind. The fool folds his hands and ruins himself. Better one handful with tranquillity than two handfuls with toil and chasing after the wind.* (NIV)

As the Seeker reflects on work, he realizes that the driving motivation in people is not the desire for pleasure: envy and ambition are the forces behind much of man's activity. The KJV translates verse 4 this way: "Again, I considered all travail, and every right work, that for this a man is envied of his neighbour. This is also vanity and vexation of spirit." A man pursues a right and good work and does so in an honorable manner. His primary goal is to help the people in his community. The more successful he is, the more the people he has helped will envy him. Envy can even destroy a person physically, "A heart at peace gives life to the body, but envy rots the bones" (Prov. 14:30, NIV).

Great souls will continue to do what is right, but shallow people need very little excuse to stop. Verse 4 describes the envious reaction of those who receive or observe good works. Verse 5 underscores the base motivation of envy by showing what happens to those who do good works but receive no acclaim for them. Some people tire of the unrewarding rat race and resent being unappreciated by the people they help, and they simply drop out. They withdraw and do not care about anything or anybody and prove they, too, were motivated by love of praise. The Seeker describes such people as fools who fold their hands. The phrase *folds his hands* means to be deliberately idle. Proverbs graphically describes the sluggard:

> Go to the ant, you sluggard; consider its ways and be wise! It has no commander, no overseer or ruler, yet it stores its provisions in summer and gathers its food at harvest. How long will you lie there, you sluggard? When will you get up from your sleep? A little sleep, a little slumber, a little folding of the hands to rest – and poverty will come on you like a bandit and scarcity like an armed man. (Prov. 6:6–11, NIV)

Many young people in the counter-culture of the sixties and early seventies discovered the truth of this maxim the hard way. They were correct to see the futility of selling one's soul for a mad race up the corporate ladder, but they went to the opposite extreme. These people withdrew from everything, including all work, and decided they could live on love alone. They soon used up all their resources and were forced to work, or to steal, or to starve. They could maintain neither their self-respect nor their physical or psychological well being. Although they were content with half a handful, they did not want to earn even that.

So what is the answer? It is quite simple. Learn to submit to the sovereign providence of God. Make your expectations realistic and potentially attainable with legitimate effort. Learn to realize that what matters is not how much you have but how much you enjoy what you have. The truth of verse 6, "Better one handful with tranquility than two handfuls with toil and chasing after the wind" is repeated in the New Testament Scriptures; "Godliness with contentment is great gain" (1 Tim 6:6, NIV). True contentment grows out of true godliness. The emphasis in Scripture is on our *being* something, and not on our *doing* something.

God has given me the privilege of traveling many places and meeting many different people. As I have traveled, two things have amazed me. First, some of the most contented and joyous people I have ever met have very little of this world's goods, and some of the most discontented were the most wealthy. Second, some of the poorest were the most greedy, grasping, and arrogant, and some of the wealthiest were the most generous, loving, and truly humble. Stuart Olyott, in his exposition of Ecclesiastes, presents a balanced approach to work and wealth.

> Work undoubtedly brings some reward, but too much of it brings nothing but trouble. It is better to have modest earnings and a restful mind than to make huge gains, with their accompanying anxiety.

> Who can count how many over-ambitious executives have learned the truth of these words, without ever reading them here? And who among us does not know a score of wives who look back with longing to the days when their now successful

husbands had less responsibilities? Less anxieties and less money—but more time to enjoy what really matters in life. Those were the days of an almost infinitely greater peace of mind, which stand in stark contrast to their present dissatisfied restlessness.[12]

The godliness of which Paul writes (1 Tim 6:6) is essential for contentment in the workplace. A good friend of mine applied for a job selling insurance. The insurance company administered a psychological test that indicated that sales was the last profession my friend should pursue. Even though he had already been successful as a salesman in a small specialty company, the insurance company trusted the test and did not hire him. A close friend finally secured him a job as a salesman with a company who did not require a psychological test. Within five years, he was sales manager of a regional office. Today he is vice president of the entire company. How could the insurance company's psychological test have been so wrong? Many of the questions in the test were designed to find someone whose chief goal was to make money and to get ahead. In other words, the company wanted someone who was willing to sell his soul for success and money, regardless of the consequences. A conscientious Christian whose chief goal is to glorify God would answer some of those questions quite differently from a person who wanted to get to the top as soon as possible. There are few large corporations where a child of God can follow his Christian conscience and at the same time "play ball by the corporate rules." Notice I did not say *none* but *few*.

---

[12] Stuart Olyott, *A Life Worth Living* (Welwyn, England: Evangelical Press, 1983), 34.

We should adopt "Better one handful with tranquility than two handfuls with toil and chasing after the wind," not as a slogan, but as a consistent way of life.

SOME ADVANTAGES OF COMPANIONSHIP

The Seeker is still looking for meaning and purpose, and he keeps arriving at the same conclusion; life is a thoroughly unpleasant experience. His thesis remains the same; life is "Vanity of vanity, all is vanity." He cannot reconcile his daily world with the idea of a sovereign, good God. No view that pictures God as holy, just, and good seems compatible with the real world, *under the sun*. On the surface, the idea of chapter 3:1–8, that God ordains every event, seems to contradict faith and love in such a God. It appears that either God is blind or impotent, or he is indifferent to the creatures he created.

In our last chapter, we examined several of the Seeker's observations: (1) tyranny and injustice rule even in the halls of justice; (2) ambition and the desire to be the object of envy drive people to sell their souls to the god of this world; and (3) human beings are never contented. The Seeker now shows that people will continue to be slaves to work and money, even when there is no purpose or reward, because they neither enjoy their wealth nor share it with anyone.

> *Again I saw something meaningless under the sun: There was a man all alone; he had neither son nor brother. There was no end to his toil, yet his eyes were not content with his wealth. "For whom am I toiling," he asked, "and why am I depriving myself of enjoyment?" This too is meaningless – a miserable business!* (Eccl 4:7–8 NIV)

Here is a picture of the workaholic with an unquenchable desire for more and more, even when there is no justification, need, or rational explanation for his actions. The man has no son or brother, no one to whom he can leave his wealth. He may have accumulated more than he could spend in a hundred lifetimes, yet he continues to occupy every waking hour acquiring more. He is a man who has everything and nothing at the same time. His work is marked by futility. Contrast this with Paul, who could say, "As having nothing, and yet possessing all things." The same words mean the opposite when they describe the miser. Charles Bridges has summed it up well. The emphasis is Bridges'.

Solomon's mind was in constant exercise. We find him returning from one side to another, only to fasten upon some new illustration of the world's vanity. The slothful fool sits with his folded hands—preferring quietness at any cost. Contrasted with him, we have the covetous fool—full of active energy. He has chosen money for his God. The miser—how well does he deserve his name! the wretched slave of Mammon, grown old as a toiling, scraping, griping drudge. He cannot plead as an excuse the necessary claims of a large family. He is alone, and there is not a second; yea—he has neither child nor brother. Yet so long as he can add one farthing to his hoard, he cannot bear the thought of giving up his toil. There is no end to his labor. Labor indeed it is without rest or satisfaction; however he may heap up his treasure. His eye is not satisfied with riches. Still he craves more. The less need the more raking. 'He hath enough for his back, his calling, the decency of his state and condition; but he hath not enough for his eye.' (Compare Prov. 27:20 and Hab. 2:5–9). All is sacrificed—even to the bereaving of his soul of common good. And for whom all this labor? "He heapeth up riches, and knoweth not who shall gather them" (Ps 39:6). [13]

The miser never stops to smell the roses; but his plight is greater than that. He never asks the logical question, "Why am I doing all this? Why am I amassing a fortune and not spending a nickel on myself?" Such a person would have to be intelligent, practical, methodical, careful, and persistent or he would have been incapable of amassing his fortune. Yet the same man acts foolishly when it comes to his personal life. He does not use his abilities to recognize that he is toiling for nothing and for nobody. Howard Hughes is a classic illustration. He had so much money that he did not know what to do with it, and yet he died as a recluse. He might as well have been a pauper.

On the opposite side of the miser is the man who spends his wealth entirely upon himself. He owes no one, including God, anything. Comparable to the rich fool in Luke 12, the covetous person never asks, "Why did God bless me with so much?" How different is the attitude of men and women possessed by sovereign grace! They know that not only have they been purchased by a price and thus belong to another, but also all they possess, including their wealth, belongs to the one who purchased them. A Christian who resembles a miser or a covetous person is a sorry sight indeed.

The Seeker makes a subtle point in verses 9–12. Verse 8 ends by stating: "This also is vanity and an unhappy business" (ESV). By adding the words "unhappy business" ("miserable business" in the NIV and "heavy toil" in the

---

[13] Charles Bridges, *Ecclesiastes, A Geneva Series Commentary* (Carlisle, PA: Banner of Truth, 1961), 89.

KJV) to the refrain "all is vanity," the Seeker emphasizes that both the miser and the covetous person are in for a lonely and unhappy life. Neither can establish and maintain true friendships and therefore both are doomed to lonely despair. Verses 9–12 describe the advantages of companionship over self-imposed loneliness. The miser cannot ask the question, "For whom am I toiling?" (v. 8) because he would then have to admit that he was "depriving [him]self of enjoyment." The loneliness described in verses 9–12 is inevitable for both the miser and the coveter.

Companionship is better than loneliness, yet loneliness is the inevitable result of certain choices. Isolation and solitariness bring their own sets of problems. Escape from competition is only a temporary solution. What lasting profit have you gained if you wind up with no family, not even an heir, no one to comfort you (4:1–3), no rest (4:46), and no companions to help you (4:7–12)?

Walter Kaiser addresses this situation:

> The Seeker has a proverb for this situation, as well: "two are better than one" (v. 9). Society, not the solitary life, and perhaps marriage, not the single life of celibacy, are to be preferred. For in such intimacy and shared life there is assistance (v. 10), comfort (v. 11), and defense (v. 12). In each of the proverbs of verses 9–12, the advantages of companionship are emphasized. [14]

Let us look at the verses carefully.

> *Two are better than one, because they have a good return for their work: If one falls down, his friend can help him up. But pity the man*

---

[14] Walter C. Kaiser Jr., *Ecclesiastes, Everyman's Bible Commentary,* (Chicago: Moody Press, 1979), 73.

who falls and has no one to help him up! Also, if two lie down togeth-
er, they will keep warm. But how can one keep warm alone? Though
one may be overpowered, two can defend themselves. A cord of three
strands is not quickly broken. (Eccl 4:9–12, NIV)

The Seeker sets these verses against the background of
the futility of miserliness and covetousness in verses 7–8.
Stuart Olyott has summed up this point well:

> It is a fact of life that wealth often makes a man a miser, so
> that he withdraws from the company of others. The picture of
> verse 8 is of a man who is so caught up with greed that he
> chooses to work alone, rather than to share his profits with an-
> yone. Without partner or helper, he gives himself to amassing
> wealth—wealth which he will be unable to leave to anyone, for
> he will have no one to leave it to!
>
> What futility! Ever working, yet never satisfied, such a man
> never stops to ask what the point is in gathering so much
> wealth (7–8). His lifestyle deprives him of one of the few joys
> this world has to offer—companionship. There are such bless-
> ings in having friends. You accomplish more, have help avail-
> able when in distress, and enjoy warmth, protection and secu-
> rity (9–12). If fellowship with two is that good, how much bet-
> ter is fellowship with three! A cord with three strands is consi-
> derably stronger than one with only two.[15]

The Seeker lists four advantages to companionship. First,
there is a natural reward from doubling up – "Two are better than one, because they have a good return for their
work" (v.9). If we understand this, we will see that two can
live more cheaply than one. This verse does not teach that
the total cost for two people living together will not be as

---

[15] Stuart Olyott, *Welwyn Commentary Series: Ecclesiastes, A Life
Worth Living* (Hertfordshire, England: Evangelical Press, 1983),
34, 35.

much as one person living alone, but that two people living together will _each_ spend less than if they were living alone. In our culture, two combined will spend twice as much for food, but only half as much for rent, light, phone, etc. If married, they will each pay less combined income tax than if they were single. A group insurance plan saves an individual person money.

Second, a friend can give needed help when difficulty comes – "If one falls down, his friend can help him up. But pity the man who falls and has no one to help him up!" (v. 10). Imagine falling into a ditch, especially on a dark night on a lonely road, and not being able to get out. If you were hurt badly, you might die before someone found you. However, the principle has a far wider application. When you slip in judgment or make bad decisions, you often need a friend to pull you out of a bad situation. The presence of friends eases unpleasant circumstances beyond your control. It is comforting to have a friend by the bed when you wake up from an operation.

Third, in some situations, survival may depend on cooperation with others – "if two lie down together, they will keep warm. But how can one keep warm alone?" (v. 11). One writer suggests that you cannot understand this verse unless you grew up in Montana. In the Eastern world of the Seeker, it was common practice for travelers, even strangers, to sleep close to each other for warmth. Again, the verse would expand the warmth as understanding and sympathy from a close friend in the time of adversity, trial, temptation, and grief.

Fourth, there is strength in numbers – "Though one may be overpowered, two can defend themselves. A cord of three strands is not quickly broken" (v. 12). The truth of this proverb is self-evident. Not only is the more the merrier true, but also the more the safer. The cord with three strands reminds me of an object lesson I used to teach children the power of temptation. I would have a boy put his hands down at his side, proceed to tie a piece of thread around his arms, and ask him to flex his arms and break the thread. He, of course, could do it with ease. I then doubled the thread and he was still able to break it. Then I started talking about repeated temptations and yielding to them more and more. All the time, I was wrapping the thread around the boy's arms. Finally, after there were about twenty-five strands of thread, I asked him to flex his arms. He could not break the thread. Continuance in sin soon forms habits that cannot be broken. A single strand of rope may be broken easily, but three strands woven together may be too strong to break.

The Seeker is not suggesting that companionship in itself is the answer to man's problem of despair and meaningless. Do we not all know older couples who sit in silence before the television set and seem to speak only when they want to say something nasty to the other person? Companionship, without question, is better than loneliness, but it still is not a full answer. It is the same with marriage and singleness. I often tell single girls who are desperately looking for a husband, "For every single girl who wishes she were married, I know ten married women who wish they were single!" The fruits of companionship are good or bad in direct proportion to our personal feelings for the companion. Some companions add to the aggravations of life as well as create more costly liabilities.

The Seeker moves to another problem he has observed *under the sun*:

> Better a poor but wise youth than an old but foolish king who no longer knows how to take warning. The youth may have come from prison to the kingship, or he may have been born in poverty within his kingdom. I saw that all who lived and walked under the sun followed the youth, the king's successor. There was no end to all the people who were before them. But those who came later were not pleased with the successor. This too is meaningless, a chasing after the wind. (Eccl 4:13–16, NIV)

Verse 13 grows out of verses 9–12 and continues to warn about self-sufficiency that grows out of a person's position and power, giving him a know-it-all attitude. The section shows the futility of seeking popularity and men's applause as a goal in life. This is an impossible goal, since popularity depends on fickle sinners like us. "What have you done for me today?" is still the cry of the mob. Any leader will testify that today's yes-men freeloading off your table may become tomorrow's enemies if they are not recognized or sufficiently rewarded for all they do for you. Some of what is supposedly done for the glory of God seems to have much selfishness mixed with it.

The Seeker's point in 4:13–16 is clear.

1. He compares a poor but wise young man with an old and foolish king who no longer takes advice.
2. The young man, despite his background, replaces, by popular demand, an old king.
3. Everyone loved the new young king.

4. The next generation did not like the king who had now grown old.

5. The cycle is complete.

The Seeker varies the order and puts the conclusion before the problem. The old and foolish king apparently was not always foolish. There was time when he knew how to take advice, but in his old age, his power went to his head. He was king, and kings can do as they please. He started well, but allowed position and authority to corrupt his thinking. A friend of mine used to say, "It is not what you say when you put your armor on, it is what you say when you take it off." The final, and true, judgment will be based not on how we started, but on how we finished.

The old and foolish king was born to the throne. He is contrasted with a young and wise man who came from a prison background to the throne. The Seeker may have been thinking of Joseph, the son of Jacob. Joseph grew in power until he was next only to the king. Like Joesph, the young wise man lost his popularity. A generation that knew not Joseph arose. Today's heroes may well be tomorrow's unknowns.

In all of this, the Seeker subtly acknowledges the sovereignty of God as well as the power of true wisdom. The young man was nobody from nowhere, and he became king, not with a sword and revolution, but by wisdom. The reigning king, with every earthly power at his disposal, still lost his throne.

The Seeker is not disparaging old age. Scripture is very clear about respecting the elderly. Leviticus 19:32 says, "Rise in the presence of the aged, show respect for the elderly and revere your God. I am the LORD." However, when the elderly act in the manner of the old and foolish king, we must do the opposite. Proverbs is quite clear, "The hoary head is a crown of glory, if it be found in the way of righteousness" (Prov. 16:31, KJV). We must remember that word *if*. It is a terrible sight to see an elderly sinner acting out his pathetic shame. It is not a sin to get old, but there is no inherent glory in being old. Glory consists in a gray-headed saint walking in righteousness. The NIV mistranslates this verse, "Gray hair is a crown of splendor; it is attained by a righteous life." It sounds as though you acquire gray hair by living a righteous life. Charles Bridges comments:

> Generally in the OT wisdom is reckoned to lie with increasing age and experience, and the elderly were honored accordingly (Lev. 19:32). But it is also realized that the aged may lose their wisdom (Job 12:20) and the young may be wiser than their elders (Psa. 119:100). Elihu's is the balanced position, giving his elders the first hearing but not regarding them as infallible, since the Spirit of God may give wisdom beyond one's years (Job 32:4–11). [16]

One of the saddest aspects of these verses is the end of the young man. His end is common for many who rise to power. They win their way to the top from the worst of backgrounds. They usually have the advantage of the bad example of their predecessor and their own personal experiences, and yet they do not learn essential lessons. In the end, they become merely one more old and foolish king. Their folly is another example of "vanity, emptiness, a striving after the wind."

---

[16] Bridges, p. 95.

Chapter 5 is a remarkable chapter that introduces a new vanity. The Seeker has provided multiple illustrations to prove his thesis that everything *under the sun* is vanity. Does that include the worship of God? Is worship also nothing but useless meaninglessness? The Seeker has admitted the vanity of life *under the sun*. He has shown that only God can give life that includes an assurance of God's sovereign control over all things. He has faced injustice and various forms of isolation, and has emphasized the need for assurance of acceptance with the God who alone can give us eternal companionship. Can we know this God? Is he approachable? The answer is yes, but there are some warnings that we must heed. Let us examine the Seeker's advice.

First, "Guard your steps when you go to the house of God" (5:1a). Watching your steps includes more than walking. It encompasses hearing, speaking, and observing. In the context of the Old Covenant, the house of God was the temple. In the context of the New Covenant, the building in which the church meets does **not** replace the temple. The dwelling place of God is Christ; our Lord is the place where God meets with people. The New Covenant corollary to the temple is any place where God's people meet with him, through Christ. This includes, but must not be confined to, attending public corporate worship. It would apply to personal time spent with God as well as meeting with the saints to worship God in Christ. The idea is that approaching God by the right means, with the right attitude, and for the right purpose is essential. We should prepare ourselves spiritually exactly the same way we would prepare ourselves physically when going to meet a person of importance. Would we have lunch with the president of the company without first shaving, bathing, combing our hair, or wearing clean clothes? Of course not! Why then do we go into the presence of God armed with our own merits or with unconfessed sin, unfulfilled vows and neglected duties?

Verse 1b answers: It is because we act like spiritual fools. "Go near to listen rather than to offer the sacrifice of fools, who do not know that they are doing wrong." An offering of praise and worship with an unprepared heart, apart from the person and work of Christ, compares to "the sacrifice of a fool." It is more than just foolishness; it is sin against God. We are doing wrong when we do not guard our feet. God says that he hates worship if our heart is not in it. "The LORD detests the sacrifice of the wicked, but the prayer of the upright pleases him" (Prov. 15:8). We who live in the New Covenant era know that we are upright only because Jesus Christ gave us his uprightness. We guard our feet when we approach God through Christ. Any other approach is foolishness.

Verses 2 and 3 remind the reader of the necessity of letting God be God. "Do not be quick with your mouth, do not be hasty in your heart to utter anything before God." Do not go into God's presence and start telling God what he should do and not do. Who are we to challenge God by telling him what he should, or should not, allow? We further compound the sin when we call it prayer.[17]

---

[17] If you struggle with the relationship between God's sovereignty and prayer, please see our booklet, "The Sovereignty of God and Prayer." Available from New Covenant Media, 5317 Wye Creek Drive, Frederick, MD. 21703

What we utter before God must come from the heart, and therefore we must not be rash with our mouth, never let our tongue outrun our thoughts in our devotions; the words of our mouth, must always be the product of the meditation of our hearts. Thoughts are words to God, and words are but wind if they be not copied from the thoughts. Lip-labour, though ever so well laboured, if that be all, is but lost labour in religion. (Matthew Henry, BibleSoft CD.)

Our Lord reproved the Pharisees for their hypocrisy in worship.

> *"You hypocrites! Isaiah was right when he prophesied about you:* *"'These people honor me with their lips, but their hearts are far from me. They worship me in vain; their teachings are but rules taught by men.'" Jesus called the crowd to him and said, "Listen and understand. What goes into a man's mouth does not make him 'unclean,' but what comes out of his mouth that is what makes him 'unclean.'"* (Matt 15:7–11, NIV)

James gives the same exhortation, "My dear brothers, take note of this: Everyone should be quick to listen, slow to speak …" (James 1:19).

Verse 2b gives another reason for exercising care when approaching God. "God is in heaven and you are on earth, so let your words be few." Remember the great distance between God and us. When we speak to God, we are not discussing something with an equal. We are not telling God something he does not already know. We are approaching the enthroned God of the universe who knows and ordains everything. Let our words come from our hearts and make sure our hearts are in submission to God's authority.

Submission to God's authority in the New Covenant age begins with recognition of our neediness and helplessness apart from Christ. Apart from Christ, we have no words to offer God. We cannot offer him a list of our own good deeds as incentive for him to hear us or grant our requests. If it were not for Christ, our words before God would be few indeed. Because of Christ, we can approach God boldly (Heb. 10:19–22). Boldly does not mean arrogantly; we must come with humble hearts that know their own capability for blackness. *Our* words as we approach God are few; *Christ's* words on our behalf are infinite, stemming as they do from his righteousness.

In 5:3, the Seeker compares the wild, distorted visions in dreams to the hurried and confused words of a fool attempting to pray. "As a dream comes when there are many cares, so the speech of a fool when there are many words." A man so filled with business matters that he cannot sleep without wild images in his dreams is like a double-minded man who worships because it is a duty. His thoughts and words concentrate not on God, but on his own business. Under the Old Covenant, a person could physically enter the house of God, yet spiritually and emotionally remain at his place of business.

In the New Covenant era, a person may meet with the saints, or set aside time at home to be with God, but remain detached and uninvolved in true worship. Unless we meet God in Christ, we cannot enter the house of God at all, much less worship him in spirit and in truth. We may think we are prepared spiritually and emotionally to meet God by going over a checklist of duties performed and rules obeyed, but that is not how we gain access to the house of God. We meet

God in the same manner as the publican who prayed, "God, be merciful to me a sinner" (Luke 18:13). We who have been rescued from sin and its eternal consequences know that God has been merciful to us in Christ, and our hearts swell with gratitude and adoration. If we approach God in this manner, we will avoid foolish prayers.

In our next chapter, we will look at the Seeker's observations on vows (5:4–7). This subject is sometimes misunderstood. The misuse of vows has ruined some sincere people, and the proper use of them has helped others.

CHAPTER ELEVEN: VERSES: 5:1–6

BE CAREFUL WHAT YOU VOW

In Chapter 5, the writer, at first glance, seems to depart from his main thesis. A closer look, however, reveals that he is still writing from within in his "meaningless, meaningless" philosophy. He retains his broad framework of the vanity of all of life and applies it to a particular area he has yet to address: worship. He exhorts his readers to continue to go to the house of God to worship, but cautions that to do so in a wrong manner or with a bad motive is worse than meaningless; it is actually sin.

> *Guard your steps when you go to the house of God. Go near to listen rather than to offer the sacrifice of fools, who do not know that they do wrong. Do not be quick with your mouth, do not be hasty in your heart to utter anything before God. God is in heaven and you are on earth, so let your words be few. As a dream comes when there are many cares, so the speech of a fool when there are many words.* (Eccl 5:1-3, NIV)

We previously have noted six points that could easily cause us to forsake our confidence in a wise sovereign God. The Seeker lamented (1) injustice in the halls of justice; (2) the inescapable fact that humans and beasts alike die; (3) that people are severely oppressed; (4) that people are motivated by rivalry; (5) that human beings are separated from each other and from God because of sin; and (6) that popularity, even when deserved, is very short-lived. Do not these six observations indicate that God cannot possibly have a good plan and purpose for every person and everything? These realities seem to turn the theology of sovereignty on its ear. Why not be honest and just give up our faith? Un-happily, many have done just that. They have not done so outwardly, but they have inwardly. These people refrain from formal, theological atheism, but engage in a "practical atheism" that thinks and acts as though God is not really in control. Do not be seduced into either outright unbelief or pious religious hypocrisy. Continue to go to the house of God and worship God as he has revealed himself in his Word.

As we mentioned in our previous chapter, we are not to limit this exhortation to "going to church" for public wor-ship. In the New Covenant era, God dwells in Christ; we meet with God in Christ. We must guard our steps whenev-er we meet with God: in any place and at all times. We can-not emphasize too strongly that we must always remember that we meet with God at the mercy seat. There is no other place where God will meet with sinners. We need frequently to remind ourselves that we wear a robe without seam or spot, hand-woven by our Older Brother. The words of the old hymn, "What can wash away my sin?/ Nothing but the blood of Jesus," are our song, and we need to sing it to our-selves daily.

To guard our steps means first to approach God only through the righteousness of Christ, and second, to be con-scious of what we are doing and saying. If ever we must choose our words carefully, it is when we speak to God. Carefulness refers not to grammar, to how long we speak, or even to content in one sense. Since our words reflect our thoughts, carefulness begins by training ourselves to think God's thoughts after him. Carefulness continues as we speak from our hearts and sincerely feel and mean exactly what we are saying. A simple "God be merciful to me a poor sinner" outstrips many of the "deep-voiced pastoral prayers" that would never use "you," but only "thee" and "thou."

When we do meet with God in the context of public corporate worship, we must remind ourselves of two important points. First, the only profitable hearing is what we remember and practice. No matter how delighted and thrilled we are with what we hear, if we do not remember it and put it into practice, we are worse off for hearing it. Our Lord has warned us, "Take heed how you hear." We are too often ready to ask curious questions, but unready to listen to practical truths. I am reminded of Mark Twain's response when asked, "How do you handle passages of Scripture that you do not understand?" Twain replied, "Oh, they don't bother me one-tenth as much as the ones I do understand."

Second, we can make our Father's house a house of merchandise without anyone selling or buying a single thing. The most powerful truth ever preached goes right over the head of the man or woman who is thinking about tomorrow's business deal. We would be horrified in a church service to see someone passing out sale's slips and other people passing money in return, but is that any worse than doing the same thing mentally?

The Teacher continues his exhortation to carefulness by urging his readers to let their words be few. We must not misunderstand his instruction here. Charles Bridges makes excellent comments on verse two.

> The *few words* here directed are words well-weighted—well chosen and ordered. They contrast strongly with the "vain repetition" of the heathen such as the frantic orgies of Baal—the

Romish Paternosters—of the Pharisees' long prayers—
"thinking they shall be heard for their much speaking." But
God hears us not the sooner for many words; but much the
sooner from earnest desire, to which let apt and sufficient
words minister, be they few or many. The *fewness of words* is
not the main concern; but whether they be words of the
heart—'whether they be gold or lead'—what life there is in
them. For nothing is more unacceptable to God, than to hold
on speaking, after we have left off praying. So long as the heart
and the tongue flow together, never suppose your Lord will be
weary of your many words. [18]

An illustration may help us grasp the significance of these
texts. Imagine a group of four men, planning to go to the
Super-Bowl in Florida. It is a two-hour drive from their
homes. "We must leave no later than 9:00 AM. If someone is
not here, we are leaving without him. We don't want to miss
the kick off." During the two-hour drive, the entire conversation is about football. All four men know all the football
players' names and stats. "I hope so-and-so (the quarter-
back) is really on today," says one man, and all agree. It
would be hard to describe the anticipation and expectancy
of these four men. During the game, they shout until they
are almost too hoarse to talk. The seats are hard and there is
occasional rain, but no one utters a word of complaint. The
game goes into two overtimes, but no one grumbles about
how long the game is taking. On the way home, the men re-
hash the game at least five times. "I will never forget that
amazing one-handed catch in the third quarter." "You're
right. I believe that turned the whole game around."

---

[18] Charles Bridges, *Ecclesiastes, A Geneva Series Commentary* (1961; reprint, Carlisle, PA: Banner of Truth Trust, 1981), 102, 103.

Ten years later, if you asked these four men to describe one of their most memorable experiences, at least three would describe that football game. You would be amazed at how much and how accurately they could describe what happened at that game.

Now imagine those same four men, each with their wives, on the way to a church service. One man says to his wife, "Let's stop and get a cup of coffee. We will only be a couple of minutes late for church." During the service, one man goes to sleep and his wife keeps nudging him. One wife, sitting next to another wife, whispers, "Do you see that hideous dress that Mary is wearing?"

After the service, the four couples all go out to lunch together. The talk among the four men soon turns to the amazing football game they saw ten years ago. The women talk about clothes. The only one time anyone mentions the church service is when someone comments that he thought the sermon was a little too long. No one would have ever imagined these people had just come from a meeting with the King of Kings! Of course it is quite possible they did not in reality meet with God. Attendance is not engagement. Far too often, we attend a church service out of habit or duty, without sufficient carefulness of thought.

I once heard Allen Redpath say, "I always go to the church an hour early on Sunday morning. One of the things I do is stand in the foyer and pray, 'Oh, God, sanctify the conversation in this hallway before and after the service.'" Why is it that we anticipate with joy, become emotionally worked up, and remember and talk about a football game that took place ten years ago, but we dare not even whisper "amen" in a church service? How is it possible to meet with the King of Kings for an hour or more and remain unaffected, and yet go wild over a football game?

In verse 3, the author compares the dumb and distorted words a fool may utter, even in the presence of God, with images of wild dreams. When our minds are occupied and controlled by business, pleasure, anxiety, and the like, our dreams may be wild and disorganized. Our subconscious feels and says things in dreams our conscious mind would not dare say aloud. Dreams bypass our inhibitions. The words of a fool in the presence of God are just such a revelation of the fool's heart.

The Seeker now introduces the subject of vows and warns against failure to keep a vow made to God. He is not condemning a person for taking a vow. He is condemning rash vows that are not kept. He is applying the theme of carefulness specifically directed at words in verses 1–3 to the subject of a particular kind of words: vows. The broad theme ties verses 4–6 to verses 1–3.

> *When you make a vow to God, do not delay in fulfilling it. He has no pleasure in fools; fulfill your vow. It is better not to vow than to make a vow and not fulfill it. Do not let your mouth lead you into sin. And do not protest to the [temple] messenger, "My vow was a mistake." Why should God be angry at what you say and destroy the work of your hands?* (Eccl 5:4–6, NIV)

The subject of vows requires careful study. One of the issues involved in vows is the question of what controls the conscience. We usually think of the exhortation to fulfill a vow as an absolute. It does not matter what the vow was, who made it, who and what was involved, or the possible consequences. Many people believe and teach that any and every vow to God is sacred and binding and must be fulfilled, regardless of the cost or consequences. The story of Jephthah is a classic example of a good man whose conscience forced him to carry out a rash vow. It was a vow he should have never made nor fulfilled. Here is the story:

> And Jephthah made a vow to the LORD: "If you give the Ammonites into my hands, whatever comes out of the door of my house to meet me when I return in triumph from the Ammonites will be the LORD's, and I will sacrifice it as a burnt offering." Then Jephthah went over to fight the Ammonites, and the LORD gave them into his hands. He devastated twenty towns from Aroer to the vicinity of Minnith, as far as Abel Keramim. Thus Israel subdued Ammon. When Jephthah returned to his home in Mizpah, who should come out to meet him but his daughter, dancing to the sound of tambourines! She was an only child. Except for her he had neither son nor daughter. When he saw her, he tore his clothes and cried, "Oh! My daughter! You have made me miserable and wretched, because I have made a vow to the LORD that I cannot break." "My father," she replied, "you have given your word to the LORD. Do to me just as you promised, now that the LORD has avenged you of your enemies, the Ammonites. But grant me this one request," she said. "Give me two months to roam the hills and weep with my friends, because I will never marry." "You may go," he said. And he let her go for two months. She and the girls went into the hills and wept because she would never marry. After the two months, she returned to her father and he did to her as he had vowed. And she was a virgin. From this comes the Israelite custom that each year the young women of Israel go out for four days to commemorate the daughter of Jephthah the Gileadite. (Judges 11:30–40, NIV)

Teachers and preachers often use this passage to show what a great and godly believer Jephthah was. In reality, he was basically a good man with bad theology. He was godly in the sense that he was zealous for Israel to possess all the land that God had given them, and in the sense that the Spirit of the Lord came upon him, and enabled him to have victory in battle much as it did upon Samson. However, Jephthah also collected a loyal band of "worthless fellows," so it would seem that he was not too choosy about the moral character of his companions. He was canny, shrewd, and politically ambitious, as his exchange with the elders of Gilead indicates. Nor did he have any qualms about killing his fellow Israelites. He was a man much like other men, with a mixed character, whom God used to make his name famous. Our concern is with his wrongly trained conscience. The Word of God did not control his conscience, or he could never have done what he did. His conscience forced him to disobey a clear commandment of God in order to carry out a rash and impetuous vow. In Hebrews 11:32, the writer of the letter includes Jephthah as a man of faith, despite what he did to his daughter.

Let us look at what happened. Israel had forsaken the true and living God and had turned to the false gods of the nations around them. God, in turn, had forsaken them and for eighteen years had given them over to their enemies: the Philistines and the Ammonites. The Israelites confessed their sin and repented, and sought Jephthah as their military leader against the Ammonites. Jephthah made a vow: if God gave him victory over the Ammonites, he would offer (sacrifice as a burnt offering) the first thing that came out of his house to meet him upon his return.

Jephthah may have made the vow carelessly, without thinking of the possibilities, or he may have felt that the situation was serious enough to warrant a calculated risk of human sacrifice. The Mosaic law, under which Jephthah lived, allowed for burnt offerings as the fulfillment of a vow, but the sacrificial victim was to come from the livestock of the herd or the flock (Lev. 21:18–20). A priest had to be involved in the ritual (Lev. 1:5–9). Additionally, the law of Moses forbad human sacrifice (Lev. 18:21). It was one of the detestable practices of the Canaanites that the children of Israel were to eschew (Deut. 18:9–10). Jephthah had no right to make that kind of a vow, and having made it, he had no right to perform it. His action neither glorified nor pleased God.

Two issues are involved. First, there is the legitimacy of the vow. Is a vow, regardless of its nature or consequences, inherently sacred and therefore essential to be performed? The answer is no. Numbers, chapter 30 offers examples of when a vow is not binding. If a vow were inherently sacred, no circumstances would be mitigating. Second, when is a vow, made in sincerity before God, wrong and therefore not to be carried out? Among other criteria, any vow that forces an individual deliberately to disobey the revealed will of God is always wrong. The question in Jephthah's case is this: Does the duty to carry out a vow carry more weight than the duty to refrain from performing a human sacrifice? Jephthah had no right to murder his daughter as an act of obedient faith in order to fulfill his vow. It does not matter how sincere Jephthah was or how deeply he believed it was his duty.

It should be obvious that any vow that is contrary to God's Word cannot bind a right conscience. A vow cannot make that right which is morally wrong. What is contrary to the law can never be a legitimate engagement to the Lawgiver. [19]

---

[19] Ibid., 107.

Jephthah is a classic illustration from the Old Testament of a man who loved God, but followed a misguided conscience. The New Testament provides us with Saul of Tarsus, who vowed to God to destroy the fledgling church, but later refused to continue to carry out that vow. A contemporary example might include a man who stands at his murdered wife's grave and vows to God that he will not rest until he has put to death the man, along with his entire family, who was responsible for his wife's death. Is he obligated to God to carry out that vow? A literal interpretation of Ecclesiastes 5:4–6 would say not only "yes," but also that God would honor the man's obedience to his vow. We must recognize the difference between obeying the Word of God and sincerely following our conscience.

Look more closely at the New Testament illustration of this principle. In Acts 24:16, Paul stated that his goal in life was "to strive to always to keep my conscience clear before God and man." In Acts 23:1, he testified that he had attained that goal, even as a Pharisee. "Paul looked straight at the Sanhedrin and said, 'My brothers, I have fulfilled my duty to God in all good conscience to this day.'" Saul of Tarsus, in good conscience, could severely persecute Christians. In fact, that is exactly what he did.

> *"I too was convinced that I ought to do all that was possible to oppose the name of Jesus of Nazareth. And that is just what I did in Jerusalem. On the authority of the chief priests I put many of the saints in prison, and when they were put to death, I cast my vote against them. Many a time I went from one synagogue to another to have them punished, and I tried to force them to blaspheme. In my obsession against them, I even went to foreign cities to persecute them."* (Acts 26:9–11, NIV)

Saul, like Jephthah, honestly believed in his conscience that he was obeying GOD, when in reality he was openly disobeying God's revealed will! History is full of records of godly men and women, sincerely obeying consciences trained by a wrong theology, performing acts contrary to God's revealed will. Calvin engineered the death of Servetus, and John Cotton whipped and imprisoned Baptists and Quakers in New England: these are just two examples of godly men performing ungodly deeds out of sincere obedience to a theology of sacralism – a wrong view of church and state – that is incompatible with New Testament teaching.

The Christian community needs a good book on conscience, law, and Christian liberty. We must have a clear understanding of the difference between an *absolute*, which has no exceptions, not even one, and a *principle* that is almost always unchanging, but does have an occasional exception. Exceptions do not destroy a principle; they merely prove you are dealing with a principle and not an absolute. An exception to an absolute either destroys the absolute or proves it was not an absolute in the first place. The only thing that can determine an absolute from a principle is the clear Word of God.

A sincere belief in the rightness of an action does not guarantee that the action is right in the eyes of God. Sincere men and women who made vows to their God have committed many of the world's greatest atrocities. The radical Muslim terrorists of our generation are a classic example. They are dedicated to what they believe is right, with a passion that knows no boundaries. Yet their course of action is controlled by a religion of hate. They can, and do, commit the worst of crimes and think they are doing what pleases God. Someone has rightly asked, "Why does the God of terrorists always tell his devotees to hate and kill, and never to love and forgive?" As long as men and women continue to take vows before God to destroy all who disagree with them, our world will know no peace or security.

Although there are many dangers that accompany vows, a vow is not inherently negative. We must consider the teacher's exhortation in its context. We should not be careless with any of the words we direct to God, and that includes vows. A carefully considered vow can be positive and helpful, depending on its nature and purpose. I remember hearing A.W. Tozer preach a sermon entitled "Five vows every Christian should take and keep." The one that impressed me the most was this; "I vow to never again call anything 'mine,' but to view everything as having been loaned to me by God and for which I am eternally responsible."

In the next chapter, the Seeker moves from the vanity of careless words to the vanity of wealth.

CHAPTER TWELVE: VERSES 5:7–20

WEALTH CAN BE A CURSE

The Seeker, in Ecclesiastes 5:8–20, contemplates the vanity of wealth. As with vows, wealth is not inherently negative, but neither does it live up to its reputation for producing happiness. It is true that even though wealth is the cause of some men's misery, it enables them to be very comfortable in their misery, thereby masking its danger.

The various proverbs of this section are bound together by the theme of poverty and wealth. We have reference to 'the poor' (5:8), 'money' (5:10), the increase of 'good things' (5:11), 'the rich man' (5:12), 'riches' (5:13, 14), 'riches and wealth' (5:19; 6:2), the 'poor man' (6:8).[20]

Verses 8 and 9 state the plight of the poor:

If you see the poor oppressed in a district, and justice and rights denied, do not be surprised at such things; for one official is eyed by a higher one, and over them both are others higher still. The increase from the land is taken by all; the king himself profits from the fields. (NIV)

The poor here are the victims of oppression who have no one to defend their rights. The rich get richer and the poor get poorer. Honest government with many checks and balances to assure equality and justice is a great blessing to any society. Such is a rare thing indeed. In most cases, government comprises an endless bureaucracy of officials whose appointments were the result of political rewards rather

---

[20] Michael A. Eaton, *Ecclesiastes, An Introduction & Commentary* (Downers Grove, IL: IVP, 1983), 100.

than integrity and ability. At each level, the presiding official has his hand in the till. Even the king must get his cut in
such a situation. Financial security corresponds to position
on the bureaucratic ladder. The Seeker offers no advice or
cure for this situation, but merely states, "That's the way it
is. Don't be surprised." Sinclair Ferguson, in *The Pundit's
Folly*, puts it in contemporary terms:

> But what does this kind of upward mobility cost? At the
> end of the day we find that we have spent all our spiritual re-
> sources on financing the journey upwards; on arrival we have
> sold everything of lasting value. [21]

Charles Bridges offers a different, more positive view on
these verses.

> Gradation of rank is indeed the ordinance of God, evil only
> when the higher abuse their elevation. Yet there is a level,
> where, "the rich and poor meet together" (Prov. 22:2). The
> curse of the ground is so far mitigated, that while "bread" is
> still "eaten in the sweat of the face" (Gen. 3:17) there is profit—
> directly or indirectly—*for all*. The many live by it. The highest
> cannot live without it. *The King himself is served by the field.* He
> is more dependent upon the laborer, than the laborer is on
> him. He has more need of the laborer's strength, than the la-
> borer has of his royal crown. Agriculture was an ordinance be-
> fore the fall. "And of all the arts of civilized man, it is tran-
> scendently the most essential and valuable. Other arts may
> contribute to the comfort, the convenience, and the embellish-
> ment of life. But the cultivation of the soil stands in immediate
> connection with our very existence. The life itself, to whose
> comfort, the convenience, and the embellishments of life other

---

[21] Sinclair Ferguson, *The Pundit's Folly* (Carlisle, PA: The Banner of
Truth Trust, 1995), 22.

arts contribute, is by *this* to be sustained, so that others without it can avail nothing. In their dependence on *the field* all are equal. The prince and the peasant are alike *served of it.* [22]

In verses 10–17, we learn that (1) Wealth does not necessarily bring satisfaction. (2) Possessions cannot give security to those who trust in them. The more possessions one has, the more insurance one needs to protect those possessions. (3) Wealth cannot give peace and contentment. (4) We may amass wealth to our detriment and lose it to our sorrow.

Verses 10 and 11 address money, goods, and two related problems: (1) All the money in the world cannot satisfy a covetous person. (2) Wealth attracts freeloaders who easily become dependents. Notice these two adages.

Whoever loves money never has money enough; whoever loves wealth is never satisfied with his income. This too is meaningless. (NIV)

Poverty is a burden, but wealth also has its own set of problems. A greedy person's discontentment will increase in direct proportion to the accumulation of his personal wealth. Human desire outruns acquisitions, no matter how large the acquisitions are. Charles Bridges points out that getting things and enjoying those things are two different propositions.

The tempter may paint a brilliant prospect of happiness. But fact and experience prove, that *he that loveth silver* or any worldly *abundance* will be satisfied neither with the possession nor *with the* increase. The appetite is created—not satisfied. The *vanity* of this disease is coveting what does not satisfy when we have it. Hunger is satisfied with meat, and thirst with drink.

---

[22] Bridges, 112.

But hunger or thirst for this world's wealth is as unsatisfied in the end, as at the beginning. "Could you,"—says a lively expositor—"change the solid earth into a single lump of Gold, and drop it into the gaping mouth of avarice, it would only be a crumb of transient comfort, a cordial drop, enabling it to cry a little louder, 'Give—give.' So true it is, that a man's life"—his real comfort in life—"consisteth not in the abundance of the things which he possesses." (Luke 12:15.) "Nature is content with little, grace with less, but lust with nothing." [23]

Ecclesiastes teaches us that God himself must not only give the wealth, he must also give the ability to enjoy it. Great wealth and influence without a heart to use both for the glory of God will destroy a man, both in this life and in eternity. Greed and contentment are incompatible; they are as different as night and day.

Greed is not restricted to those who own goods; those who use goods can be greedy as well.

As goods increase, so do those who consume them.

You never know how many "close and dear" relatives and friends you have until you win the lottery. One uncle, named Sam, is quick to take a personal interest in your wealth and will consume (legally steal) a large share of it. Wealth creates other problems, besides those who take advantage. The more wealth increases, the more staff is required to manage it. These must be honest and efficient people. And where are such to be found? Even if we solve the problems of taxes, dependants, and staff, one key question remains:

---

[23] Ibid., 113.

And what benefit are they to the owner except to feast his eyes on them?

If one who possesses wealth does not use it to benefit others, what good is the wealth? A person can only sleep in one bedroom at a time, and can only consume so much food. A man who shares his wealth with friends has some people, granted many who may be parasites, slapping him on the back and telling him how wonderful he is. A man who hoards his wealth has no one with whom he can share anything.

"What benefit are they to the owner," asks the Pundit, "except to feast his eyes on them?" Possessions cannot talk to you, love you, or guide you! Either their pleasing beauty will wear off or your eyes will grow dim to their luster before you are blinded by death. What lasting security can they give you then? You came from your mother's womb with nothing; you will go to earth's womb with nothing. How can possessions give you security? You *know* you cannot take them with you."[24]

The Seeker next compares the effects of relative wealth on two different men. Ironically, great wealth can easily destroy a person's peace and sense of security.

The sleep of a laborer is sweet, whether he eats little or much, but the abundance of a rich man permits him no sleep. (NIV)

The author does not ask the logical question, "Which of the two men is better off?" It is not a question of one man being physically tired from physical labor, while another man cannot sleep because he is too well rested from a life of leisure. The rich man may work equally hard or he may spend hours strenuously exercising in a private gym that

---

[24] Ferguson, 23.

boasts every piece of modern equipment. The rich man cannot sleep because wealth consumes him to the place where he cannot enjoy life. The sleep that is sweet to the laborer is not something the rich man can buy, no matter how much he is willing to spend. The laborer does not lie awake worrying that he might dig a hole too deep or commit some other mistake; but the rich man tosses and turns in his bed while he repeatedly reviews the vital decisions he must make tomorrow, where just one mistake can destroy him.

The Seeker now looks at another aspect of the vanity of wealth. He describes the fleeting nature of riches and the effect upon a person who gains and loses a great amount of wealth.

> *I have seen a grievous evil under the sun: wealth hoarded to the harm of its owner, or wealth lost through some misfortune, so that when he has a son there is nothing left for him. Naked a man comes from his mother's womb, and as he comes, so he departs. He takes nothing from his labor that he can carry in his hand. This too is a grievous evil: As a man comes, so he departs, and what does he gain, since he toils for the wind? All his days he eats in darkness, with great frustration, affliction and anger.* (Eccl 5:13–17, NIV).

Michael Eaton catches the true sense of these verses in his summary, "Wealth—loved and lost (5:13–17)."

> We now pass to those who have had wealth and lost it. First the tale is presented; we see wealth acquired (13) and lost (14a), and man's inability to pass anything on (14b) or take anything with him (15). Then follows a grim view of the life of the one who loved and lost his wealth (16ff). [25]

The Seeker's grief is not only an evil; it is a "grievous" evil. It is painful or sickening (verse13).

---

[25] Eaton, 103.

Hoarded wealth helps no one, and it causes great harm to its owner. Not only does his greedy heart prevent him from enjoying his wealth himself; it also prohibits him from experiencing the great opportunity to be a source of blessing to others. During the greedy man's lifetime, his wealth did not help him in any eternal sense, and in eternity, his greed will harm him; it will be the just grounds for punishment from God. Sometimes, but not always, the ungodly lose all even in this lifetime. Such is the case in verse 14.

> ... or wealth lost through some misfortune, so that when he has a son there is nothing left for him.

The introduction of a son with no inheritance compounds the tragedy of lost wealth. The Teacher does not tell us whether the misfortune was the man's own fault or if events beyond his control caused it. Perhaps he destroyed his health from immoral living or from excessive work. Perhaps the misfortune was of a different nature and came from outside sources. The automobile business, overnight, put the buggy makers out of business. Advances in computers and digital equipment in many fields have made things such as large photo film almost obsolete. The Seeker's point is the same, regardless of whether the loss is from a trip to Los Vegas, investment in phony stocks, or a terrorist attack. Neither hoarded wealth nor lost wealth matter when we die.

> Naked a man comes from his mother's womb, and as he comes, so he departs. He takes nothing from his labor that he can carry in his hand.

Many people misquote verse 15. The verse does not say that we take *nothing* with us when we die. It says that we take nothing in *our hand*. We take nothing tangible that we can hold in our hands: there is no material possession that I may clutch and say, "This is mine." However, we all take intangible things with us into eternity. A person's character, his conscience, and the record of his life go into eternity with a person. Neither death nor eternity has the power to change a person's life or character. Death merely confirms for all eternity the truth about us. Revelation 22:11–12 is clear on that point.

> *"Let him who does wrong continue to do wrong; let him who is vile continue to be vile; let him who does right continue to do right; and let him who is holy continue to be holy. Behold, I am coming soon! My reward is with me, and I will give to everyone according to what he has done."*

Those who give their hearts to wealth as their God will discover their nakedness in the sight of the true and living God. A person's greed will be an eternal noose around his neck.

> *This too is a grievous evil: As a man comes, so he departs, and what does he gain, since he toils for the wind?*

One thing is sure. *Nobody*, and that really means *nobody*, leaves the world a dime richer than when he entered it. So why beat your brains out living for riches? What profit or final advantage is there? At the end of your life, you have gained nothing from it. Add to that futility grief, pain, sorrow, anger, and sickness, which no amount of wealth can keep you from experiencing. That which keeps you from enjoying all that you own is the failure to see them as gifts from God. You can find neither delight nor satisfaction in God's gifts while rejecting the giver of the gifts. Looking for contentment in things is as futile as chasing the wind. You will exit this world just as you entered it. Eaton comments:

> The Hebrew for "as," or "just as," in verse 16 is emphatic and may be translated "quite exactly as." What a man has in

his hand at birth signifies what capital he brought with him—
nothing. What he may take with him when he leaves exactly
corresponds. His accumulation was futile. [26]

Verse 17 details the price tag that accompanies greed.

*All his days also he eateth in darkness, and he hath much sorrow
and wrath with his sickness.* (KJV)

Darkness symbolizes misery. Preoccupation with wealth
inevitably leads to a gloomy outlook on life. We may eat a
delicious meal in beautiful surroundings, but if our heart is
not happy, we cannot enjoy the experience. *Sickness* points
to the results of physical strain and the natural results of
stress. This sickness probably grows out of the emotional
strain of constant discontent. *Sorrow,* or vexation, refers to
the cares, anxieties, and frustrations that constantly tear at
mind and heart. *Wrath* describes rage over thwarted ambi-
tions and schemes. The physical cost of greed is amazing.
The spiritual cost is beyond description.

In verses 18–20, the Seeker reminds us of the only cure for
greed.

*Then I realized that it is good and proper for a man to eat and
drink, and to find satisfaction in his toilsome labor under the sun
during the few days of life God has given him – for this is his lot.
Moreover, when God gives any man wealth and possessions, and
enables him to enjoy them, to accept his lot and be happy in his work
– this is a gift of God. He seldom reflects on the days of his life, because God keeps him occupied with gladness of heart.* (NIV)

As he looks at the bitterness of life, the Seeker recalls the only remedy for it. "Then I realized" could be written, "I realized again" or "I was again reminded." The Seeker always

---

[26] Ibid., 103.

returns to the same basic truth. Apart from knowledge of God and his Word, life is meaningless.

Whatever he may call the path which he walks, no unconverted person has yet succeeded in taking himself off the path of futility. Even the richest among them is bankrupt. How very different is the person who lives for God! These words of the Seeker, written from a spiritual point of view, most powerfully underline the contrast.

He does not view the blessings that he enjoys as merely the earned rewards for his labor—but as gifts from the hand of a sovereign God. Food, drink, all good things, life, riches, wealth, our various faculties, the power to rejoice, gladness of heart—all these things come from God's hand. The godly person reasons that God has given him these things that he might enjoy them, and he is able to do so because he sees all as symbols and pledges of God's favor (18–19).

No doubt the believer, like other men and women, has his fair share of difficulties. But he dos not get totally absorbed by them, because he has other things to think about. [27]

The ESV introduces verse 18 with the word *behold*. "Behold, what I have seen to be good and fitting is to eat and drink and find enjoyment in all the toil with which one toils under the sun the few days of his life that God has given him, for this is his lot." With the word *behold*, the Seeker invites his readers to review the evidence and arrive at his conclusion: there is another life besides merely under the sun. The Seeker uses the expression "to eat and drink" as a symbol of a contented and happy life. The Apostle Paul echoes this sentiment in his words to Timothy:

But godliness with contentment is great gain. (1 Tim 6:6, NIV)

---

[27] Olyott, 40.

Many people, including many Christians, do not see the tight link between *over the sun* and contentment. You cannot be a truly godly person without having the joy of the Lord's presence. True godliness and discontentment cannot coexist in the same heart any more than true contentment can be found apart from godliness. Our society is convinced that they will find contentment in things.

> Man must get enjoyment, not possessions. And that capacity to enjoy, no matter how great or small, is a gift from God. It is much better to receive wealth as a gift from God, along with the God-given ability to enjoy it, than to see wealth as an end in itself. [28]

A. W. Tozer said, "You can own five cars, just so none of them owns you."

For secular humanity, life is drudgery, but not so for the children of God. Our life is not a series of meaningless events, but is the working out of a plan and a purpose that God has ordained for us. We sing with understanding and feeling:

> What ever my lot, Thou hast taught me say,
> "It is well, it is well, with my soul."

We must be careful not to have an unbalanced view of wealth. Our Lord taught us that riches can, but not necessarily must or will, shut us out of heaven (Matthew 19:23), and Paul said "the love of riches has drowned some men in destruction and perdition" (1 Timothy 6:9,10). Paul also said, "God gives us richly all things to enjoy" (1 Timothy 6:17). Is God sending mixed signals about riches? Bridges comments:

---

[28] Kaiser, 77.

The Seeker gives the true balance. Wealth is not essentially evil. The evil is in their abuse—as we have said—in their love, not in their possession. The true difference is not in the gift, but the *power* to use it—*to eat thereof.* The gift may belong to the ungodly. The *power* is the exclusive privilege of the Christian. He 'is not the slave of his worldly goods, but truly the master of them.' [29]

Bridges describes the life of fellowship with God that a Christian enjoys, and contrasts that with the outlook of the lost man:

And what of the ungodly? His days drag heavily. *The remembrance* is clouded. The road before him, dark and wearisome. But what with him, who lives in God's grace? God answereth him in the joy *of his heart* by the comfort of his Spirit. With him, time flies on with angel's wings. *The remembrance of the days of his life* are 'few and evil' (Genesis 42:9). The glowing anticipation melts away the past. For how soon will every spring of sorrow be dried up forever (Isaiah 35:10)! How bright does the eternity of joy contrast with the 'affliction but for a moment' (2 Cor 4:17)! 'Pleasures' ever new are his portion 'at God's right hand for ever more' (Psalm 16:11). [30]

As I prepared this chapter, I looked back over fifty-five years of ministry. I have preached in hundreds of churches and met thousands of believers. I have met some very godly and truly contented people who were poor and some who were wealthy. I have met some who were neither contented nor truly godly in the biblical sense, some of whom were poor, as well as some of whom were wealthy. I have no

---

[29] Bridges, 121.

[30] Ibid., 121.

doubt that the wealthy ones who were godly would have been just as contented if they had been poor. Likewise, I am sure the poor ones who were not contented would have been just as discontented if they had won the lottery. It is not what I own, but what owns me. That which truly defines me is my living relationship to the Lord Jesus Christ.

CHAPTER THIRTEEN: VERSES 6:1–12

SOME GREAT SAINTS DIED IN POVERTY

The Seeker, in the latter half of chapter five, contemplates the vanity of wealth. He compares riches and poverty, and concludes that true contentment for any man, whether rich or poor, comes only from recognizing and living in the world *over the sun*. In chapter six, the Seeker continues to develop this idea, expanding the concept of the vanity of wealth to include all forms of success. He shows that prosperity may not always be good. In chapter seven, he sets forth the opposite and accompanying truth—namely, that adversity may not always be bad.

> *I have seen another evil under the sun, and it weighs heavily on men. God gives a man wealth, possessions and honor, so that he lacks nothing his heart desires, but God does not enable him to enjoy them, and a stranger enjoys them instead. This is meaningless, a grievous evil.*
>
> *A man may have a hundred children and live many years; yet no matter how long he lives, if he cannot enjoy his prosperity and does not receive proper burial, I say that a stillborn child is better off than he. It comes without meaning, it departs in darkness, and in darkness its name is shrouded. Though it never saw the sun or knew anything, it has more rest than does that man even if he lives a thousand years twice over but fails to enjoy his prosperity. Do not all go to the same place?* (Eccl 6:1-6, NIV)

Chapter six of Ecclesiastes begins with a series of sketches that show some of the limitations of money and what it procures: possessions and prestige. The old saying, "Money is not the only thing, but it is miles ahead of whatever is second," is not always true. Wealth, regardless of how we measure it or how much of it we possess, cannot guarantee contentment. If God gives a man everything that the heart could desire and does not give him a heart to enjoy it, then it would have been better for that man never to live. What profit is a life of discontentment, even if lived in the lap of luxury? How many people do you know that have all that money can buy, and yet cannot seem to enjoy what they have? They live jaded, empty lives while surrounded by every modern status symbol.

The Seeker, in 5:18–20, depicts a man who lives under the blessing of God because God gave him contentment. In 6:2, God gives another man wealth, but not the ability to enjoy it. Additionally, this man has fame and recognition. These too, he is unable to enjoy. The author does not explain what has happened to prevent the second man from enjoying his wealth. The scenario includes a bitter irony: a stranger will enjoy his wealth. Neither the man nor his children will benefit from the man's prosperity.

The reader can imagine various reasons why the man in 6:2 cannot enjoy the prosperity given by God. He may die young – cut off in the prime of his life. However, even if he lives a long life and has many children, there is no guarantee of any true happiness. He has all the symbols of fame and security but (v. 3) his life may be unsatisfactory. The key thought in this section is in the words, "God does not enable him to enjoy." Repeatedly, the Seeker pounds home that lesson in the book of Ecclesiastes. Enjoyment does not reside in possessions; it is a gift that God alone can give. If he withholds it, no amount of effort is going to extract it from any other source. This truth is the exact opposite of the message constantly bombarding us today from every form of advertising.

The text raises the question of why God would give prosperity, but withhold the ability to enjoy it. The Seeker has already answered that question in 2:25, 26 where he says,

> "... for apart from him, who can eat or find enjoyment? To the man who pleases him, God gives wisdom, knowledge and happiness..." (Eccl 2:25–26, NIV).

Notice the Seeker's wording: "to the man who pleases him." Do not misunderstand this to mean that performing certain religious exercises or joining a church is a way of pleasing God. The way to please God is to have faith, to believe him, to take him at his Word and act on that Word. This is what pleases God: obedience based upon faith. God freely gives such a person the gift of enjoying all things as a gift from God. This is why a thankful heart is vital to the Christian life (1 Thess 5:18).

Regardless of what wealth, possessions and honor a person has, if he does not have contentment, he has missed the boat. Eternally, his condition is worse than that of a stillborn child. Michael Eaton comments:

> Despite family, longevity and fame, a man's life may so miscarry as to incur lifelong dissatisfaction and an unmourned death. The *soul* in the KJV, *his soul is not filled with good*, is the whole inner life of man, and is used here as his capacity for feelings, inclinations, enjoyment, and satisfaction. To die unburied was the mark of a despised and unmourned end, *(cf. Jer.*

22:18f. and Eccl 8:10. Better to miscarry at birth than to miscarry through life.[31]

The Seeker compares the dissatisfied rich man of verse 3 with a stillborn child in verse 4. The child comes into the world without any realization of life. It departs in darkness, or the realm of the dead. It has never seen the sun, or anything *under the sun*, and it will never know any existence of reality. However, the stillborn child has more rest than the discontented rich man. The child does not have to fight a meaningless and irksome life of despair *under the sun*.

In verses 3 through 6, the author raises the subject of long life. Normally, we view long life as a blessing from God. However, if one's life is a prolonged time of misery, no one can view it as a blessing from God. It is really just a waiting period for death—and death is the common destination of all, no matter how long a given individual takes to get there. In verses 7 through 9, the Seeker returns to a theme he has addressed earlier: the vanity of work, wisdom, and ambition.

> *All man's efforts are for his mouth,*
> *yet his appetite is never satisfied.*
>
> *What advantage has a wise man over a fool?*
> *What does a poor man gain by knowing how to conduct himself before others?*
>
> *Better what the eye sees than the roving of the appetite. This too is meaningless,* (Eccl 6:7–9, NIV).

We must not take verse seven to mean the only reason any man works is to satisfy stomach hunger. Many people

---

[31] Michael A. Eaton, *Ecclesiastes, An Introduction & Commentary* (Downers Grove, IL: IVP, 1983), 106.

with full bellies have empty hearts and souls. We have appetites other than hunger that exert stronger influences on us. However, the main point is that no amount of labor, regardless of what it attains, can ever satisfy the human heart. Remember the words of our Lord, "Man shall not live by bread alone."

A wise man (verse 8), may, in one sense, be no better off than the fool, because his very wisdom gives him a greater capacity to see the potential of man, as well as the sin of man, that makes realization of that potential impossible. Wisdom, as we saw earlier, carries its own set of problems. Likewise, a fool may learn how to ingratiate himself in the eyes of others, yet he remains a fool. What has he really gained that is worth having? What price has he paid to gain so little?

Charles Bridges points out that verse 9 repeats the theme and message of the Book of Ecclesiastes as well as the whole of Scripture.

> *The sight of the eyes* is the reality before us. *The wandering of the desire* is the longing pursuit of some unattainable object some phantom only imagined never reached. The fruitless search only ends in *vanity and vexation of spirit.* Better therefore to enjoy what we have in possession, than to be roving up and down in anxious weariness. For what can be more wretched, than when the false pictures of the world palm themselves upon us for realities, when shadows begin to pass away, and there is no substance to supply their place! The true good that a man can have in this life, is to enjoy that which he hath in peace and rest, and not to *wander* in the straying and unsatisfied desires after that which he hath not. The *wandering desire* "Loving to wander" is indeed our nature. But under Divine Teaching the light is clear and strong; the eye and heart are

fixed. One object fills every desire "Whom have I in heaven but thee? and there is none upon earth that I desire beside thee" (Psalm 73:25). Everything is unreal, when placed beside this glorious treasure. Our position is not so much looking up to heaven from earth, as looking down from heaven to earth. And it is when we thus realize our rightful standing in heaven (Compare Eph. 2:6; Phil. 3:20) we rise above the dying vanities of earth. "The way of life is above to the wise, that he may depart from hell beneath" (Prov. 15:24). There is no *wandering* here. But if we do not find our rest here, truly it is a sickening picture. Our comforts are dashed with bitterness. Our whole sky is darkened with despondency.[32]

Earlier, in 1:9, 10, the Seeker wrote that there was "nothing new under the sun." Now, in 6:10, he states the same thing in slightly different terms. His long and serious search for truth and reality always hits the same wall. There really is nothing new under the sun.

> That which hath been is named already, and it is known that it is man: neither may he contend with him that is mightier than he. (KJV)

To give something a name is to note it worthy of study or give it a specific character. However, everything worth recording has already been named and recorded. *That which has been,* the whole of what can be obtained from all sources using every method, wisdom, history, pleasure, honor, power, riches, fame, all, *has already been named.* The Psalmist said it better than we could,

> LORD, make me to know mine end, and the measure of my days, what it is; that I may know how frail I am.

---

[32] Charles Bridges, *Ecclesiastes, A Geneva Series Commentary* (Carlisle, PA: Banner of Truth, 1961), 127–28.

Behold, thou hast made my days as an handbreadth; and mine age is as nothing before thee: verily every man at his best state is altogether vanity. Selah.

Surely every man walketh in a vain shew: surely they are disquieted in vain: he heapeth up riches, and knoweth not who shall gather them.

And now, Lord, what wait I for? my hope is in thee. (Ps 39:4–7, KJV)

The Psalmist and the Seeker in Ecclesiastes express the same hope and confidence in the sovereignty of God. The Seeker is telling us that God has decreed that no human effort, regardless of how sincere and exacting, can find true happiness. We must receive enjoyment, in faith, as a gift of God. God made it that way. Proud and self-sufficient, fallen humanity does not like those terms and is ready to fight with God. We must learn three things from this text:

1. God has decreed all things, including the creation of humanity. God has already known whatever has come to be before it happened. Before human life appeared on earth, it was named in the mind and thought of God.

2. God knew everything about human beings before he created them. There were no surprises, including humanity's fall in Eden.

3. The Seeker insists that all was decreed in spite of humanity. Human beings may not like the way God operates, but they cannot argue with God.

Man's original dignity, being made in the image of God, serves to highlight more clearly his present degradation. All things known and named are varying shades of the same vanity. No matter how high man esteems himself in his own eyes, or is held in admiration by fellow creatures, the stamp of vanity is indelible. *It is known that it is man,* at best, but man. Bridges explains:

> His religion is self-wrought. Whatever it be, it never brings him close to God. It always therefore leaves him short of peace with God. Man is its center. What is lacking is the teaching of humility. "Remember," speaks Bishop Taylor in his own eloquence, "what you were before you were begotten? Nothing. What were you in the first regions of your dwelling, before your birth? Uncleanness. What were you for many years after? Weakness. What in all your life? A great sinner. What in all your excellencies? A mere debtor to God, to your parents, to all the creatures."
>
> A being, thus fraught with infirmity and corruption, a very worm in weakness and helplessness, can he *contend* with his Maker, infinitely *mightier than he* (Isa. 45:9)? Can he impeach him and call him to account? "Nay, but, oh man, who are thou that replies against God?" (Romans 9:20). Learn the lesson of prostrate submission. Take thy proper place, "laying your hand on your mouth" (Job 40:4), and your mouth in the dust. To contend with God is to add madness to folly. To submit to God's sovereignty is your security and your rest.[33]

The more we know, the more visible becomes the vanity and futility of life. Arguing with God will only aggravate the problem and add to the vanity. Add up all the things that on the surface appear to be positive and you discover that man is none the better. Look at and combine all his words of rationalizing, boasting, and questioning; together they give no light or hope.

> *The more words, the more vanity, and what is man the better?* (Eccl 6:11, RSV)

---

[33] Bridges, *Ecclesiastes*, 130.

In verse 12, the Seeker asks two questions. (1) Who really understands life and knows what is good for man, and (2) who can know what the future holds?

For who knoweth what is good for man in this life, all the days of his vain life which he spendeth as a shadow? For who can tell a man what shall be after him under the sun? (Eccl 6:12, KJV)

Where is the person who, without question, knows what is good for him? How many times have you and I been willing to do almost anything to get something we thought would simplify life or make it more enjoyable, and when we got it, we were soon trying to figure out how to get rid of it? Likewise, where is the person who can accurately predict the future?

There is a sense in which a child of God can answer both of these questions as they concern the most important things in our existence, both in the present and in the future. We know for sure who we are, where we came from, why we are here, and where we are going when we leave here. We know where to find the Bread of Life that satisfies the soul in its hunger to know truth and reality. We drink from a well of water that quenches that deep thirst to know God and fellowship with him.

Walter Kaiser, in his commentary, includes the following excellent review of chapter six:

"Never judge a book by its cover," goes the old saying, and men should never get confused about the true state of others' affairs by looking merely at their outward welfare. A man may possess wealth, honor, numerous children, long life and virtually every outward good that anyone could possibly imagine; yet he can still be a very broken, dissatisfied, and unhappy person.

Indeed, this is a weight that weighs heavily on men (6:1): God may grant a man wealth, possessions, honor, and virtually anything his heart wants without also granting him the ability to enjoy any of it (6:2). Therein lies the point of Solomon: things are not always what they seem to be. Prosperity without the divine gift of enjoyment is nothing. In fact, God-given wealth without the God-given power to enjoy it is a major malady. Worst of all is that a stranger, not even his own kin, consumes the whole estate from which a man had only joylessly partaken portions.

So immense is this deprivation of enjoyment that even if the case just mentioned were reversed and, instead of being childless and leaving his possessions to a total stranger, that same man was blessed with an abundance of children; and if, instead of departing from this earthly scene quickly and letting a stranger receive a bonanza of goods, he lived for an unusually long number of days; still, if he were not given the divine gift of enjoying it all, death at birth would have been preferable to what had happened to such a man (6:3). A stillborn baby is free from all the suffering of the joyless rich man and has more rest than he does (6:4, 5).

After all the concessions made in verses 3–5, we see that even if an inordinate number of days were offered to this man, they must come to an end. Then he, too, must go to the same place as the stillborn child (6:6). That "one place" is, as seen in 3:20, the grave. What then? If even the longest life eventually terminates having yielded no enjoyment, not to mention any prospect of anything to follow, what is the benefit, or advantage, of all those years? Although others may have looked on with envious eyes, the truth is that the extension was not what it appeared to be; it was a compound sorrow.

Whereas the man's labor was continually aimed at his insatiable desire for pleasure, he never arrived (6:7). No man, be he wise, poor, or rich can satisfy his desires on his own (6:8). True, making do with what we possess is better than striving for what we do not have, for all the wishing for things we want is worthless. (6:9).

The reason riches fail to yield any happiness rests on the unalterable ordinance of God (6:10). Mortal man, the creation of God, cannot set aside or overcome that divinely established connection between earthly things and the dissatisfaction with those things apart from God. Try as man will to wrestle and contest God's decision to link these two things—the more he talks, the more vapid, empty, and unsatisfactory the situation becomes (6:11). All words are useless; man might just as well acknowledge his limitations and begin immediately to fear God. The ordinance of God dictates the capacity of worldly things to yield enjoyment; in fact, it must be observed that often worldly prosperity only increases the emptiness and dissatisfaction. We might ask, in the words of Paul in Romans 9:20, "Who art thou, oh man, to talk back to God?" Do you know what is good for man? (6:12). Does any man know what the future holds? Of course, no one knows except God. Therefore, no one can say what will be the real advantage of one thing or another for himself or others.

If every one of the above cases has shown the inadequacy of judging the fairness and goodness of the plan of God by observing only external features, then the providence of God may not have so many exceptions as we may have thought as we began to apply the truth of 3:1—that there is a time and season for everything under heaven—especially when compared to the apparent success of the wicked. Prosperity may not always be what it seems. Therefore, let us seek to know God, to be content with such gifts as He gives us, and to receive the accompanying gift of enjoyment from His hands.[34]

In chapter seven, the Seeker depicts situations where a particular choice is far better for us than the opposite choice. Just as prosperity is not always good, it is equally true that adversity is not always bad. Many of the best things that ever happened to us grew out of hard and painful situations.

But ... that is the next chapter.

---

[34] Walter C. Kaiser Jr., *Ecclesiastes, Everyman's Bible Commentary* (Chicago: Moody Press, 1979). 80–82

ADVERSITY CAN BE PROFITABLE

In Ecclesiastes 6:1–12, the Seeker demonstrated that prosperity in itself neither proves the blessing of God, nor is it necessarily a good thing. The Puritans often said that God curses his enemies with riches. They clearly understood that having wealth and power without a heart to use both for the glory of God would prove in the end to be an eternal curse. The companion truth of 6:1–12 is set forth in 7:1–14. Just as prosperity is not always accompanied by good, so suffering and adversity is not necessarily a sign of God's disfavor. Actually, adversity is often a greater good than is prosperity. The Seeker raised the question of what is good in 6:12. Of course, a child of God knows that "God works *all things* together for his good" (Romans 8:28), but an *under the sun* philosophy cannot grasp this truth.

Having asked the question of what is good, the Seeker now answers with proverbs that show some things that will be good for us regardless of either the surface appearance or the way the world may view those same things.

7:1a – "*A good name is better than fine perfume …*" (NIV). The writer uses a play on the words *name* and *perfume*. The Hebrew for name is *shêm* and the Hebrew for perfume is *shemen*. A good *shêm* (name) is better, gives a better smell, than the best *shemen* (perfume). Some of the silliest television ads today are about perfume. You are assured that just a small squirt of a particular perfume and those of the opposite sex will be falling all over you. The purpose of perfume in our culture is to make people notice you and to make a favorable impression. In the ancient world, perfume served several different functions. It was used as a cosmetic in the same way that deodorant is today, as well as for moisturizing the skin, both important considerations in the hot, dry climate of Palestine. Additionally, ancient people used perfumed ointment for funeral, medicinal, and ritual purposes. Perfumed ointment was costly and strong, in some cases retaining its scent for over three thousand years.[35] The Seeker recognized the value of perfume; he also realized that a good name is worth more. A good name, like perfume, will attract people to you, but with distinct differences. A good name continues to attract even after the perfume smell fades or turns rancid. People will drive past flashy restaurants to go to a small place, out of the way, that has good food. So a good name not only attracts, it keeps on attracting. You may never be able to afford Chanel No. 5, but you can have a good name that attracts the best of people and lasts beyond your lifetime.

7:1b – *"and the day of death better than the day of birth."* The writer begins to introduce a series of things that, on the surface, are not at all what they are in reality. Fallen human beings view the day of death as the end of everything. In reality, death is the beginning of everything worthwhile. Birth is viewed as the first day of your life and death as the last day of your life. In reality, death is the first day of forever. Death does not end the dreams and hopes of a child of God. Death is the first day of the rest of eternity. Birth is the beginning

---

[35]*Wycliffe Bible Encyclopedia*, vol. 2, (Chicago, Moody Press, 1975), s.v. "Ointment."

of an experience of struggle, pain, and hopelessness. Death is the end of pain, shame, and suffering.

7:2 – *"It is better to go to a house of mourning than to go to a house of feasting, for death is the destiny of every man; the living should take this to heart."* When we face death, we face reality. When we stand by the grave, we are forced to say, "Death is the final destiny of all people, including me!" Looking into the casket or the grave is like looking in a mirror and saying, "That is my end also." We are no longer dealing with side issues, but with the fact of all facts, the certainty of death.

Going to the house of feasting is a delight. Remember that there is a time to go to the house of feasting, just as there is a time to go to a funeral. Both have their times and their proper responses. Do not try to turn a funeral into a birthday party or a wedding into a funeral. A believer will take this to heart and will learn from all experiences. However, the lessons learned at the graveyard will be more important to his eternal well-being than those learned at the junior prom will be.

7:3 – *"Sorrow is better than laughter, because a sad face is good for the heart."* Sorrow, even when blessed by God, will not necessarily lead to laughter. It does, however, lead to spiritual growth. Sorrow is good for the heart, even if painful to the flesh. On the other hand, we cannot sustain laughter indefinitely in a world of sin, but will find that our countenances change with a change in circumstances. We need only compare the expression on people's faces as they enter a party and see the looks on the same faces as they walk to their cars after the party ends.

7:4 – *"The heart of the wise is in the house of mourning, but the heart of fools is in the house of pleasure."* This is a variation of verse 2. This seems to be upside down. How can sorrow, grief, and pain ever be the cause of gladness and godly wisdom? Talk to godly Christians who have gone through difficult trials who, at the same time, have enjoyed the presence and comfort of God the Holy Spirit. A fool will laugh away reality, but a wise person will learn through the difficult times. It has been my joy to know many saints who went through heart-wrenching experiences and testified, "In the hottest furnace, I knew my Lord was with me." They also said, "I would not trade all the things God taught me through the trial, even if I could avoid all the pain."

7:5, 6 – "It is better to heed a wise man's rebuke than to listen to the song of fools. Like the crackling of thorns under the pot, so is the laughter of fools. This too is meaningless." No person would enjoy listening to careful and honest criticism as much as he would enjoy a songfest. Likewise, it would be more fun to listen to Jay Leno bring down the house with some hilarious one-liners than it would be to sit in a counseling session, having your attitude and actions analyzed and reproved. The first, however, will not help a struggling marriage; the second just might save it. It does not take long for the fire to consume crackling thorns; neither does it take long for the laughter that was designed for pure entertainment to stop.

7:7 – *"Extortion turns a wise man into a fool, and a bribe corrupts the heart."* Using bribery or extortion seems, at the time, an easy means of getting something you want, but both bribery and extortion have a devastating effect on your heart and life. Usually, the person who resorted to bribery or extortion was smart enough to get more than he needed by honest work. However, the temptation for easy money may turn even the wisest of people into fools who say, "I will not get caught." Bribery not only corrupts the self-image of those who submit to it, it usually makes them a captive of the man to whom they paid the bribe. The price you pay for silence or dishonest gain is far greater than the benefit you get from the bribe.

7:8 – *"The end of a matter is better than its beginning, and patience is better than pride."* I used to play golf once a week with a deacon in the church where I was pastor. If I said, "Herb, I feel like I'm really on today," he would always reply, "It is not what you say when you put your armor on, but what you say when you take it off."

Patience in waiting for God's timing is better than fretting over the elusiveness of things. Inability to control our emotions is one proof of foolish immaturity. How many things have we started with great zeal, only to become discouraged and quit? We had no patience. We lost sight of how worthwhile the goal was and lost the will to persevere. Pride may start a matter; patience will carry it through to completion.

7:9—*"Do not be quickly provoked in your spirit, for anger resides in the lap of fools."* The man who can control his spirit is, according to Proverbs, stronger than a general who conquers a city. I know of nothing that has destroyed as many relationships as have words spoken in anger. Often times, the lost patience and perseverance described in verse 8 are the direct result of losing our temper with someone essential to the success of a particular endeavor.

7:10 – "*Do not say, 'Why were the old days better than these?'*
For it is not wise to ask such questions." Nostalgia can easily
lead us away from reality and toward depression. It is easy
to imagine a situation that never really existed. Selective
memory often forgets bad things and magnifies the good.
This makes honest evaluation impossible, because we have
distorted our memory of the real "good old days." The
Children of Israel were ready to go back to Egypt where
they had enjoyed onions, leeks, and garlic. They conveniently forgot the tyranny and hardship of making bricks without
straw, and other grievous indignities arising from slavery.

My grandma used to say, "I would love to go back to the
good old days, provided I could take my air-conditioner,
refrigerator, and TV." I remember those good old days
when we had no running water in the house; we had to go
outside to a pump. We had to walk several hundred feet to
an outside toilet with holes cut in a wooden bench. We used
Sears Roebuck catalogues or corncobs for toilet paper. We
put bricks in the oven of the wood stove, then wrapped
them in towels and put them at the end of our beds to keep
our feet warm enough to go to sleep. The "good old days"
had a few problems and some "not so good memories."

God never gives you grace to cope with the problems of
the generation in which you live while you are pining for
another generation either gone by or coming in the future.
Godly wisdom always faces the reality of the present. The
Bible does not allow us to run from facts, but openly tells of
the problems, and then says, "But my grace is sufficient."

7:11 – "*Wisdom, like an inheritance, is a good thing and benefits those who see the sun.*" We can solve many of our problems with money. Money, especially money from an inheritance, is a good thing, provided we see it as a gift from God. However, we cannot solve the deepest problems we face with money, no matter how much money we throw at them. Godly wisdom will sometimes give you answers and security that no amount of money can give you.

7:12 – "Wisdom is a shelter as money is a shelter, but the advantage of knowledge is this: that wisdom preserves the life of its possessor." Both money and wisdom can shelter you from many things. Money may secure medical care that prolongs your physical life by twenty years or more. It will indeed shelter you from much adversity, aggravation, and discomfort. However, the wisdom that comes from God will shelter you eternally in the presence of God. Godly wisdom excels anything money can buy.

7:13 – *"Consider what God has done: Who can straighten what he has made crooked?"* The phrase *made crooked* covers difficult times, painful experiences, mistreatment, sicknesses, and persecution – whatever we endure in our lifetime. First, we are to consider all of these things as the work of God and not as accidents or misfortunes. Whatever circumstances exist, whether good or bad, in some way must be traced back to a sovereign God. The moment we do that, the question becomes, "Who can straighten out what God has made crooked?" The writer repeats this admonition in the next verse.

7:14 – *"When times are good, be happy; but when times are bad, consider: God has made the one as well as the other. Therefore, a man cannot discover anything about his future."* Both the good times and the bad come from God's sovereign hand. We observe and acknowledge God's work, but we cannot predict it, explain it, or in any way control it. The unsaved person hates any suggestion that he is not the captain of his fate and the master of his soul.

7:15 – *"In this meaningless life of mine I have seen both of these: a righteous man perishing in his righteousness, and a wicked man living long in his wickedness."* Life is full of anomalies that do not make sense to our finite minds. Have we not all been amazed, and from a human point of view, confused, at the recent Supreme Court hearings? We have not only watched good people from two different sides sincerely express opposite opinions, we also saw dishonest people willing to distort the truth to advance their agendas. If we ask, "Why does God allow it?" the Seeker will answer, "God is sovereign." God has designed life under the sun in such a way that rebels can never second-guess him, nor can they frustrate his purposes. Just when the sinner thinks he has it all figured out, God will pull the rug out from under him. It is painful to learn that you do not control the future.

The Book of Ecclesiastes contains an exhaustive study of the values of different worldviews and lifestyles. The Seeker, in verse 15, begins a new section with his oft-repeated statement, "I have seen everything" and his conclusion is still the same, ours is a meaningless life apart from God's revelation. In Chapter 6, the Seeker learned that prosperity is not always good. In chapter 7, he shows the opposite is also true. Adversity is not always bad. Some of the most blessed times we ever went through were those when we had very little and faced great odds.

We must note two important things in verse 15. First, phony righteousness abounds; and second, true wisdom is a scarce commodity. Living to be old is no proof of righteousness. The best of men and women often die young and the worst of wicked people often live to a ripe old age. Look around the world at the many dictators who are both old and powerful. Likewise, being very religious is no evidence that you really know God. Many of the terrorists who are active in the world today are very religious people. They are more than willing to sacrifice everything, even their lives, for their religious beliefs.

7:16–18 – *"Do not be overrighteous, neither be overwise—why destroy yourself? Do not be overwicked, and do not be a fool—why die before your time? It is good to grasp the one and not let go of the other. The man who fears God will avoid all* [extremes]." These words often are greatly misunderstood. They are the favorite verses of both antinomians and legalists. One interpretation sees this verse as teaching moderation in all things, or Aristotle's Golden Mean. Do not be an extremist. Do not go overboard. In this view, the Seeker seems to be saying, "Be a good person, but not so good that you do not have any fun. Enjoy sowing your wild oats as a rite of passage, but do not go too far." Who has not heard people saying, "I believe in religion, but I am not a fanatic," and by fanatic, they mean bringing religion into real life.

I am glad that God taught me early in my ministry that truth does not lie in the middle as most people think. Truth usually lies in taking both of the extremes at the same time. The mindset that promotes moderation at all cost marks the person who actually believes nothing and is willing to listen to anything. When we read the New Testament, we are confronted with a person who claims to be God and who seems to have all of the credentials to prove it. We conclude that Jesus is God. We continue to read and discover that Jesus sleeps, eats, weeps, and acts exactly like a man. We conclude that Jesus is a man. The contemporary exponent of moderation in all things will say, "Let's not go to an extreme. Let's not be strict literalists. To say Jesus is both God and man at the same time would involve a clear contradiction. It is obvious that no one can be God and man at the same time."

So what conclusion does moderation propose? We must tone down both of the two extremes. We must say that Jesus certainly is God-like and is therefore half God. Jesus is also is truly manly, so he is half man. We have now reconciled both of the teachings and avoided both extremes by saying that Jesus is half God and half man. Unfortunately, we wind up with nothing. We have denied the clear biblical facts that Jesus is, without any question, "God of God and Man of Man." We have lost an able Savior, one in our nature who is also God, and we have lost a human Savior who, in our humanity, can truly understand and sympathize with us. We have lost both the absolute deity of Christ and his absolute humanity. We have lost the Christ of the New Testament Scriptures.

We could show the same thing with God's absolute sovereignty and man's moral responsibility. We may not be able to reconcile some statements, but regardless, we dare not deny God's absolute sovereignty to do what he chooses, when he chooses, and to whom he chooses. Likewise, we dare not deny that the sinner is completely responsible for every one of his actions.

These verses warn against the extremes of self-righteousness and of self-indulgence. Proverbs says, "The righteous are bold as a lion" (Prov. 28:1); unfortunately, the self-righteous are even bolder. The New Testament Scriptures denounce this attitude of pharisaism. In God's sight, self-righteousness is as wicked as adultery or murder. It destroys churches and individual lives. This attitude of heart manifests itself in a harsh judgmental attitude, bigotry, pride, pompousness, cold and critical disdain, sarcastic words, a vengeful attitude, and vindictive actions. I am always amazed to see church people act more ungraciously than do lost people. This is especially true in a church fight. The reverse attitude (self-indulgence) is just as bad. The foolish person will cast off all moral restraints, often using the excuse that he is not under the law but under grace. New Covenant Theology has a few adherents that seem to think that any kind of self-discipline that uses specific rules to help keep them on track must be wrong. Some people combine the two attitudes; they eschew all rules, claim to "follow the Spirit," and to be spontaneous. At the same time, these people demonstrate a self-righteous attitude by criticizing others.

Both of these lifestyles are self-destructive. The Seeker asks the legalist, "Why should you destroy yourself in your hypocrisy and self-righteousness?" "Why should you die before your time?" he asks the self-indulgent. Both of these theologies and lifestyles lead their exponents to deny their basic humanness as well as the gospel of sovereign grace. From a human standpoint, they both may die prematurely. One may die from not taking care of himself and the other may die of ulcers. Soft living is as dangerous as wild living.

7:18–19 – *"It is good that thou shouldest take hold of this; yea, also from this withdraw not thine hand: for he that feareth God shall come forth of them all. Wisdom strengtheneth the wise more than ten mighty men which are in the city* (KJV)" The Seeker gives us the right attitude or world and lifeview. Ray Stedman has commented on this text.

This is the consistent position of Scripture, Old and New Testament alike. We are not to withdraw from the world in an attempt to escape its evil; we are not to gather our robes of righteousness about ourselves and look down our noses with disdain at those who live morally unrighteous lives. It is good to take hold of true righteousness, but it is also good not to withhold oneself from the world. Be out of it, but live in it, be in touch with it. Do not seek to avoid it, to hide in a spiritual cocoon, but do not go along with its unrighteous and hurtful attitudes and practices.

The godly way to live, of course, is "He who fears God shall come forth from them all." We have seen this phrase, "The man who fears God" many times in this book. "To fear God" is the full-orbed truth. It means not only to respect God, but to acknowledge his presence in your life; not merely at the end of your life someday, but now. To fear God is to know that he sees all that you do, and that it is his hand that sends circumstances into your life. The knowledge of God's power, wisdom, and love, his willingness to accept you, to change you, to forgive you, to restore and stand by you, are all part of fearing God. "To fear God" is to know how to live in the midst of the world and yet not be self-righteous, priggish, smug and complacent. That kind of wisdom "gives strength to the wise man more than ten rulers that are in a city." It is better to learn to live that way than to have ten influential friends in high places who can bail you out![36]

The Seeker is constantly realistic. His world and lifeview is not rose-colored, but consistent with his real and meaningless life. He not only sees that individuals are depraved, he also sees that the entire race of humanity is depraved. We live in a world deeply infected by sin. There is no righteousness, or any hope of righteousness, apart from the grace and power of God.

7:20 – *"There is not a righteous man on earth who does what is right and never sins."* We are all tempted to say, "That is, all but me. I am the exception." The Bible constantly shuts your mouth and says, "All, INCLUDING YOU, have sinned and come short of the glory of God." The Seeker proceeds to show us how we can prove for ourselves that he is correct.

7:21, 22 – *"Do not pay attention to every word people say, or you may hear your servant cursing you – for you know in your heart that many times you yourself have cursed others."* This is especially true when the words were spoken in anger or frustration. If all husbands and wives believed that their spouses meant everything they said, most marriages would not last much over a week. If all bosses took seriously what some of their employees said about them, they would cry themselves to sleep or fire every employee. Remember that you too have made regrettable remarks when you were stuck in traffic or when a store clerk could not answer your questions. Do not forget those brutal words you hurled at your spouse.

---

[36] Taken from a taped sermon by Ray Stedman, preached at Peninsula Bible Church, Palo Alto, CA, 1982.

I remember what a professor in Bible School told a tearful student who had confided to him that some students were lying about her. He smiled and said, "You should thank God they are not telling the whole truth about you."

The Seeker closes this chapter by asserting that he looked hard and long to find righteousness. Godly wisdom that leads to true righteousness is indeed hard to find.

7:23 – *"All this I tested by wisdom and I said, 'I am determined to be wise' – but this was beyond me."* In the early part of this book, we saw the intensity and thoroughness of the Seeker's search for truth and reality. He first looked inside himself. He determined that he himself would be wise and learn the secret of life. Repeatedly, he pitifully confesses, "I could not find the answers. The truth was far beyond my comprehension. It was all too deep for me." The Seeker's honest confession is the very thing that unsaved people cannot admit. They believe they can, and often feel they do, understand both themselves and the reality around them.

7:24 – *"Whatever wisdom may be, it is far off and most profound—who can discover it?"* The Seeker feels hopeless in all his efforts to understand either himself or life itself. This is a bitter pill to swallow. A lost man is confident of one thing— he alone really understands himself. How often have we heard a person say, "Nobody understands me?" Of course, the person does not realize that he is saying, "I alone understand me." If Scripture is clear about one thing, it is clear that the one person that you really do not understand is yourself! Do you want proof of this fact? Look at the next verse.

7:25 – *"So I turned my mind to understand, to investigate and to search out wisdom and the scheme of things and to understand the stupidity of wickedness and the madness of folly."* Have you ever said, "Why was I so stupid as to do that?" Do you know a single soul who has not cried out in despair, "Why do I think and act as I sometimes do, in spite of the fact that I know better?" Were you not admitting the truth of the Seeker's lament?

Have you ever seriously tried to understand the mystery of evil? Not just in the Garden of Eden sense, but in your own breast? What did you find in your investigation? Whether you looked at the world or in your heart and family, what did you find? Could you rationally explain selfishness, greed, and ungratefulness? If you are honest, you will admit the Seeker was right. You found bitterness and death, and the only key that unlocked any truth or reality to you were the Words of God.

7:26–28 – *"I find more bitter than death the woman who is a snare, whose heart is a trap and whose hands are chains. The man who pleases God will escape her, but the sinner she will ensnare. 'Look,' says the Teacher, 'this is what I have discovered: "Adding one thing to another to discover the scheme of things – while I was still searching but not finding – I found one [upright] man among a thousand, but not one [upright] woman among them all."'"* The male chauvinist loves these verses. Is the Seeker really antiwomen? It certainly sounds that way on the surface. However, if we take everything the Seeker says at face value, men are only one-tenth of one percent (verse 28, I found one [upright] man among a thousand) better than women. One in a thousand is not good enough odds to warrant boasting. Before we try to understand the Seeker's words, we must remember that the same man extols womanhood in the Book of Proverbs, especially in chapter 31.[37] This chapter is known the world over for exalting godly womanhood as an example of a person who lives a life well pleasing to God. I think we must understand the Seeker's words in the light of his own personal experience, which was not even remotely close to a godly monogamous marriage.

In the ancient world of the Seeker, men had power and money to use to coerce others to submit to their wills, but women had only guile. The Seeker probably had seen more men brought into captivity through the wiles of a woman than vice-versa. Verse 26 is not to be limited to a prostitute or a kept mistress, even though it surely includes them. In the course of his life, the Seeker learned several things about both women and men. He never found a single relationship with a woman that he could label as true love. He was caught in constant sexual seduction. He went looking for love, but found only sexual gratification. He found a thrill, but never found a woman to support, sustain, help, encourage, and strengthen him in such a way that made him feel that life was worth living. However, we must ask, "Where was he looking for such a woman?" Only an idiot would expect to find such a woman among the hundreds of women in his harem. The Seeker's lament is the same sorry tale of both men and women who today are trying to find love and hope in a bar or brothel or a new affair.

Some have suggested that the Seeker was bisexual, and they use his comment about finding one man in a thousand

---

[37] Solomon did not write Proverbs 31, but he was the editor who included it in the Book of Proverbs.

with whom he could really relate to support their thesis. This is textually insupportable. Getting to know a man by working with him, going hunting and fishing with him, and enjoying his companionship as a friend, is not the same thing as nightly choosing one of a hundred women in your harem to be your bed partner for the night. A mere sexual partner can never give another person the kind of relationship for which the Seeker was searching.

The Seeker's immediate sexual involvement with a woman made it impossible to get to know her as a person. He had no such problem with men, because he did not base his relationship with men on sex. There may well have been more than one woman in his harem who was exactly what the Seeker wanted and needed. However, the sexual situation of a harem would have made it next to impossible to discover her. One thing this passage should teach both men and women, and especially young people, is that sex outside of marriage greatly diminishes the hope that two people will ever really get to know each other. I have heard people ridicule schools that do not allow unsupervised dating. Some have a "six inch rule." There is no body contact, including no handholding. A serious date consists of spending several hours in the lounge talking to each other. Those who endured what some have called a "torture chamber" experience usually were grateful later, since they married someone they really knew and not a stranger. They discussed things in the lounge that they never would have discussed alone in a parked car. A couple under these conditions developed a relationship that would be difficult to develop if that relationship involved sex outside of marriage.

7:29 – *"This only have I found: God made mankind upright, but men have gone in search of many schemes."* Everyone wants to tell God how to run his world. When a troubled young person shoots up a high school and kills innocent students, everyone cries, "Where was God?" The problems of the world are not with God, they are with man. Every single problem in this world, in one way or another, can be traced to humanity's deliberate rejection of the wisdom of God. Human beings have chosen to go their own way, and God sometimes says, "Go right ahead." The first chapter of Romans describes this as "God gave them up" to their lusts and sins.

Every day we read about a new scheme that promises to bring meaning, peace, satisfaction, and other good things into our lives. I am reminded of something I said in an early chapter. I remember watching a little boy blow big soap bubbles while his little sister chased them in glee. Of course, the moment she caught a bubble and touched it, the bubble would break. Finally, in desperation, she said, "Bubba, make one that will not break." That is what people are saying today. "Where do I find a relationship that will stand the strain of real life? Where do I find the truth that explains life and gives the strength to conquer my sin and selfishness?" Like the Seeker, they continue to look in the wrong place and to keep finding out that "all is vanity." Everything a lost man touches is like a bubble.

GODLY WISDOM IS PROFITABLE

I am deeply indebted to the late Ray Stedman for many of the seed thoughts in this chapter.

In the last chapter, we noticed that sorrow sometimes blesses a believer's walk with God. Of course, the world would totally disagree. Donald Trump and his devotees would laugh in scorn at most of the things written in our last two chapters. Their definition of what constitutes success and what is good would be far different from that proposed by the writer of Ecclesiastes. The philosophy of "he who dies with the most toys wins" cannot conceive of sorrow being better than laughter or the day of death being better than the day of birth. People with this mindset spend large sums of money and go to great lengths to have highly paid entertainers dull their senses to the very realities about which the Seeker writes.

The Seeker used scenes of sadness in the early part of chapter 7 to set the stage and to prepare his readers for the argument we covered last time. Walter Kaiser has caught this truth in his remarks about 7:1–6.

> In verse 1, Solomon points to those things that are more abiding than the rich man's mirth. A good reputation (name) has an influence (the aroma of the perfume) beyond its owner. The day of a man's death also has a lasting influence, for afterward his life can be held forth as an example if his name has merited it.

The second proverb, in verse 2, is not much different from what our Lord said in the Sermon on the Mount: "Blessed are they that mourn" (Matthew 5:4). There is a mellowing that takes place in affliction and sorrow. To be in the presence of sickness and death has a tendency to bring us into the really crucial issues of life. Likewise the third proverb, in verse 3, 4, teaches that there is a lesson to be gained and a work to be accomplished by sorrow.

Contrariwise, the prattle and laughter of fools (verses 5, 6) is useless, hollow, and bothersome. We, with David, should much more prefer the kind smiting and rebuke of the righteous (Psalm 141:5).[38]

Although we finished chapter 7 in our last chapter, we did not come to the end of the Seeker's on-going argument. Ecclesiastes 8:1 is an example of a poor chapter division. The first verse of chapter 8 belongs with chapter 7. The Seeker brings his argument in chapter 7 to a fitting climax with his description of the value of true, godly wisdom. Previously, he has shown that wisdom is good and enables a person to cope with uncertainty and injustice. He now describes true, godly wisdom and explains what it can accomplish. Here is his description of a wise man.

> *Who is like the wise man? Who knows the explanation of things? Wisdom brightens a man's face and changes its hard appearance.* (NIV)

This verse is full of intriguing ideas that merit close examination. We will unpack the four characteristics the Seeker uses to describe the person who learns, in a daily practical sense, that true wisdom is a gift of God. This kind of wis-

---

[38] Walter C. Kaiser, Jr., *Ecclesiastes, Everyman's Bible Commentary* (Chicago: Moody Press, 1979), 83, 34.

dom enables a child of God to walk with God in conscious fellowship and know and experience what it means to "fear the Lord" in a biblical sense.

First, the wisdom of God, put into practice, will make an individual a very unique person— *"Who is like the wise man"?* Who indeed? The media, sometimes subtly and other times flagrantly, constantly urges us to mimic the latest fad or fad maker. On the one hand, they promote individuality; we are urged to make a statement and to be different. In the next breath, they espouse conformity: we are pressed to imitate some famous person in our hairstyle, clothing, attitude, conversation, and so forth. Few people realize that if they succeed, they have managed only to become a cheap imitation of another person.

One of the most wonderful things about sovereign grace is that it makes you a new creation. You are never more aware of your unique true self as when you see your self in Christ. His grace will make you different from anyone else as it changes you to become more and more like him. The children of God are not cheap copies of the famous people in this world. Every believer is a spiritual original created by the Holy Spirit. Who indeed is like a child of God? Who is the truly eternally wise person?

Second, the Seeker reminds us that the "godly wisdom which is from above" (James 3:17) opens up the secrets of eternity to a child of God. *"Who knows the explanation* [true interpretation] *of things?"* The expected answer to that question is, "The child of God who has been given the Spirit of truth and wisdom knows all he needs to know, have, and enjoy eternal life." Someone has said, "Children with faith in

Christ on their knees can see further than can philosophers on their tiptoes."

This is what Paul means in 1 Corinthians 2:14–16.

> *The man without the Spirit does not accept the things that come from the Spirit of God, for they are foolishness to him, and he cannot understand them, because they are spiritually discerned. The spiritual man makes judgments about all things, but he himself is not subject to any man's judgment: "For who has known the mind of the Lord that he may instruct him?" But we have the mind of Christ.* (NIV)

A child of God is capable of passing moral judgment on all things. He may never earn a PhD, may not be able to spell the phrase *Theory of Relativity*, and may be unaware of the great scientist who first propounded it. However, any child of God could give Einstein the answers to the ultimate issues of life. We know the answers to, "Who am I, where did I come from, and where I am going?" We know these answers, not because we are smarter than Einstein or anyone else, but only because our teacher is so wise. Actually, our teacher knows everything.

Third, the truly wise person, or child of God, will enjoy his relationship with God to the degree that it will literally give a visible joy—"Wisdom brightens a man's face." The KJV says, "a man's wisdom maketh his face to shine." Ray Stedman has made some excellent comments on this phrase.

> Grace is what makes the face shine, not grease. Grease is what they put in cosmetics to make the face shine or to take away the shine as the case may be, but it is grace that does it

from within; grace makes the face shine because it is joy visibly expressed on the human face."[39]

That which is inside a man's heart will ultimately manifest itself in the countenance.

Fourth, experiential knowledge of salvation changes the countenance on believer's face because radical conversion changes the disposition of a person. The RSV translates verse 1, "... the hardness of his countenance is changed." The Puritans often said, "Even your dog will realize that something has happened to you when you get converted."

I never cease to be amazed at watching a hard and cruel individual come under the influence of the Holy Spirit. When God's spirit applies the gospel of sovereign grace to a sinner's heart, even the strongest of men will weep like a child as he asks his wife and children to forgive him for past cruelty.

Very few people have ever exceeded John Newton in his life of sin and shame. Newton had a godly mother who taught him Scripture in his childhood. He fell into the worst of company and wound up working on a ship as a slave trader. He barely escaped death on several occasions. At one point, he was the slave of a ship captain's African slave wife. She kept Newton in chains tied to an old ship anchor. The woman placed his food in the sand and made him crawl and beg like a dog for scraps. She set water just out of his reach; after he would struggle in vain to reach it, she would kick it over. He finally escaped and found his way to the coast

---

[39] Taken from a taped sermon by Ray Stedman, peached at Peninsula Bible Church, Palo Alto, CA 1982.

where a slave trading ship picked him up. During a vicious storm in which everyone, including Newton, had relinquished hope of life, Newton was converted. He later became one of England's greatest preachers. He was also a prolific songwriter, known best for his hymn "Amazing Grace." His hymns often included aspects of his personal testimony, as we see in this excerpt from Hymn 57 of the Olney Hymns, subtitled "Looking at the cross."

> In evil long I took delight, unawed by shame or fear;
> Till a new object struck my sight, and stopped my wild career.
>
> I saw one hanging on a tree, in agonies and blood;
> Who fixed his languid eyes on me, as near his cross I stood.
>
> Sure, never till my latest breath, can I forget that look;
> It seemed to charge me with his death, though not a word he
> spoke
>
> A second look he gave, which said, "I freely all forgive;
> This blood is for thy ransom paid, I die that thou may'st live."

Few saints have affected the lives of as many people as John Newton has. However, the whole point of Eccl 8:1 is to show that regardless of who we are in the eyes of the world or the circumstances in which God's sovereign providence has placed us, we are still the unique objects of God's personal love and care. It is wonderful to quote Romans 8:28 and know it is not merely a platitude to hang on the wall, but a factual, personal promise from our heavenly Father to us as individuals.

Ecclesiastes 8:2 begins a new section. As I studied these verses, I was amazed at how relevant they were to our situation today. The Seeker here deals with government authority and people's response to it, a controversial issue for us today. I remember when all young men had to register with the government and be prepared to be drafted into the armed services whether they liked it or not. There is talk of reinstating the draft. If it happens, I am sure someone will challenge it in court. We will probably hear again the same chants we heard last time: "Hell no! We won't go," from the anti-war crowd, and the "It's not wacky to wear khaki," from the pro-war crowd. If we understand the scope of Scripture, we should not be surprised that the Bible would be so contemporary.

Government can be, and often is, corrupt and cruel. However, according to Paul in Romans 13, government is ordained of God. We must learn how to respond properly to government. We who live in America and are used to personal rights and liberties find it difficult to understand many parts of the world where people do not enjoy similar privileges. In the early sixties, I visited Saudi Arabia. Women could not appear in public without a head covering and a long dress. A few feminists went downtown wearing shorts and no head covering. In less than fifteen minutes, they were in jail. Their husbands had to bring them full-length bathrobes before they could get out. If they repeated the offense, they were on the next airplane out of the country. The Seeker sets his advice wisdom in Ecclesiastes 8:2 in the context of authority:

> Obey the king's command, I say, because you took an oath before God.

One mark of godly wisdom is loyalty to God-ordained responsibilities and relationships. The Seeker suggests three reasons why people should obey their government or authority structure. First, they are citizens of that government. That is what is meant by, "because you took an oath." Every citizen of the United States has taken an oath in one form or another. If you came here as an immigrant and became an American, you took an oath of loyalty to this country. If you were born in America, you have taken an oath every time you have saluted the flag. You said, "I pledge allegiance to the flag of the United States of American, and to the Republic for which it stands." The Seeker's text urges obedience to the king's word, or government's decree, as if it were an oath to God. Of course, it is impossible to make an oath to God that would be sinful; the same would apply to government.

Obeying the government's word may be inconvenient, difficult, and sometimes downright unfair. Still, we must obey it unless we can redress it at a hearing or in court. If a zoning law makes it impossible to change something in your home, you may not go ahead and change it. The government may call you for jury duty on the date you planned to go on vacation. Hopefully, they will excuse you, but if they refuse, you will have to reschedule your vacation. Paying taxes when the government uses that money to support things in which you do not believe is indeed a burden. There are times when we would all would agree with Will Rogers, when he said, "We ought to be grateful that we don't get as much government as we've paid for!" One pundit said, "Congress is at its best during its recess."

In verses 3 through 5, the Seeker adds a second reason why we should obey the government.

> *Do not be in a hurry to leave the king's presence. Do not stand up for a bad cause, for he will do whatever he pleases. Since a king's word is supreme, who can say to him, "What are you doing?"*

Whoever obeys his command will come to no harm, and the wise heart will know the proper time and procedure. (NIV)

We are to obey because if we do not, the government has both the authority and power to make us obey. Paul writes, in Romans 13:4, that government "does not bear the sword in vain." We do not have a king over us in America but we do have a head of state as well as other authority structures that we must obey.

When you read the opening statement of the Constitution and the final paragraph of the Declaration of Independence, you see that we take an oath to honor and obey government, and that government has the authority to compel us to do so if we refuse.

I remember an instance when I was in boot camp in the Navy. When ordered by a Petty Officer to do something he did not like, a young rebel defiantly said, "You can't make me do that." The Petty Officer looked at him for moment, smiled, and said, "Son, you are right. I cannot make you do that, but believe me, I can sure make you wish that you had done it." So it is with government.

Having said all of the above, we much add a word of caution. Charles Bridges has given us the "balance of truth" in the area of obedience to government.

> Yet no earthly sovereign can claim the right of absolute obedience. "The law of the land ought not to be made our standard of moral right and wrong." (Dan. 3:16–18; 6:10. Acts 4:19; 5:29). The Babylonish confessors and the Apostles of Christ showed themselves to be servants of God by their very act of disobedience to man. The service of man must ever be subordinated to the supreme claims of the service of God. To God, *the oath* of allegiance is bound indissolubly. Soul and body are

alike the purchase of the Son of God. (Ps 119:106, with 1 Cor 6:19, 20.) When therefore man's command is contrary, we must shew respectful but unflinching determination. "The case" — as a valuable Christian writer determines — "does not admit of argument. The course is distinct and clear. The will of God is the simple and absolute rule. Whatever is not in exact consistency with this is sin. God alone is worthy of homage. His law is the supreme and only guide, from which there is no appeal, and which admits of no rival." The throne must be for the Great King. The second place would be, as if we cast him out, and "would not have him reign over us."[40]

Let us look at the specific phrases in the verses. "Do not be in a hurry to leave the king's presence." To leave the king's presence without his consent was to show disrespect. There is a correct protocol in dealing with government and we are foolish to try to avoid or deny it. Some writers apply this to God as the King of kings. It would then mean, "Do not try to find some place where you can hide from God, for that is impossible." The Psalmist is quite clear that God's eye follows you no matter where you flee. You can make your bed in hell, but God is there (Psalm 139:7, 8).

"To stand up for a bad cause" before the king is folly. It is bad enough to sin, or to become involved in a bad cause, but it is surely utter folly to "stand," or remain in it. The wise thing is to repent of the bad cause and seek forgiveness. Nobody tells the king what he should or should not do; this is especially true when the would-be advisor has done wrong.

---

[40] Charles Bridges, *Ecclesiastes, A Geneva Series Commentary* (Carlisle, PA: Banner of Truth, 1961), 185, 186.

Surely, no sensible person would try to get the king to side with him in a bad cause.

When the king speaks, be quiet because "he will do whatever he pleases." Since a king's word is supreme, who can say to him, "What are you doing?" It is not wise to openly question the wisdom of the king's action. Again, some would apply this to our Lord. He speaks with the voice of the greatest of all Kings. It is folly to challenge the words of God. In chapter 12, we will learn about the "words of the Shepherd" that are to be nailed in our consciences. When we question authority, we often do not know all the variables involved. This is true in civil government, just as it is in the kingdom of God. If we could see the big picture, and be willing to see the greater good for the whole community, we might be a little slower to say, "What are you doing?"

"Whoever obeys his command will come to no harm, and the wise heart will know the proper time and procedure." We should do all we can to escape further harassment. David said, "My soul is among lions." Spurgeon, commenting on that phrase said, "If your soul is among lions, it is wise not to pull his whiskers." It is the height of ignorance to challenge those in authority when you need them to act on a request that you have made of them. There is a time to ask a favor of the king or even to suggest an alternative course of action. The Seeker adds, "the wise heart will know the proper time and procedure" to make such a request. In a world of sin, discretion is often the better part of valor and wisdom.

In verse 6, the Seeker expands the idea of wise timing.

For there is a proper time and procedure for every matter, though a man's misery weighs heavily upon him.

There is a time to obey an authority even when you do not agree. There is a time to smile and say, "yes, sir or ma'am" to someone incompetent who holds his job only because of family connections. Verses 5 and 6 are not teaching that we must compromise any moral convictions. Many sincere people cannot tell the difference between compromise and acting wisely within the accepted protocol. The wise heart will understand the difference. The world is a giant massage parlor and we must learn to navigate in it without going against our conscience before God. One of the first things that true wisdom will teach us is that we must be realists and idealists at the same time. Again, the wise person will know both when and why to act accordingly. We will know when to take a half of loaf instead of contending for the whole loaf and getting nothing. Likewise, we will know when we must plant two feet on the truth and say, "Here I stand. I can do no other, so help me God," knowing our stance may even mean death.

I am sure your mind went back to chapter 3 of Ecclesiastes as you read the above. The wise person must understand, absorb, and put into practice the lessons of that chapter. There must be a constant reminder of the sovereign providence of God. There is a time to protest and a time to shut up. There is a time to take a stand and a time to say, "We must wait." In chapter 3, the Seeker spoke of a time for birth and death, for joy and sorrow, war and peace, and here he reminds us that every matter has its time and place. There will be times when we cry, "It is not fair"—and we will right. However, even though it is not fair, it will sometimes have to be endured in patience. We live in a world of sin where evil often triumphs. We must see sin and its awful effects and realize there is no law that can cure the problem. Grace enables us to "keep on keeping on." Verse 6 is true whether there are good times or bad times. This verse is the Romans 8:28 of the Old Testament—*For there is a proper time and procedure for every matter*, yea, even *though a man's misery weighs heavily upon him*, meaning even in the worst of times, God still controls both each event and its timing.

The Seeker continues to discuss wisdom in the context of obedience to authority; he uses the metaphors of wind and war to make his point clear.

> 8:7-8: *Since no man knows the future, who can tell him what is to come? No man has power over the wind to contain it; so no one has power over the day of his death. As no one is discharged in time of war, so wickedness will not release those who practice it.*

All of life is an unknown. No wizard or wise man can predict the future. This is even truer in times of war. In avoiding a bullet or bomb, you may step on a land mine. No man can defeat or conquer death, but death will conquer all men—"*No man has power over the wind* [spirit, or life] *to contain it.*" John Gill has some excellent comments on these verses.

> This life a man has not power over to dismiss or retain at pleasure; he cannot keep it one moment longer when it is called for and required by the Father of spirits, the Creator of it; he has not power "to restrain" it, as in a prison, as the word signifies; whence Aben Ezra says, that the spirit or soul in the body is like a prisoner in a prison; but nothing that attends a man in this life, or he is in possession of, can keep the soul in this prison, when the time of its departure is come; not riches, nor honours, nor wisdom and learning, nor strength and youth, nor all the force of medicine; the time is fixed, it is the appointment of God, the bounds set by him cannot be passed,

(Ecclesiastes 3:2; Hebrews 9:27; Genesis 47:29; Job 14:5). The Targum is, "no man has power over the spirit of the soul to restrain the soul of life, that it might not cease from the body of man"; and to the same sense Jarchi, "to restrain the spirit in his body, that the angel of death should not take him;"

Neither [hath he] power in the day of death; or "dominion"; death strips a man of all power and authority, the power that the husband has over the wife, or parents over their children, or the master over his servant, or the king over his subjects; death puts down all power and authority: it is an observation of Jarchi's, that David after he came to the throne is everywhere called King David, but, when he came to die, only David (1 Kings 2:1); no king nor ruler can stand against death any more than a beggar; no man is lord of death any more than of life, but death is lord of all; all must and do submit to it, high and low, rich and poor; there is a day fixed for it, and that day can never be adjourned, or put off to another; and as man has not power to deliver himself in the day of death, so neither his friend, as the Targum, nor any relation whatever; and [there is] no discharge in [that] war; death is a warfare as well as life, with which nature struggles, but in vain; it is an enemy, and the last that shall be destroyed; it is a king, and a very powerful one; there is no withstanding him, he is always victorious; and there is no escaping the battle with him, or fleeing from him; a discharge of soldiers in other wars is sometimes obtained by interest, by the entreaty of friends, or by money; but here all cries and entreaties signify nothing; nor does he value riches, gold, or all the forces of strength (see 2 Samuel 12:18; Job 36:19); under the old law, if a person had built a new house, or married a wife, or was faint hearted, he was excused and dismissed; but none of these things are of any avail in this war (Deuteronomy 20:5, 6, 8); captives taken in war are sometimes dismissed by their conquerors, or they find ways and means to make their escape; but nothing of this kind can be done when death has seized on the persons of men.

Some render it, there is "no sending to" or "in [that] war"; there is no sending forces against death to withstand him, it is to no purpose; there is no sending a message to him to sue for a peace, truce, or reprieve; he will hearken to nothing; there is no sending one in the room of another, as Jarchi observes, "a man cannot say, I will send my son, or my servant;" no surrogating is allowed of in this case, as David wished for (2 Samuel 18:33). Aben Ezra interprets it, no armour, and so many interpreters; and so the Targum; "nor do instruments of armour help in war;" in this war: in other wars a man may put on a helmet of brass and a coat of mail, to protect and defend him, or throw darts and arrows; but these signify nothing when death makes his approach and attack; *neither shall wickedness deliver those that are given to it*; or "the masters of it"; that is, from death; neither Satan the wicked one, as Jerome, who is wickedness itself, and with whom wicked men are confederate, can deliver them from death; nor sinners the most abandoned deliver themselves, who have made a covenant with it, and an agreement with hell (Isaiah 28:15, 18); such who are masters of the greatest wicked craft and cunning, and who devise many ways to escape other things, can contrive none to escape death; nor will riches gotten by wickedness deliver the owners of them from death; (see Proverbs 10:2 11:4).[41]

---

[41] _The Collected Writings of John Gill._ CD-ROM, 2000, AGES Software, Inc., P.O. Box 216, Rio, WI, 53960.

ARE MEN NO BETTER THAN ANIMALS?

Many philosophers and other wise people have tried to define the meaning of life in one sentence. The Seeker found that the secret of true life is significance, meaningfulness, and a sense of contentment about one's life. Human beings lost all sense of significance when they sinned in the Garden of Eden. They are now alone in God's universe with no knowledge of either who they are or why they exist. They have convinced themselves that they are only animals on top of the evolutionary scale. To describe a person as only an animal and not as a creature created in the image of God is to rob the individual of every ounce of significance. Modern psychology has demonstrated that we understand more about ourselves as we learn about the environment in which we were born and raised. If this is true on a physical level, it is even more salient on a spiritual level. Man only knows who he really is when he knows the God who created him. Our personal significance is tied to our origin as creatures and to our relationship with our Creator. Modern man's dilemma is that he wants to be autonomous from his creator but he cannot stand the isolation of not knowing what it is all about. He wants to be alone but hates his loneliness.

The Seeker continues to remind us that we find a life of significance only when we bow our minds and wills to a sovereign God. In chapters 8 and 9, the Seeker connects wisdom with humility before God. Humanity exhibits foolish arrogance by assuming it is able to understand and solve all of life's problems and difficulties. The Seeker warns us that life is too complicated to justify such conceited optimism. Some of the problems humanity faces are beyond understanding, let alone solving.

Our last chapter ended with Ecclesiastes 8:8. The Seeker had framed wisdom in the context of obedience to authority, and humility in the context of the certainty of death. Beginning at 8:9, the Seeker underscores the reality of universal evil. It does not matter in what direction we look; we will behold people manifesting their sin.

All this I saw, as I applied my mind to everything done under the sun. There is a time when a man lords it over others to his own hurt. (NIV)

Some translations render "to his own hurt" as "to their own hurt." Thus, it can refer to the hurt of either the oppressor or the oppressed. It probably refers to the latter. Millions suffer great hardships because of the tyranny of dictatorships, although governments and individuals, over time, often reap what they sow. Their suppression of people sometimes returns to bite them. The primary point is that tyranny is a universal sin. John Kenneth Galbraith, the famous economist said, "Under capitalism man exploits man; under communism it is exactly the reverse." Government is ordained of God, but nonetheless, it still is filled with evil because evil men run governments. We cannot restrict the tendency to want to be the boss, and to lord it over other's consciences to the secular realm alone. This same tendency manifests itself among religious people. We see an example of this today in the Muslim extremists who attempt to use the sword to impose their religion on the world.

In verses 10 and 11, the Seeker points out two evils that accompany wickedness in high places.

Then I saw the wicked buried. They used to go in and out of the holy place, and were praised in the city where they had done such things. This also is vanity. (Eccl 8:10, ESV)

A pompous funeral and a eulogy filled with lies for a person known for wickedness creates unimaginable harm. It is a grievous sin to exalt and glorify a known reprobate and never to mention any of his evil deeds. Adding religion to the list of "wonderful things" this person did compounds the sin. How can we teach children who are victims of wickedness that honesty, integrity, and kindness are worthwhile and will be justly rewarded if we praise the dead who have committed that wickedness? Nothing destroys the motivation to do right as much as glorifying a wicked person at a funeral. The adage "It pays to be honest" sounds like a joke at the funeral of a Mafia member. Derek Kidner has summarized it well.

There are few things more obnoxious than the sight of wicked men flourishing and complacent. Yet wickedness respected and given the blessing of religion (10a) is even more sickening. In the spectacle here, the sycophants have not even the excuse of ignorance. The villains are being honored at the very scene of their misdeeds—and they are no longer alive to cast their spell of fear or favor over anyone. So, incredibly enough, the admiration must be genuine, making it very clear that popular moral judgments can be totally astray, swayed by the evidence of success or failure, and construing heaven's patience as its approval. The dictator or corrupt tycoon may have bent the rules, it will be said; but after all, they got things done, they had flair, they lived in style.[42]

The worst part of the charade is that everyone knows the truth. They all know what the villain was really like. It is almost like a case of mistaken identity.

The Seeker highlights a second evil in verse 11:

When the sentence for a crime is not quickly carried out, the hearts of the people are filled with schemes to do wrong. (NIV)

What an honest, accurate observation on human life! We find abundant examples today of delays in justice that encourage criminals and permit crime to increase. When justice is delayed or circumvented in any way, when judges release criminals on technicalities even though it is clear that they are guilty of outrageous crimes, then more crime ensues. The Seeker offers a clear picture of the evil that can be present in government; nevertheless, he finds cause for patience in the promise that follows. There is a fixed day of judgment when the truth will be revealed and openly acknowledged. You may be able to buy a wonderful funeral and have your name put on a great building because you financed it, but nothing but the truth will meet you in eternity. Verses 12–14 assure us that no matter how things appear *under the sun*, the wicked will be punished and the good rewarded.

Although a wicked man commits a hundred crimes and still lives a long time, I know that it will go better with God-fearing men, who are reverent before God. Yet because the wicked do not fear God, it will not go well with them, and their days will not lengthen like a

---

[42] Derek Kidner, *A Time To Mourn & A Time To Dance* (Downers Grove, IL: InterVarsity Press, 1976), 76.

shadow. There is something else meaningless that occurs on earth: righteous men who get what the wicked deserve [righteous men treated as wicked men], *and wicked men who get what the righteous deserve* [obvious criminals treated as righteous]. *This too, I say, is meaningless.* (NIV)

Life often seems to be upside down. Neither wicked men nor righteous men usually get what they deserve in this life. The righteous are often the victims of unfair treatment and the wicked many times get away with the worst of crimes. Psalm 73 describes the lament of a godly man suffering at the hands of the ungodly. When you are the victim of injustice, you can dwell on it until you become deeply resentful and allow it to eat you up. You can sulk and even plot revenge, but such attitudes will never produce any good results. Instead of becoming angry and frustrated, you can bow your heart to God's sovereignty, even when you have no clue as to what God is accomplishing. Be assured of this, eternity will put the situation right.

However, eternity will not only judge the wicked in truth, verse 13 says their *days will not lengthen like a shadow.* This is an interesting statement. This refers to a person's influence after his death. Life "prolonged like a shadow" is not real life at all. It is amazing the lengths to which people with big egos will go to be remembered in history. However, history usually reveals the true character of individuals. How many roads, bridges, and buildings have undergone name changes when certain skeletons came out of the closet after death?

In verse 15, the Seeker returns, as he has many times before, to the same true conclusion:

So I commend the enjoyment of life, because nothing is better for a man under the sun than to eat and drink and be glad. Then joy will accompany him in his work all the days of the life God has given him under the sun. (NIV)

Ray Stedman clarifies a potential misunderstanding of this verse:

Do not misunderstand. That is not justification for living it up now, for saying, "Eat, drink and be merry for tomorrow we die." That philosophy is based upon the lie, the illusion that enjoyment comes from pleasant circumstances. If this book is teaching us any one thing, it is telling us that that is not true. Enjoyment does not come from happy, pleasant circumstances, where everything is going the way we like it. That is what the world believes; that is what underlies all the television commercials of our day, the magazine ads, etc. No, according to this book, enjoyment is a gift of God which can accompany even difficult and hard circumstances; that is why he encourages us to it. True enjoyment, true contentment does not come from having everything the way you like it. It comes no matter what you are going through, as a gift from the God of glory, who, in relationship with you, is able to give you peace and contentment in your heart in the midst of the pressures, the problems and the dangers of life.

Surely this is what the apostle Paul meant in Philippians: "I have learned the secret both how to be abased and to abound," (Philippians 4:12).What secret? He tells us: "I can do all things through Christ who strengthens me," (Philippians 4:12 RSV). It is that inner strengthening, by a relationship with the Living God, which is the secret of contentment, whether you are abased or whether you abound; the realization that a loving Father is working out strange and inscrutable purposes, which you cannot always guess at or estimate, through the difficult problems and circumstances which you are undergoing.[43]

One of the difficult things about Scripture is that it is completely honest with reality. It not only teaches us that we must take life the way it is, it also gives us a true picture of life as it really is. The glory of the Scriptures is that they do not try to evade real life; they do not put a veil over it, doll it up or dress it up and put a bow on it to make it look different. Scripture faces life just the way it is. Life is not a rose garden; it is vale of tears that always ends in death. The Bible does not always provide answers to our "why" questions, but it does tell us that God has everything under control. Scripture assures us that the world is not a run-away train with neither conductor nor engineer. God is working everything together for his own glory and the good of his redeemed people. Stedman comments:

> The answer to life is found by those who know how to walk before God, to love him, to fear him, to trust him, and to rest their lives in his hands. This does not excuse us from the struggles of life, or from the need to make decisions, but it does reassure us that those who walk that way will find a source of contentment and satisfaction that is the gift of the God of grace.[44]

Some commentators feel that verses 16 and 17 belong with chapter 9. It does seem that the Seeker is giving a summary and starting a new section. Consider 8:16, 17 and 9:1 together.

---

[43] Taken from a taped sermon by Ray Stedman, preached at Peninsula Bible Church, Palo Alto, CA, 1982.

[44] Ibid.

*When I applied my mind to know wisdom and to observe man's
labor on earth — his eyes not seeing sleep day or night — then I saw all
that God has done. No one can comprehend what goes on under the
sun. Despite all his efforts to search it out, man cannot discover its
meaning. Even if a wise man claims he knows, he cannot really comprehend it. So I reflected on all this and concluded that the righteous
and the wise and what they do are in God's hands, but no man knows
whether love or hate awaits him.* (NIV)

One tenet repeated over and over in this book is the fact
that even though every person knows that God is there, no
one really knows God himself in a personal way apart from
God revealing himself. The Seeker insists that a person
could say awake every night, use the entire time searching
for truth, and still not find it. Human beings could use every
waking hour of every day in pursuit of ultimate reality and
find nothing. With all of our genius, logic, computers, philosophers, drugs, medicine, psychology, and every other resource we have, we are forced to agree with the Seeker's
conclusion: "No one can comprehend what goes on under
the sun. Despite all his efforts to search it out, man cannot
discover its meaning. Even if a wise man claims he knows,
he cannot really comprehend it." We hear Paul echo this as
he explains humanity's inadequacy to understand truth.
God has rejected the wise and noble of this world, and has
chosen to reveal himself to the nobodies (1 Cor 1:26–31).

The Roman Catholic Church uses Ecclesiastes 9:1 to prove
that assurance of salvation cannot exist. Their exegesis,
however, fails to consider the entire verse: the statement includes the phrase *under the sun*. No person whose vision is
limited to what is comprehended *under the sun* can know
anything certain about eternity. However, the child of God
knows for sure that the eternal and unchanging love of God

awaits him. The lost person has more than sufficient evidence to know that God exists, and as Creator, Lawgiver, and Judge will demand an account from everyone. Psalm 19 and Romans 1 make this clear. We refer to that as the witness of nature. All creation, day and night, screams at humanity about God's eternal power and Godhead, but human beings deliberately close their ears and eyes, and will not follow any revelation that God gives. However, Scripture is also clear that there is not enough truth in creation's witness to bring people to a saving knowledge of Christ. There is nothing in the bright shining sun, the moon, or the stars that will teach a sinner "Jesus loves me, this I know." Only the child of God who believes the Bible can say that because he can add, "For the **Bible** tells me so." The ungodly laugh at the Bible and then wonder why they do not understand truth and reality.

Having shown that all people, apart from God's electing love and grace, share a common ignorance of the truth, the Seeker adds that all also share a common destiny. In 9:2–3, he reflects that the rich and the poor, the wicked and the good, the religious and the irreligious all die.

> *All share a common destiny–the righteous and the wicked, the good and the bad, the clean and the unclean, those who offer sacrifices and those who do not. As it is with the good man, so with the sinner; as it is with those who take oaths, so with those who are afraid to take them. This is the evil in everything that happens under the sun: The same destiny overtakes all. The hearts of men, moreover, are full of evil and there is madness in their hearts while they live, and afterward they join the dead. (NIV)*

The Seeker's primary point goes beyond the fact that death is the inescapable event that levels all humanity. That certainly is true and these verses teach it clearly. However, because that fact is so clear to all, a sinner who lives his entire life with no thought of preparing for a sure death is nothing short of insane. How else can we explain such obvious stupid behavior? People do not act so foolishly in any other area of their lives. We will not drive a newly purchased car off the lot until we make sure we have insurance. We will not buy a washing machine without making certain it has a warranty. We usually will have regular medical check-ups. Yet the same people will not take even a moment to secure their eternal state in grace. Human beings will carefully plan for the future in every part of their lives except for their souls. Nothing but spiritual madness can explain such irrational behavior.

Death not only levels all people, it ends all opportunity for securing eternal life. As long as a person is alive, there is hope that God will open his heart with the truth. When death separates the soul from the body, then all hope of being born-again and trusting Christ for salvation is forever gone. There is no second chance. Many adages underscore the finality of death. A dog would be no match for a lion in any kind of contest, but "even a live dog is better off than a dead lion"!

Earlier, the Seeker had insisted that the dead are better off than the living. Here he is not contradicting that sentiment, but is establishing a different point. There is indeed a sense in which the dead are better off than the living, but there also are some advantages to still being alive. Again, as you read verses 4–6, do not forget to qualify them with *under the sun*. Also remember that even though this is a truth that includes the godly, it is also true that the godly will have a blessed part in all that is good for all eternity while the ungodly will experience all that is shameful and dishonorable.

> *Anyone who is among the living has hope—even a live dog is better off than a dead lion! For the living know that they will die, but the dead know nothing; they have no further reward, and even the memory of them is forgotten. Their love, their hate and their jealousy have long since vanished; never again will they have a part in anything that happens under the sun.* (NIV)

Both the godly and the ungodly know and experience reality after death. The Seeker is not at all suggesting annihilation of the wicked. The phrase *under the sun* controls the thought. Once a person dies, whether he is godly or ungodly, that person can no longer experience anything in *this world*: the world *under the sun*. All people experience conscious blessing or cursing for all eternity.

The Seeker links verses 7 and 8 to verse 1 of chapter 9, "the righteous and the wise and their deeds are in the hand of God" (ESV). Verses 7 and 8 presuppose the person addressed is righteous and wise: a child of God. Only a child of God can have a truly joyful heart and realize that his joy comes from the assurance that *"God favors what he does."* We should not disassociate these words (God favoring our works, or what we do), from justification. Before God justified us, our works were as filthy rags in his sight. Once God accepts us in Christ, our works are pleasing in his sight. It is this assurance of God's approval, or acceptance, that gives a believer the joy and assurance of eternal salvation. Believers can go about all of life knowing a heavenly Father is watching over them.

> *Go, eat your food with gladness, and drink your wine with a joyful heart, for it is now that God favors what you do. Always be clothed in white, and always anoint your head with oil.* (NIV)

In Scripture, to be clothed in white is to be washed in the blood of the Lamb. To have the head anointed with oil is a picture of the gift of the Holy Spirit. When we consider all of these things from verse 7 and 8, we see that the Seeker refers to a justified child of God. The exhortation to *"eat your food with gladness, and drink your wine with a joyful heart"* is only possible in this *"meaningless life,"* (v. 9) because we have peace with God (Rom. 5:1). We are to remind ourselves always that we are clothed in white. This signifies recognition and acceptance by God. We find real significance by realizing who we are in Christ. God approves us as perfectly accepted in Christ. If we want to find significance in life, if we want to find deep meaning, peace, and contentment, this is the basis for it: Believe that what we have has been given to us by God, and then enjoy it all as a gift of God. We must constantly keep looking at the righteousness with which we have been clothed in Christ. McCheyne said, "Take one good long look at your sin and then take ten-thousand looks at Jesus Christ." If we look around us and see all that is happening *under the sun*, or look inside at our own hearts, we indeed will be depressed and devoid of all joy. If we look to Calvary and drink the wine of grace, we will have a joyful heart.

In Ecclesiastes 9:9, the Seeker concludes that a person can realize that he is in the hand of God, but it is impossible to discern from the events whether he is in God's favor. Instead of trying to figure out God's providence or judging God's thoughts toward us by things that are happening to us in our daily lives, we must look past the *under the sun* mentality and see our Savior seated at the right hand of God.

In verse 10, the Seeker almost sounds as though he believes in annihilation. "Whatever your hand finds to do, do it with all your might, for in the grave, where you are going, there is neither working nor planning nor knowledge nor wisdom." His point is not that existence and consciousness no longer continue after death; rather, he is making the same point as our Lord made. "As long as it is day, we must do the work of him who sent me. Night is coming, when no one can work" (John 9:4). Everything we can possibly do to affect our state in eternity must be done while we are living in this life. If there is any status or classification in eternity, what we do or fail to do in this life establishes it. My mother used to say, "Whatever is worth doing is worth doing right." The Seeker is saying that if you cannot do something with all your might, you probably should not be doing that in the first place.

Stedman concludes that the Seeker's message is clear.

> We are not to seek after comfort, but significance. What are you living for? That is his question. What are you dying for? What is the purpose of your existence? I would urge every one of us individually to come to an answer to that. Why are you here? What is it all about? If life has any purpose at all, it must be found in what happens now. The attempt of this book is to bring us to the answer to that, to help us to see what that purpose is.[45]

The following excerpt from Dorothy Greenwell's "Songs of Salvation" expresses the appropriate attitude of every believer toward the providential circumstances of his life.

---

[45] Ibid.

I am not skilled to understand
What God hath willed
what God hath planned
I only know at his right hand
Is one who is my Savoir.

(Dorothy Greenwell, 1821–1882)

As long as I keep looking to that throne of grace, I will know something of the joy of the Lord. I will be able to sing with assurance, even sometimes through tears:

When peace like a river attendeth my way
When sorrows like sea billows roll
What ever my lot, Thou hast taught me say
It is well, it is well, with my soul.

(Horatio G. Spafford, 1828–1888)

This world will still appear to be upside down and meaningless; wickedness, tyranny, and utter confusion will still reign; the righteous will still suffer at the hands of the wicked; but we will bless the Lord and wait in hope. We will echo the prayer of Habakkuk, recorded in Habakkuk chapter 3.

LIVING LIFE SKILLFULLY

We ended our last chapter by showing the need to be diligent in whatever our hands find to do. This assumes that what our hands find to do is legitimate in the sight of God. We often hear a zealous person described as "really deeply committed. He is out and out for his belief." However, we need to ask, "But exactly to what is he committed? For what is he out and out?" The terrorist, the liberal, and the new moralist are all deeply committed to their views; unfortunately, they are committed to the wrong thing. A.W. Tozer once said, "I do not care how loud the band or how large the parade, before I get in it I want to know two things. Who is leading it and where is it headed?"

It is amazing how many people think that sincere belief is the ground for all to be well in eternity. Scripture is quite clear that is not the case. Righteousness, not sincerity, is the condition for eternal life. A sincere, but unrighteous person who dies will not be changed by death. Nor is there anything in the process of death that makes a person who sincerely disdained holiness in life want to be holy. Death gives us no new desires. Death puts us into a realm where we receive in full the true desires of our hearts. There is nothing in death that changes our natures or desires. We cannot love sin in this life and then obtain a hatred for it in the life to come. We should set the words of Revelation 22:11 before our minds every morning.

> *He that is unjust, let him be unjust still: and he who is filthy, let*
> *him be filthy still: and he that is righteous, let him be righteous still:*
> *and he that is holy, let him be holy still.* (KJV)

Most people agree with the adage, "We grow too soon old and too late smart." Age seems to increase faster than wisdom does. By the time we learn what we need to know, it is often already too late to use it! Mr. I. C. Herendeen, the publisher of A.W. Pink's books and a dear friend, used to say, "John, I do not know why God does not teach us some sense when we are young. Usually, when we just about get a handle on things, God says, 'That is it! Time to check out!'" The book of Ecclesiastes teaches us that we can learn some important things before it is too late. There is a godly wisdom that will safely guide us through life, even if it will not enable us to avoid all the hurt and pain of life. Ray Stedman has said it well.

Many people make the mistake of thinking that wisdom will deliver them from all pressure and struggle, but it will not. We learn in this book that struggle, pain, pressure, and sorrow are all part of the learning process. But by discovering and obeying the wisdom of God, your life will not be rendered bitter, angry, and resentful by such pain. You will not find yourself plunged into a morass of self-pity and depression; you will not find your life ravaged and torn apart, all your dreams collapsed at your feet. The wisdom of God will lead you into fullness and liberty and inward peace in the midst of the pressures and dangers of life. That is the message of the book of Ecclesiastes, as it is the message of the whole Bible. Beginning in chapter 9, verse 11, the Seeker tells us that the first and probably most difficult lesson of all to learn is that natural gifts in themselves are not enough to handle life; natural abilities and diligent effort alone will not lead us into truly successful living.[46]

The Seeker now turns his attention to another thing he has observed *under the sun*. At first glance, he seems to be contradicting not only what he said previously, but also what is clearly observable by anyone on a day-to-day basis. I think we can add the word *always* to verse 11 to clarify his observation, since it obviously is implied.

> *I have seen something else under the sun: The race is not* [always] *to the swift or the battle* [always] *to the strong, nor does food* [always] *come to the wise or wealth* [always] *to the brilliant or favor* [always] *to the learned; but time and chance happen to them all.* (Eccl 9:11, NIV)

Normally, the fastest runner wins the race unless he trips over an unseen soft spot in the ground. The stronger army usually wins the battle unless an unforeseen tornado destroys most of its men and equipment. Usually, a wise person gets ahead, but the most brilliant college professor, may, under some circumstances, be forced to work at McDonald's. The Seeker's point is that time and change happen to all people regardless of their ability, power, or efforts, and neither time nor change is under humanity's control. Human beings cannot outwit God's sovereign providence.

In verse 12, the Seeker is talking about more than death. It is certainly true that no one knows the hour of his death, but it also is true that no one can predict many of the evil times that befall him.

---

[46] Taken from a taped sermon by Ray Stedman, preached at Peninsula Bible Church, Palo Alto, CA, 1982.

Moreover, no man knows when his hour will come: As fish are caught in a cruel net, or birds are taken in a snare, so men are trapped by evil times that fall unexpectedly upon them. (Eccl 9:12, NIV)

How often does a new invention force some businesses that have operated for a hundred years to close? How often does a physical examination show that we are the picture of health, and five weeks later, the doctor diagnoses us with cancer? We say, "But I had no indication of this happening." A fish or a bird may imagine that it is free without realizing that it is moving into the captivity of a snare or a net. Just so are people trapped by time and circumstance when they least expect it. Who can estimate the unforeseen evils that resulted from the 9/11 tragedy? How many hopes, dreams, and careful plans were destroyed in a moment? The whims of fashion on the one hand and the dislike of change on the other create constant tension. How often has a bad court decision had an adverse effect on innocent people who had no way of anticipating what happened? In other words, no matter how smart, industrious, wealthy, and well connected we are, the doctor may still say, "The x-ray shows it is cancer and it is inoperable. You have three months to live." We dare not try to live by sight and human wisdom alone. We must live by faith in the promises of an unchanging God. We must not trust our gifts and abilities and forget the main lesson – all things are from the hand of God. Charles Bridges has caught the truth of these verses.

It is natural indeed to believe, that the race would *be to the swift,* and *the battle to the strong;* that prudent *wisdom* would obtain a competent provision, and courtly *skill* would be the way to favor. But it is not always so. The racer makes an incautious step. "The fortunes of war" (so called) may take an unfavorable turn. Men of wisdom continue to be poor, and gifted with no very successful *favor*. Oh! Christian–do you not find it hard to possess gifts, and not rest in them?–to have riches and not trust in them?–to have wisdom and skill, and not to glory in them?–to exercise simple dependence upon God, as if we had and were nothing? Far is he from discouraging the use of means. He would only direct us in the use of them not to "sacrifice to our nets." (Hab. 1:16)[47]

In verses 13–16, the Seeker is impressed with a clear observable fact. Wisdom often does not garner reward, even from those who greatly benefited from the wise person. The language of the ingrate is "What have you done for me today?" People whose outlook on life is fashioned by an *under the sun* philosophy do not appreciate wisdom. The Seeker notes both the power of wisdom and the ingratitude of those helped by the wise person. Possibly this incident of a wise, poor man saving a city impressed the Seeker because it brought wisdom and poverty together. Rich, powerful, self-made people are usually embarrassed to have to admit that a nobody saved them. Better to be a wise and generous nobody than a rich and powerful ingrate.

> *I also saw under the sun this example of wisdom that greatly impressed me: There was once a small city with only a few people in it. And a powerful king came against it, surrounded it and built huge siege works against it. Now there lived in that city a man poor but wise, and he saved the city by his wisdom. But nobody remembered that poor man. So I said, "Wisdom is better than strength." But the poor man's wisdom is despised, and his words are no longer heeded.* (Eccl 9:13–16, NIV)

---

[47] Charles Bridges, *Ecclesiastes, A Geneva Series Commentary* (Carlisle, PA: Banner of Truth Trust, 1961), 227.

What should we learn from this particular observation by the Seeker? First, learn to evaluate the true worth of a person by his wisdom and willingness to help in time of need. Do not despise the day of small things by refusing a wise person's gift, since wisdom is indeed a gift of God.

Second, prepare yourself for disappointment because it is sure to come. Work as hard as you can for the best interest of others, but never work for their favor, approbation, or reward. Never let the praise of people be your motivation to action. Humanity's approval is a hollow and useless reward.

Last, do not be weary in well doing. Some of the people whom you help the most may become your enemies. Continue to do right regardless of their attitudes. There is a day when God will balance the record books and make known the truth in every detail. In that day, all that will matter is God's approval.

In the light of possible and probable disparagement of unostentatious wisdom, how shall we consider the Seeker's next comment?

The quiet words of the wise are more to be heeded than the shouts of a ruler of fools. (Eccl 9:17, NIV)

One writer said, "This is a very remarkable verse in these days of 'mobocracy.'" There seems to be a bit of inconsistency between this verse and the previous remark concerning the slighted and quickly forgotten words of the wise man. In this verse, the wise man's words are highly regarded. Both Bridges and Stedman have excellent comments on this text.

The words of the wise man have just been spoken of as slighted, and not remembered. Here however considerable weight is subscribed to them. Though the case of the foregoing verse is of frequent occurrence, yet exceptions may be found.

The words of the wise, spoken in quiet and unobtrusiveness, may be little thought of at the time, and yet may command attention, when circumstances bring them out. Often will they drown the senseless clamor of him *that ruleth among fools.* Noisy popularity indeed has its influence for a moment. But the real and solid good are the words that are heard in quiet. Popular oratory in the pulpit may stimulate excitement. But it needs much unction and humility to give it practical influence. We are directed to behold our Lord's ministry as words heard in quiet–"Behold my servant!–He shall not strive or cry; neither shall any man hear his words in the street." (Matthew 12:18–19.) Yet this implies no heartlessness, but the "doctrine" dropping as "the rain upon the mown grass"–upon hearts made ready to receive its Divine influence (Deut. 32:2; Psalm 72:6).[48]

This text (v. 17) is simply saying that the insights of Scripture, heard in the inner self, quietly, before God alone, are more effective to solve problems than worldly rhetoric or propaganda, better than the ideas of some prominent opinion maker who says things that are popularly received but are contrary to Scripture. In Scripture, rulers are not always governors and kings; they are opinion-makers, shapers of the minds of men. Yet what they say is often merely what foolish people around them want to hear. The words of wisdom heard in quiet are much more effective than such empty propaganda.[49]

The Seeker continues to extol wisdom, even though it is limited. Wisdom is far better than ignorance. One poor person's wisdom may save a city just as another's wickedness may destroy it. War is probably one of humanity's most

---

[48] Ibid., 232.

[49] Stedman.

stupid actions. Using wisdom to seek peace and security is one of its highest acts.

In verse 18, the Seeker introduces the idea of one person's folly destroying much good.

> *Wisdom is better than weapons of war, but one sinner destroys much good.* (NIV)

One negative or selfish person may easily destroy the efforts of many. This is never more evident than when sincere people are seeking to reach a necessary consensus for the good of all, and one person blocks it all with selfish demands. This is true in family life, public life, international life, and even church life. Any time it is essential to negotiate to bring different parties together for the mutual good of both, you will see one or more individuals willing to disrupt the entire preceding to assure they get what their personal selfishness demands. The attempted negotiation may fail simply because one or more of the leaders were not willing to think of the greater good of the community.

In Chapter 10, the Seeker compares the merits of wisdom over folly and stupidity.

> *As dead flies give perfume a bad smell, so a little folly outweighs wisdom and honor.* (Eccl 10:1, NIV)

One wonders how the dead fly got into the perfume in the first place. Maybe a careless attendant left the lid off the jar while he went to the toilet. Maybe the boss turned the job over to an unqualified employee because he wanted to go play golf. Regardless of the cause, it is foolish to blame the fly; "That stupid fly ruined my perfume." Did you ever see someone curse and kick a flat tire? "That tire made me late for an important meeting." Do not blame the tire! A bit more care and planning might have avoided the problem. Likewise, we can avoid the "little follies" in our life if we are more watchful and disciplined in our Christian walk. One thing is certain; it is far easier to poison a pure well than to purify a poisoned well. It takes only a little bit of stupidity to destroy a lot of wisdom. It is far easier to blame than it is to mend – to tear down the house than to build it up again.

In verse 2, the Seeker uses the term *right hand* (KJV) figuratively to describe a place of honor, strength, and blessing. A person whose heart inclines toward these virtues is a wise person.

> *The heart of the wise inclines to the right, but the heart of the fool to the left.* (NIV)

The fool, by way of contrast, follows a path of deceit and stealth. Even when a fool does the right thing, he usually does it for the wrong reason.

> *Even as he walks along the road, the fool lacks sense and shows everyone how stupid he is.* (Eccl 10:3, NIV)

The Seeker advises applying wisdom to potentially explosive situations.

> *If a ruler's anger rises against you, do not leave your post; calmness can lay great errors to rest.* (Eccl 10:4, NIV).

Our first impulse when the boss is mad at us is to flee. We resign in anger or fear. The Seeker recommends that we maintain our calm and responsibility. A calm attitude may give us a chance to explain. Even kings may be inclined to be more objective in the light of loyalty. Running from problems does not solve them.

As the Seeker contemplates the anger of rulers, he reflects on other evils that those in authority often commit.

> *There is an evil I have seen under the sun, the sort of error that arises from a ruler: Fools are put in many high positions, while the*

rich occupy the low ones. I have seen slaves on horseback, while princes go on foot like slaves. (Eccl 10:5–7, NIV)

It is the duty of leaders to appoint the best and most capable people to places of authority. Unfortunately, this is not usually the case. The politician appoints his in-laws (who in reality are often outlaws) to leadership posts. The community suffers when incompetent people run any government agency. Too often, these people are in leadership only because of being a relative or personal friend of the ruler. When nepotism places an uneducated, but conceited, person in an office with authority, he may deliberately "stick it to the rich" out of pure envy.

Commentators offer differing explanations for verses 8–11. One view sees the Seeker warning against overthrowing the government, even despotic governments. A second view suggests this is a discussion of the difficulty of governing the masses. A third view sees it as a reminder that life is determined by what some call fate and not by the wisdom of men. Others see in these verses a description of the unenviable end of upstarts who try to buck the system. What is clear is that seeking to deal with perceived wrongs may prove disastrous in the end. When we urge major change, we had better be moved and controlled by godly wisdom, and not by the flesh.

Verses 8–9 warn against plotting evil against another person. All four illustrations teach the same point.

Whoever digs a pit may fall into it; whoever breaks through a wall may be bitten by a snake. Whoever quarries stones may be injured by them; whoever splits logs may be endangered by them. (NIV)

A vindictive attitude has its own built-in problems. Haman, in the book of Esther, is a classic example of a man who dug a pit and fell into it himself. This is where the saying, "He dug his own grave" comes from. Every wall was built with a purpose in mind. It kept some out and closed others in. It functioned as protection of some kind. In tearing it down, you might discover a worse situation than if you had left it standing. When a society, or an individual, tears down moral walls in the name of freedom, they may discover the snake of depravity ready to bite and devour. The Seeker mentions injuries from quarrying stone and splitting logs to show that what appear to be perfectly safe activities may hide problems. Accidents occur in every endeavor.

In verse 10, the Seeker expands his illustration of splitting wood to address how wisdom applies to our endeavors.

If the ax is dull and its edge unsharpened, more strength is needed but skill will bring success.

A wise person will sharpen the ax because he knows it will save effort. Thoughtfulness and careful planning bring more success than does brute force. Far better to take the time to get correctly prepared than to jump into a project without knowing what you are doing. In the spiritual realm, we whet the blade of the ax through fervent prayer and earnest seeking to ascertain the will of God.

In verse 11, the Seeker recognizes the dangers of mistaking procrastination for preparedness.

If a snake bites before it is charmed, there is no profit for the charmer.

Here the Seeker sees the opposite danger from that addressed in verse 10. A person who is able to handle a difficult situation (a charmer) fails to do so because of tardiness. The snake bites before the charmer gets there. Often, individuals with great gifts and abilities fail because they are

slack in fulfilling their obligation. The theme in these two
verses is success. We do not succeed because of wisdom
alone, but we will certainly fail without wisdom. We cannot
outwit God's providence, but a diligent use of ordained
means will enable us to cope with whatever comes.

Verses 12–15 compare the fool and the wise man.

> _Words from a wise man's mouth are gracious,_
> _but a fool is consumed by his own lips._
> _At the beginning his words are folly;_
> _at the end they are wicked madness —_
> _and the fool multiplies words._
>
> _No one knows what is coming —_
> _who can tell him what will happen after him?_
>
> _A fool's work wearies him;_
> _he does not know the way to town._ (NIV)

Walter Kaiser offers helpful comments here.

Appropriately enough, there now follows a series of proverbs on using the tongue wisely while fools prattle away emp-
tily (10:12–15). Wisdom is still the only proper guide to joyful
enjoyment in life, despite life's pitfalls and inexplicable twists.
Wisdom will temper, guard, and guide our actions–that is, true
wisdom found in the fear of God. And the instrument of this
wisdom will be the tongue, or words, of a wise man. His
words are gracious in content, winsome in spirit, affectionate
in appeal, and compliant and affable in tone.

On the other hand, the words of a fool work his own defeat
and destruction–they "swallow him up" (10:12b). He is his
own worst enemy. His words may be portrayed in a sort of
gradation, where at first he is guilty of no more than mere sil-
liness or nonsense; but as he goes on from one folly to the next,
he ends up in all sorts of extremism. There is nothing by which
he can measure or guide his speech–it becomes sheer madness

(10:13). He simply talks too much (10:14a), a constant stream of foolishness.

The rhetorical question about the fool's lack of knowledge of the future, of his deficiency in the area of some teacher who should tell him of the future (10:14a), is a valid reminder of a Solomonic theme. The same question has been asked in 3:22, 6:12, 8:7, and in part in 9:12 to prepare the true seeker after God for the grand conclusion of 12:14: God–He alone–will bring every deed in judgment, whether good or evil. Foolish babblers are a dime a dozen, but revelation that is "in the know" is difficult to come by unless a wise man (12:9–11) teaches words of truth about man's future.[50]

According to James (3:4), the tongue is the small rudder that controls great ships. The fool's talk quickly reveals his stupidity. Someone has said, "It is better to remain silent and have people think you are stupid than it is to open your mouth and remove all doubt." Verse 15, *"A fool's work wearies him; he does not know the way to town"* is meant to show that the fool's dislike of work rules out any kind of competence in any of his labors. In a contemporary paraphrase of the latter half of the verse, we would say, "He does not have enough sense to come in out of the rain."

Verses 16–20 deal with folly in national life. Verse 16 proclaims woes to a nation that has unfit leadership, and verse 17 extols the blessings that come to a nation with good leadership.

Verses 18–19 describe a culture that may result from bad leadership examples.

---

[50] Walter C. Kaiser Jr., *Ecclesiastes, Everyman's Bible Commentary,* (Chicago: Moody Press, 1979), 110.

> *Woe to you, O land whose king was a servant*
> *and whose princes feast in the morning.*
> *Blessed are you, O land whose king is of noble birth*
> *and whose princes eat at a proper time—*
> *for strength and not for drunkenness.*
> *If a man is lazy, the rafters sag;*
> *if his hands are idle, the house leaks.*
> *A feast is made for laughter,*
> *and wine makes life merry,*
> *but money is the answer for everything.* (NIV)

In some cases, wrong behavior is actually encouraged by bad leadership. The only people who can afford a lazy and wine-filled life are the rich. It would appear that the Seeker thinks that money is everything. There is a sense in which only money can buy the goods of this world, and it certainly appears on the surface to be the answer to everything. A closer look at reality, however, will burst that bubble. Money cannot buy any of the things that are important in the sight of God, nor can it buy most of the things essential to true happiness in this life. It cannot buy health, happiness, or immortality. It cannot make us moral, kind, or wise. The person who has money lacks for nothing in this world that his heart desires. It is true that some people with money tend to be misers who are miserable; but they are quite comfortable in their misery. If this life is all there is, then indeed money is the answer for everything. If, however, there is an eternity where human beings cannot take one penny with them, then money is not the answer to any of the real questions.

Verse 20 is a back-door exhortation to keep your mouth shut, especially when criticizing those in authority.

Do not revile the king even in your thoughts, or curse the rich in your bedroom, because a bird of the air may carry your words, and a bird on the wing may report what you say. (NIV)

Two of my grandma's favorite expressions were, "The walls have ears" and "a little birdie told me." It would be interesting to go through Ecclesiastes and list all of our adages that have their roots in the Seeker's vocabulary.

CHAPTER EIGHTEEN: VERSES 11:1-10

BE BOLD! BE JOYFUL! BE GODLY!

The Seeker, in the first part of chapter 10, contrasted foolishness and wisdom as they pertain to individuals. In the latter half of the chapter, he lamented the foolishness of certain governments, but advised cautious restraint in criticizing such regimes. After having looked at the worst, he now begins to give direction that is more positive. In chapters 11 and 12 of Ecclesiastes, he presents three keys ideas. They are (1) be bold, (2) be joyful, and (3) be godly. We will examine them one at a time. The first, *be bold*, is in 11:1–6. There, the Seeker stresses both faith and enthusiasm, especially in the area of giving.

Cast your bread upon the waters, for after many days you will find it again. (Eccl 11:1, NIV)

The phrase *cast your bread upon the waters* was a Hebrew saying describing a stupid action. Who in his right mind would cast bread into water unless he was intending to feed the fish? The Seeker uses it to show that faith in the wisdom of God transcends human wisdom. What looks like foolishness to men is often the wisdom of God. The Apostle Paul describes the gospel itself this way.

The picture from antiquity could be that of a farmer sowing seed when the Nile River receded after its annual flood stage, leaving a foamy bed. It would appear that he was going to lose his seed. Even though it looked as though that seed would be lost forever, it would reappear in a stalk – in due course. Or it could have been a picture of a ship sailing off, loaded with grain. The merchants of that day must have considered the possibility of the ship sinking, causing them to lose everything. Of course that was a possibility, but it was more likely that the ship would return, full of gold or other goods from the sale of the grain.

The message of Ecclesiastes goes beyond business or agriculture. The Seeker, in encouraging his readers to cast their bread upon the waters, does more than turn conventional wisdom on its head. He urges boldness in the form of giving to others, especially to those in need. We are, of course, to be careful and cautious, but not to the place that we miss opportunities to do good because we are afraid to take a risk. There are no risk-free ventures in life. Likewise, it is not possible to be a true helper of the needs of others without, at times, having someone take advantage of us. However, we must not be so careful that we miss opportunities to do good. The Seeker is talking about living life before God. Better to be used wrongly on a few occasions than to miss any occasion to minister to Christ. We minister to Christ by helping his sheep. Our giving unto God may appear to be a waste of money or time, but it is an eternal investment. The Seeker's underlying message is that by giving to God, we invest in an unseen eternity.

Other Scriptures confirm the Seeker's meaning in this section. For a child of God, giving is both a duty and a joy, accompanied by a clear promise from God. This is the heart of these verses. The life of faith will have many trials, frustrations, and heartaches, but never any eternal disappointments! No man or woman who has obeyed these words will ever stand on the shores of eternity and cry "meaningless, meaningless." Even in this life, the child of God who learns to give generously, first of himself or herself, will know something of the presence and blessing of God.

Paul emphasized this aspect of God's faithfulness to the Corinthians.

> But as surely as God is faithful, our message to you is not "Yes" and "No." For the Son of God, Jesus Christ, who was preached among you by me and Silas and Timothy, was not "Yes" and "No," but in him it has always been "Yes." For no matter how many promises God has made, they are "Yes" in Christ. And so through him the "Amen" is spoken by us to the glory of God. (2 Cor 1:18–20 NIV)

Did Christ fulfill every jot and tittle of the Old Testament promises? Is the total fulfillment of every promise of God in the New Testament certain? Will our God fulfill every promise he made to us? Everyone else we know and love may prove false and faithless, but not a single promise of God will ever fall to the ground. When we give, we must remember that we are giving to the God who unfailingly will perform all that he has promised. We are to be bold in our giving to those in need, because we are actually giving to God himself. God is faithful to reward all that we do, according to his will, in his name, and for his glory.

The Seeker provides a faint foreshadowing of our Lord's words as recorded in John 12:23–26.

> Jesus replied, "The hour has come for the Son of Man to be glorified. I tell you the truth, unless a kernel of wheat falls to the ground and dies, it remains only a single seed. But if it dies, it produces many seeds. The man who loves his life will lose it, while the man who hates his life in this world will keep it for eternal life." (NIV)

Sometimes our giving may appear to be lost or wasted. If, however, we have given as unto God, then what we have given can never be wasted, regardless of what others do with it. The best way to lose something for eternity is to try to hang onto it in this life. Jim Elliot, the missionary killed by natives in South America, had uttered the following words before he died. When told by friends that he might lose his life in his missionary endeavor he said, "He is no fool to give up what he cannot keep in order to gain what he cannot lose." That is the message in these verses.

Following Christ includes giving as he gave. We cannot give our lives in sacrifice to pay for another's sins, but we can give in many ways to help make others' lives a bit easier.

Our Lord's words in Matthew 7:1 and 2 illustrate this truth.

> *"Do not judge, or you too will be judged. For in the same way you judge others, you will be judged, and with the measure you use, it will be measured to you."* (NIV)

At first glance, it may seem that this text does not address giving. A moment's reflection, however, reveals that our Lord is condemning more than unjustified criticism and judgment; he is also showing that judging includes an unwillingness to give to meet a need. Judging is more than criticizing; it is being consciously unwilling to help. When we refuse to help, we judge the person in need as unworthy of our help. By not helping, we are saying, "You deserve what you are getting." That is how God sees it. You may say, "I am not obligated," but God says that you are judging the person as not worthy of your help.

The Seeker does not encourage restraint, but gives us a biblical motive for bold, bountiful giving. Have you ever thought of giving to others as actually making a loan to God? Proverbs 19:17 says, "He that hath pity upon the poor lendeth unto the LORD; and that which he hath given will he pay him again" (KJV).

Do you believe that God is honest and will keep this promise? Do you believe that God is a good credit risk? Is his bank a secure place in which to invest your money? Does he pay good dividends? Do you want a great pension plan? Learn to give bountifully to the Lord. Giving to him beats Social Security or any retirement plan you will ever find. We must learn to trust God by investing in his enterprises.

This principle does not define the gospel as giving to the poor in order to earn merit with God. Rather, it teaches that the gospel that saves sinners also touches their pocketbooks, as well as the rest of their lives. Redeemed sinners give themselves, their time, their talents, and their money to God.

Remember what our Lord said when he referred to the righteous who would ask him at judgment, "When saw we thee hungry?" He said that he would reply, "As much as you have done unto the least of these, you have done unto me" (Matt.25:31–40). The over-cautious manner in which some Christians give would seem to indicate that they do not really believe this truth. How many Christians do you know who have suffered because they were **too generous?** How many Christians do you know who have had more than their hearts could desire, and yet were miserable and always fighting about money? How many grey-headed saints have you heard complain that they were sorry they had given so much to God?

There is yet a third, wider, application of this text that includes the "sower went forth to sow" about which Jesus spoke (Matt. 13). Dear Christian, I urge you to cast abroad the seed of the gospel. Use tracts and any and every means to spread the gospel. Take advantage of every gospel opportunity. You will rarely see the full benefits of your labor, but God sees. My brother Ernest was converted through a tract he found in the family Bible. He never knew who gave him the tract or how it got into the Bible. Somebody "cast the truth on the water" and years later, the Holy Spirit was pleased to use it. Teach your children Bible verses. Sow the seed in the morning, at noon, and at night with your children. John Newton's mother taught him Bible verses when he was three years old. Newton grew up to become a wicked man, yet he remembered those verses during a great storm, and God converted him. Cast your bread upon the water every day, in every place, for every person, at every opportunity. Paul repeats this admonition in Galatians 6:10, "as we have opportunity, do good to all people." The Holy Spirit will guide us and use us if we have hearts that want to please him.

In verse 2, the Seeker again gives advice that seems contrary to conventional wisdom.

> *Give portions to seven, yes to eight, for you do not know what disaster may come upon the land.* (NIV)

The eastern culture of the Seeker practiced reciprocity. You shared with others because you never knew when you yourself might need others to share with you. Life was uncertain, and mutual care was all you could count on in a day of disaster. Under the New Covenant, the motive for sharing rests, not in the uncertainty of temporal life, but in the certainty of eternal life, secured for us by Jesus' work on the cross. Jesus shared his great righteousness with us; how can we refuse to share anything that we have with others?

Notice that the Seeker says to give a portion – not a pittance. Generosity is a facet of boldness. The covetous will use the latter part of this verse as an excuse to hoard, but hoarding demonstrates the opposite of boldness; it is a mark of fearfulness. Ironically, people who hoard for fear of famine do not seem to realize that in a time of real famine, their lives would not be safe for a moment. Who wants a basement full of food when every neighbor is dying of hunger? You would need an army to protect you and your hoard.

If someone gave you ten gallons of milk and you had no refrigerator or freezer of any kind, what would you do? You know the milk will sour in a few days. Some people might hope that something will somehow happen to prevent the milk's spoiling. In most cases, however, the milk will sour and you will have nothing either to use yourself or to share with others. The milk would be wasted. That is exactly what is happening in our lives. We try to hoard all we can, but eternity will show that we lost it all. When you are dead, you cannot give. There is no generosity from the grave. There is an old saying that states, "Do your giving while you're living, then you're knowing where it's going."

This is the message for the godly: Today is the only day I have to live and to help. Who knows what next month will bring? Maybe the economy will collapse. Maybe the Muslims will start winning and take over. Communism may revive and recapture all it lost plus our country as well. The government may become despotic and socialize everything. The stock market may collapse and we may have a deep depression. Sickness may wipe me out. The message to me is this: I must share NOW while I am able.

This is the message for the ungodly: You think you must hoard it all so you will have enough. Remember, you will take none of it with you when you die. Consider the rich man about whom Jesus told us. He kept building bigger and bigger barns, only to hear those dreadful words, "Thou fool, this night shall your soul be required and then whose shall all this be?" (Luke 12:13–21).

Here are a few things I have observed in my lifetime.

1 You will never grow in true godly contentment until you grow in true godliness.

2 You will never grow in true godliness until you grow in obedience to God's truth.

3 You will never grow in obedience until you grow in faith.

4 Faith and obedience express themselves in giving and lead to true godly contentment.

In 11:3–6, the Seeker shows that we cannot wait for ideal times to obey God in giving. Pushing creates most opportunities. The salesperson said, "It is amazing how lucky I get when I make a lot of calls." The **power** as well as the **opportunity** to do good things always comes from first having a willing heart.

> _If clouds are full of water, they pour rain upon the earth. Whether a tree falls to the south or to the north, in the place where it falls, there will it lie._ (Eccl 11:3 NIV)

If the clouds are full of rain, they cannot help but pour it out. Likewise, if the heart is full of love, faith, and thanksgiving, it will pour out its blessings on others, just as the clouds do the rain. In eternity, we will find our reward exactly where we sowed it. God sovereignly makes every tree fall in his time and in the direction he chooses. In eternity, we will find each tree we planted exactly where it fell. The great question we must ask ourselves concerns our sowing. Are we living and sowing for time or for eternity? Are we investing in *people* or only in *things*?

Verses 4 and 5 contain a much-needed admonition.

Whoever watches the wind will not plant; whoever looks at the clouds will not reap. As you do not know the path of the wind, or how the body is formed in a mother's womb, so you cannot understand the work of God, the Maker of all things. (NIV)

If we wait for perfect conditions before we act, we will remain idle. The best forecasters often get it wrong. I love to play golf, but not in the rain. I do not know how often, as I teed off at the first hole under dark clouds, I thought, "We will never finish today without getting wet." Sometimes we did have to quit early, but more often than not, we played golf on what was just a cloudy day. I would have missed a lot of golf if I had looked at the clouds. We cannot out-guess providence. You and I do not understand God's plans and purposes.

The problem is not the weather; it is the attitude in the heart. If we really do not want to obey, we will easily find a hundred excuses. The sun's moving behind one cloud is enough to send some folk back to bed. If, however, we have a heart to obey, we will go as far as possible regardless of the circumstances. Proverbs describes a "rational thinker" who in reality shows a lack of faith.

The way of the sluggard is blocked with thorns, but the path of the upright is a highway. (Proverbs 15:19, NIV)

The sluggard says, "There is a lion outside!" or, "I will be murdered in the streets!" (Proverbs 22:13, NIV)

In verse 6, the Seeker says, "Sow your seed in the morning, and at evening let not your hands be idle, for you do not know which will succeed, whether this or that, or whether both will do equally well." (NIV)

This verse links *sowing* with seed. Verse 1 tells us to *cast* our seed. Although neither verse uses the word *pitch*, it too, expresses an action we take in sharing the gospel. We pitch a baseball, cast a fishing line, and sow seed at random. In the first instance, we know the receptor; in the others, we do not. Therefore, we perform all three kinds of actions. We cast and sow the seed with tracts; we pitch it when we witness one-on-one to an individual.

I cannot emphasize too strongly that the attitude of the heart is everything. Are we really looking for opportunities to serve and to sow, whether it is deeds or money? Or are we careful to avoid situations where we might be asked to help and cannot manufacture a good excuse not to help? I wonder how many genuine opportunities we have missed because of a wrong heart attitude. Empty words are not enough; we must actually get to work. I heard of two salespersons who were talking before their weekly sales meeting. One said, "I have three of the best contacts lined up next week." The other said, "I didn't sell anything this week, either."

Did you ever say, "Oh, if I only was younger, I would ..." or "if I only had more money, I would ..." No, you would not. If you do not do what you can with what you have now, then having twice as much would not help you do more. Do not fantasize or rationalize. Get busy! Stop looking at the weather vane and look at the one who controls the weather. Whatever you do, arrange your priorities so that money or things are not the goal in your life. Get into the swim of God's purposes and program. Start thinking and acting like you really believe there is an eternity. I remember listening to a radio talk show where the host asked a farmer why, since farming was so difficult, he did not quit. The farmer said, "I like to farm, it is great for a family. We eat well and we stay physically fit and healthy, so we keep sowing and hoping. I know I will never get rich, but I have more than enough and I can even help my neighbors sometimes."

We need to ask and honestly answer, as God sees our heart, this question: "What do I really want out of life?" We generally hit exactly what we aim at! In vital things, we have that for which we bought and paid with our time, effort, and money. The question is: Is the life we have good, or is it meaningless? Is it sweet or sour? Consider verse 7.

Light is sweet, and it pleases the eyes to see the sun. (NIV)

Is life sweet to you or is it a daily drudgery? Do you look forward to every new day, opening your eyes and facing the new day with faith and joy? What will your life be like ten years from now? What will it be like in eternity? Young man, young woman, will your life be sweet twenty years from now? Elderly person, has grace sweetened your life? Religious people often get sour when they get old. In her book, *So Who's Afraid of Birthdays,* Brethren matriarch Anna B. Mow writes:

> Many people find a sense of fulfillment in church activities and service, but when the activity ceases, they feel lost and unwanted …The values of mutual concern and fellowship are not enough in the hard places of life … a doctrinal faith may give security until we have to hold our faith instead of it hold-

ing us. When we get "protective" we lose our love and get hard.[51]

Only a personal living relationship with Christ can keep the heart true during times of difficulty or adversity. When we face trials, we need more than the church, the preacher, or our friends. Arthur W. Pink points to the example of the persecuted Madam Guyon:

> Some two hundred years ago, the saintly Madam Guyon, after ten years spent in a dungeon lying far below the surface of the ground, lit only by a candle at meal times, wrote these words.

"A little bird I am,
Shut from the fields of air;
Yet in my cage I sit and sing
To Him who placed me there;
Well pleased a prisoner to be,
Because, my God, it pleases Thee.

Nought have I else to do
I sing the whole day long;
And He whom most I love to please,
Doth listen to my song;
He caught and bound my wandering wing
But still He bends to hear me sing.

My cage confines me round;
Abroad I cannot fly;
But though my wing is closely bound,
My heart's at liberty.

---

[51] Anna B. Mow, So Who's Afraid of Birthdays: For Those over Sixty and Those who Expect to Be (Phil, PA: J. B. Lippincott, 1969).

My prison walls cannot control
The flight, the freedom of the soul.

Ah! it is good to soar
These bolts and bars above,
To Him *whose purpose I adore,*
Whose Providence I love;
And in Thy mighty will to find
The joy, the freedom of the mind."[52]

The Seeker has emphasized the uncertainty of life and urged bold action in the face of that uncertainty. In verses 8 and 9, he recommends joyfulness and thanksgiving in the life that God grants under the sun, even with its uncertainty, and directs our attention to the one event that is certain: a day of judgment.

> *However many years a man may live, let him enjoy them all. But let him remember the days of darkness, for they will be many. Everything to come is meaningless. Be happy, young man, while you are young, and let your heart give you joy in the days of your youth. Follow the ways of your heart and whatever your eyes see, but know that for all these things God will bring you to judgment.* (NIV)

This philosophy is not "have fun now, but be aware that God will get you for it later," nor is it "sow your wild oats when you are young." Fun and holiness are not opposites. I think many Christians are like the little boy who prayed and asked God to make him good. He thought for a moment and then added, "But don't make me so good that I don't have any fun." It is the devil's lie that gives you a choice between having fun and being holy. You do not have to sin to enjoy life! The truly happy people are the truly holy people.

---

[52] From A. W. Pink, *The Sovereignty of God* (Grand Rapids, Michigan: Baker Book House, 1984), 236.

Young people are able to do things, to see things, and to enjoy certain experiences of life that are only possible for a young person. I remember, many years ago, picking up three young men who were hitchhiking across the country. They were law school students and this was their last summer before graduation. They knew this was the last opportunity they would have to do this, so they did it. Remember the Seeker's comments in chapter 3; there is a time for youth to be youth, but they never have to sin to really enjoy their youth!

The uncertainty of life under the sun is a reality that both youth and maturity must face. Yet youth is also the time to dream about the possibilities that the future may hold. Uncertainty need not produce gloom or resignation; it may act instead as an incentive to attempt amazing things. Rather than viewing the uncertainty of the future as an impediment to accomplishment, youth often takes the attitude that since we do not know what tomorrow will bring, we may as well make big plans. We are only young once, so we should appreciate our youth. But because we are only young once, we should not waste that youth on the things of the world that are meaningless. Enjoy youth but do not make an idol of it! Look at verse 10:

> So then, banish anxiety from your heart and cast off the troubles of your body, for youth and vigor are meaningless. (NIV)

Youth is life "now," but it will not last. Youth is fleeting, so enjoy it while you can. Enjoy it, but do not try to hang on to it. Nothing is more ridiculous than an old woman who is heavily made-up and wearing juvenile clothing. I agree that cosmetics may help some women. Every old barn needs a little paint occasionally. However, an older woman or older man trying to look like a teenager is foolishness. I remember a friend who was asked if his wife was still as beautiful as she was twenty-five years ago. He thought a moment and said, "Yes, she is, but it takes her quite a bit longer."

Enjoy youth, but do not succumb to our culture's idolization of it. Do not try to look like something you are not. Plastic surgeries, crash diets, designer hairpieces, and dyed hair may not enhance your appearance; they may simply look silly. It is amazing that young people want to look old and old people want to look young! How amusing, because how silly, to see a three-year old dressed like a college student.

You are going to grow old whether you like it or not. Remember that fact, but do not dwell on it and ruin today or tomorrow. Visit your grandparents and say, "that is me someday." Visit the gravesites of people you knew and say, "I will be buried here in the near future." Remember both old age and death, but do not be afraid of either. Neither old age nor death is an enemy of a child of God. Do not allow yourself to think of either as a cause for fear. This meaningless life is not all there is!

Do not be alarmed if in ten years you will be thirty, or forty, or fifty. Live boldly and joyfully NOW in the day that God gave you. Live a holy life NOW in the way God tells you to live. I had a tough time when I hit seventy. I forgot that age seventy was simply *one* of the ordained times in chapter 3 for me. I started to think, "I only have a few years left." I began to make every decision in the light of three-score-and-ten. I did not buy any new clothing since I would not need it "before I died." I became depressed for the first time in my life. My wife grew disgusted with me and said, "Why don't you just die and get it over with!"

God does not want us to live in the future any more than he wants us to live in the past. In the spiritual and eternal sense, youth, in itself, is just as meaningless as is old age. God wants us to enjoy life when we are young and when we are old. I cannot emphasize too strongly that the Seeker is not in any way suggesting that youth is the time to have a fling with the world. No matter how old or how young we are, we do not have to sin to enjoy life to its fullest. The exhortation to love and obey in youth reminds us that how we live as a young person affects our life as an old person. My grandma used to say, "You made your own bed, now you have to sleep in it." This is true! However, we must never give the impression that God holds some of the sins of our youth or of our old age against us in both time and eternity. Actions have consequences, but in Christ, God forgives completely. I often say when preaching, "The most important thing about you is not what you did or failed to do yesterday. What matters right now is the direction your life is headed in as you walk out that door tonight and the depth of your resolve to live pleasing unto God tomorrow." Recognize the uncertainty of life under the sun, count on the certainty of eternity, and live bold, joyful, and holy lives.

CHAPTER NINETEEN: VERSES 12:1–10

WHEN THE PIECES WEAR OUT

In the final chapter of Ecclesiastes, chapter 12, the Seeker encourages the young, while in their youth, to remember the God who made them. They must cultivate a friendship and a walk with God that prepares them for old age. We saw a little about youth in chapter 11; in chapter 12, we find a stark and sustained comparison between youth and old age. The Seeker opens this section with the word *remember*.

> *Remember your Creator in the days of your youth, before the days of trouble come and the years approach when you will say, "I find no pleasure in them–"* (Eccl 12:1 NIV)

The writers of Scripture use this word to mean more than simply to recall. Walter Kaiser explains:

> When God "Remembered" Hannah (1 Sam. 1:19), he did more than say, "Oh yes, Hannah, I almost forgot you." By remembering her, he acted decisively on her behalf, and she who was barren conceived the child Samuel.[53]

God's remembering is nothing less than his acting to fulfill his sovereign promises. Our remembering likewise is our acting in consideration of those promises. We do not merely remember that God exists, but we seek to put into practice what he has said. We are not to wait until we are old to obey God; we are to do this while we are young.

---

[53] Walter C. Kaiser Jr., *Ecclesiastes, Everyman's Bible Commentary* (Chicago: Moody Press, 1979), 118.

George Barnard Shaw said that youth was such a wonderful thing that it was a crime to waste it on children. Youth indeed is a wonderful and exciting time. One reason is that life is simple for the young. When my wife and I were first married, we could get ready for a picnic in ten minutes. Now it takes three days and by the time we are ready, we are so exhausted that we wonder if it would not be better just to stay at home.

Life lived as a godly young person will bring joy both during the time of youth as well as in old age. It does not take much to cultivate a positive attitude in young people. They do not have a hundred things that need their attention nearly every day. Children do not stay awake at night, worried about job security and the cost of food and gasoline. A teenage girl's greatest concern may be that someone else will wear the same kind of dress as hers to the prom. Few teenagers look back over each week and say, "I find no pleasure in anything." No one, including the young person who has remembered his creator, will cry out in despair as he faces the dark days of old age, "All is meaningless. I find no delight in life or anything in it." Those dark ages will come, but they need not rob us of the comfort of the gospel.

Verses 2–7 describe more than just old age. They certainly do depict old age, but they also emphasize that youth should not try to act elderly, nor should they fear old age as an enemy. Any person is foolish to ignore old age, just as anyone is foolish to be consumed by its thought. All people are to realize that how they live when they are young will greatly affect how they enjoy old age and eternity. We covered this point in our last chapter. Young person, you will get old. Your life will radically change. That is a fact that is most foolish to ignore. It is also a fact that should not occupy your every waking thought.

The Seeker describes the days that come after youth as days of trouble. He does not intend to imply that youth has no problems and age is nothing but problems; rather, compared to youth, old age seems troublesome. It comes with limitations that are absent in youth.

Remember your Creator
in the days of your youth,
before the days of trouble come
and the years approach when you will say,
"I find no pleasure in them"–
before the sun and the light
and the moon and the stars grow dark,
and the clouds return after the rain; (Eccl 12: 1, 2 NIV)

These two verses describe a person who has no real pleasure in living. Just as clouds and rain hide the sun and the moon, so the problems of old age can easily end the hope of better days. Normally, when the rain is over, the clouds retreat and the sun reappears. The Seeker portrays a situation where the clouds remain and the sun and the moon do not return to shine and to give light. They remain covered, and there is nothing but the continual darkness of night. It is like living in a land with only night and darkness.

This can be a picture of physical, emotional, or psychological despair–or even all three. If the Seeker is speaking of physical light, then he refers to the eyes and the idea of physical sight and blindness. If he is talking in terms of emotional light, he probably means the ability to think clearly. If his concern is in the area of psychological light, then he addresses the ability to have hope for the future. Regardless of which he means, he paints a picture of gloom and despair.

In old age, we come to the place where we forget old friends. We refrain from participating in former enjoyable activities and stop attending events of which we were a vital part for years. We start getting lost on what used to be familiar roads. We lose the resilience we had in our youth. We used to view an illness as a temporary setback from which we were certain to recover. Now when a sickness occurs, it is a disaster and often becomes permanent. In youth, time was an ally upon which we could count for help because it would heal the problem, whether physical, financial, or interpersonal. Now time is an enemy that we cannot defeat. It is slowly destroying us physically, psychologically, and sometimes even financially. When we were young, we always faced the prospect of recovery from anything and everything. We knew the sun would shine again, and so we were able to smile with assurance in the face of trouble. Now, "the clouds return after the rain" and neither the sun by day nor the moon by night give light. Sometimes either pain or fear fills the night and we long for the sun to rise and give us a new day. However, there are neither any *really* new days, nor any possibility of a day that brings healing.

Chapter twelve's message to the young person repeats that of chapter 11. Live your life to the fullest NOW in such a way that you will not be sorry THEN—when that night comes. Youth is the time to live: do not worry about getting old, but still think occasionally about death. Be neither obsessed with nor forgetful of death. Verse 2 pictures winter coming. Live pleasing to God in the sunlight of summer today and you will have all you need to be warm and secure in the winter of old age. Verses 3 and 4 picture a house in decline. Some writers suggest that it is not necessary to assign a part of the body to each item mentioned in the following verses. All the text requires is that we recognize that a body, like a house, wears out piece-by-piece and ultimately decays completely. It seems far more probable that each image is analogous to a body part or life experience. Let us look at them carefully.

when the keepers of the house tremble, [The hands and arms that take care of us start to tremble with palsy or feebleness]

and the strong men stoop, [The legs and thighs that hold us up begin to wobble and cannot keep us upright. We start to bend over a bit.]

when the grinders cease – because they are few, [There is no chewing since we have so few, if any, teeth left. Eating becomes nothing but "munching" soft food. Forget about that corn on the cob.]

and those looking through the windows grow dim, [The eyes no longer see clearly.] (Eccl 12:3 NIV)

when the doors to the street are closed [The doors include the mouth and the ears through which we receive and give communication to the outside world. The mouth is silent and we no longer communicate with others; even when we do, there is little clear speech. We mostly just mumble. The ears also do not receive clear information; we grow hard of hearing. Communication with others is lost.]

and the sound of grinding fades; [Probably refers to loss of hearing. We cannot hear the wheels that creak as they grind out the grain. Or it could refer to the sound of chewing; there is no noise because there is no crunch because we have so few teeth.]

when men rise up at the sound of birds, [Sustained sleep is difficult. We rise early. Sleep is easily interrupted; a little bird can wake us from light sleep.]

but all their songs grow faint [The birds wake us, but all we hear is a sound or a noise, there is nothing distinct.] (Eccl 12:4 NIV)

when men are afraid of heights, [They hang on to the banister with both hands when going down the stairs.]

and of dangers in the streets, [They are afraid to go out and prefer to stay at home where it is safe and still familiar.]

when the almond tree blossoms, [Gray hair comes as the first proof of old age. The first tree to blossom in the Middle East is the almond tree.]

and the grasshopper drags himself along, [A picture of an old person dragging along instead of jumping like a grasshopper. They no longer walk with supple limbs and a springy step, but instead, slowly shuffles along.]

and desire no longer is stirred. [This refers to not only sexual desire. It also includes food and other things. One of the problems with old people is getting them to eat regularly. They no longer desire food, fellowship with friends, or taking a trip. They just want to sit and rock.]

Then man goes to his eternal home [Death itself will come. We wind up where we started, in the ground. Is it not amazing that creatures made to be kings and priests before God wind up as worm food?]

and mourners go about the streets. [The big question is, and then what?] (Eccl 12:5 NIV)

The writer exhorts us to remember God before death comes. He uses two images to describe the reality and finality of death or the final separation of the soul from the body. In verses 3–6, the image is that of a house, our body, in gradual decay. In verse 6, it is a once-for-all break with life, as a cord breaking or a pot smashing.

Remember him – before the silver cord is severed, [This could be a reference to the spinal cord. The spinal marrow that connects the brain and nerves is pale and silver-like.]

or the golden bowl is broken; [This could be could be the brain, because of its shape and color.]

before the pitcher is shattered at the spring, [This could be the failing heart, a pitcher-like receptacle, being pierced or broken, and all the life-supporting blood flowing out.]

or the wheel broken at the well, [This could be the entire nervous system and blood vessels.] (Eccl 12:6, 7 NIV)

Regardless of the meaning of these last four images, several things are certain. Each item pictures the inescapable reality and finality of death. The silver cord snapping, the golden bowl smashing, the pitcher shattering, and the wheel breaking all mean there will be no more supply of the water of life. Just as a rope severs in one snap, a bowl breaks in one crash, a pitcher shatters in one drop, and a wheel ceases to turn in one rotation, so death ends life and everything connected with life in one second.

What apt descriptions of the finality of death! Fanny Crosby has said it well in her hymn.

"Someday the silver cord will break,
And I no more as now shall sing;
But oh the joy when I shall wake
Within the palace of the King.

(Fanny J. Crosby, 1820–1915)

Consider the end of verse 7 — "and the dust returns to the ground it came from, and the spirit returns to God who gave it."

This is the reversal of our creation in Eden. This is the end of everything except eternity. Eternity has just become our only reality. All people will go to their eternal home. Some of those homes will be in hell and some will be in heaven.

The writer ends this section the same way he began the book.

> *"Meaningless! Meaningless!" says the Teacher. "Everything is meaningless!"* (Eccl 12:8 NIV)

How futile to live a lifetime without knowing the true meaning of life. This is the cry of a person who ignored Ecclesiastes 12:1, both in youth and in old age.

Have you ever wondered what it will be like for a lost person to wake up in an eternal hell? What will it be like to realize, in one second of time, that everything you rejected is true? How can we describe what it will be like to enter consciously into eternal damnation, knowing that this is what you willingly chose? To witness in some way the blessedness of the child of God and to realize that this is what you consciously rejected?

Have you ever wondered what it will be like for a saved person to wake up in an eternal heaven? What it will be like to realize, in a second of time, that heaven is a thousand times better than you could have ever imagined or believed?

I remember years ago visiting two elderly men on the same day. One man, I. C. Herendeen, was a godly Christian and the other man was a blasphemer. When I read the Scriptures and prayed, Mr. Herendeen cried and said, "John, I can't wait to get home." I asked him this question: "Do you have any real regrets in your ninety years of life?" With no hesitation he replied, "I wish I had been more faithful to my Savior who loved me and gave himself for me."

The other man would not talk about the gospel or about his soul. He made light of every thing I said. He laughed and swore, saying, "I have handled God so far, and I can handle him when I die." That man did not have the least concern for his soul. I cried in the car as I thought about him waking up in hell and remembering our conversation. Both of these men died within a month after my visit with them.

In verses 9–12, the Seeker sets forth his qualifications to write this book.

> *Not only was the Teacher wise, but also he imparted knowledge to the people. He pondered and searched out and set in order many proverbs.* (Eccl 12:9 NIV)

The Seeker was not a man who pursued knowledge merely for its own sake. He pursued knowledge to discover if it, by itself, could give meaning to life (Eccl1:12–18). Yet he was not interested in winning philosophical discussions; he had a genuine concern for people and their eternal destinies. He had a shepherd's heart. He shared the things that God had taught him. Three verbs, "pondered, searched out, and arranged" (or set in order), describe skill in the undertaking. The word *pondered* means to weigh carefully or to evaluate in detail. This shows the Seeker's honesty, caution, and balance in his pursuit. The word *searched* refers to his thoroughness and diligence. The word *arranged* points out the Seeker's orderliness in presenting his message. This is not work thrown together to meet a deadline. This is a thorough, careful, clear, and comprehensive presentation of truth.

> *The Teacher searched to find just the right words, and what he wrote was upright and true. (Eccl 12:10, NIV)*

The KJV translates *right words* as *words of truth*. The Teacher was not concerned with philosophy, psychology, tradition, or entertainment; his goal was truth—the unchanging truth of God. Every preacher or teacher should follow the Seeker's example in this verse. The ESV translates the phrase as *words of delight*. Michael Eaton offers an excellent comment:

> Further characteristics of his ministry are underlined. First, he realized that *pleasing words* (Lit. 'words of delight') have a penetrating effect that slapdash and ill-considered words lack. Second, his words are written *uprightly*. The two characteristics balance each other. His words are not so *pleasing* that they cease to be *upright*. Attention to form at the expense of content would loose the verdict of his God (v. 14; *cf.* 2 Cor 4:2f.) To be upright and unpleasant is to be a fool; to be pleasant but not upright is to be a charlatan. Third, his message consists of *words of truth*, on which, like other wise men, he sets a high premium (cf. Prov. 8:7; 22:21, etc.). Fourth, his ministry involved writing as well as speaking. Like law-givers (Ex. 24:4), judges (1 Sam. 10:25), kings (2 Chron. 35:4), prophets, and psalmists, the wise man was concerned to perpetuate his teaching in writing.[54]

We are aware that no amount of love, wisdom, skill, or patience can make the truth of God palatable to a lost person. Some preachers have so much tact that they have no real contact. God, through Ezekiel, warned against false prophets who, in Eaton's words, are pleasant but not upright.

> *And mine hand shall be upon the prophets that see vanity, and that divine lies: they shall not be in the assembly of my people, neither shall they be written in the writing of the house of Israel, neither shall they enter into the land of Israel; and ye shall know that I am the Lord GOD.*

---

[54] Michael A. Eaton, *Ecclesiastes, An Introduction & Commentary* (Downers Grove, Illinois: IVP, 1983), 154.

Because, even because they have seduced my people, saying, Peace; and there was no peace; and one built up a wall, and, lo, others daubed it with untempered mortar:

Say unto them which daub it with untempered mortar, that it shall fall: there shall be an overflowing shower; and ye, O great hailstones, shall fall; and a stormy wind shall rend it.

Lo, when the wall is fallen, shall it not be said unto you, Where is the daubing wherewith ye have daubed it?

Therefore thus saith the Lord GOD; I will even rend it with a stormy wind in my fury; and there shall be an overflowing shower in mine anger, and great hailstones in my fury to consume it.

So will I break down the wall that ye have daubed with untempered mortar, and bring it down to the ground, so that the foundation thereof shall be discovered, and it shall fall, and ye shall be consumed in the midst thereof: and ye shall know that I am the LORD.

Thus will I accomplish my wrath upon the wall, and upon them that have daubed it with untempered mortar, and will say unto you, The wall is no more, neither they that daubed it;

To wit, the prophets of Israel which prophesy concerning Jerusalem, and which see visions of peace for her, and there is no peace, saith the Lord GOD. (Ezek 13:9–16 KJV)

The gospel is, was, and always will be foolishness in the eyes of unregenerate people; they will hate and reject it until God opens their eyes to see its beauty and its truth. Likewise, those who preach the whole counsel of God will be reviled, vilified, ignored, and in some ages and circumstances, even put to death. However, preachers who display crude and revolting attitudes may easily add needless and hurtful offense to the gospel message. To seek to be as acceptable as possible is not to be inconsistent with faithfulness to the truth. Good sense and godly zeal encourage us to speak unpalatable truth as sweetly and persuasively as possible. We can corrupt the Word of God in the *manner* in which we preach it as well as in the way we interpret it. Paul's words to the Corinthians are appropriate here.

> *Unlike so many, we do not peddle the word of God for profit. On the contrary, in Christ we speak before God with sincerity, like men sent from God.* (2 Cor 2:17 NIV)

> *Rather, we have renounced secret and shameful ways; we do not use deception, nor do we distort the word of God. On the contrary, by setting forth the truth plainly we commend ourselves to every man's conscience in the sight of God.* (2 Cor 4:2 NIV)

It is essential that we understand and heed Paul's words. We must be fearless in proclaiming God's Word. We do not hold back because of fear of offending either friends or enemies. We do not worry if the wealthy who contribute large sums of money will be upset and stop giving, nor do we allow those who openly sin to go on without rebuke. However, there is an abundance of biblical exhortation concerning the other side of the coin. God calls us to model Christ to the world around us, and to do so in a winsome manner.

We are to preach the truth in love. When needful, we are to refrain from eating meat—and we do not call the weak brother stupid for not understanding the truth that frees us to eat all food (Rom. 14). We must take people where they are in their knowledge and teach them accordingly. Our Lord gave us a clear example when he said, "I have yet many things to say unto you, but ye cannot bear them now" (John 16:12 KJV).

We sin against people if we give them truth that they cannot possibly understand because they lack background enough for comprehension. There is a sequence to understanding truth. We do not give a new convert the Book of Revelation to study. We cannot give a two-week-old baby a piece of steak to eat, and we should not give a newborn child of God a book on our millennial view or on limited atonement. Paul, in 1 Corinthians 3 teaches that there are different stages in a Christian's ability to digest milk and meat. The preacher who ignores this fact sins against some who listen.

I remember, years ago, sharing the latest truth that I had learned from Scripture with a good friend, Bob Dittmar. We usually think the most recent thing we have learned answers all the problems in the entire Bible. Bob listened patiently and when I was finished, he said, "John, how many specific truths did you learn before you saw the last one that was essential to your learning this latest truth?" I thought for a moment and said, "Three, maybe four." Bob said, "Promise me you will not tell another soul what you just told me until you are certain they understand those three or four things!" That was great advice. Blessed is the person who can speak the truth without fear or favor, and blessed also is the person who can keep his mouth shut and not choke people with food too heavy for them to swallow or digest, and especially blessed is the person who knows the difference. That person will be like the Seeker: one who speaks words of delight and of truth.

THE CONCLUSION TO THE MATTER

This is the final chapter in my thoughts on the book of Ecclesiastes. It has been a joy for me to study this book. I appreciate the many testimonies from those who have been blessed by reading the messages as they appeared in *Sound of Grace*. I trust the same will be true of the book. Those testimonies encourage me to hope that I, like the Seeker, have been able to help others by sharing the truths that God has taught me. I stated at the end of the previous chapter that the Seeker pursued knowledge, neither for its own sake, nor simply for the personal benefit he could glean from it, but for the good of others. He was concerned for people and for their eternal destiny.

In this chapter, we will look at the final five verses of Ecclesiastes.

The preacher sought to find out acceptable words: and that which was written was upright, even words of truth.

The words of the wise are as goads, and as nails fastened by the masters of assemblies, which are given from one shepherd.

And further, by these, my son, be admonished: of making many books there is no end; and much study is a weariness of the flesh.

Let us hear the conclusion of the whole matter: Fear God, and keep his commandments: for this is the whole duty of man.

For God shall bring every work into judgment, with every secret thing, whether it be good, or whether it be evil. (Eccl 12:10–14 KJV)

Verse 10 demonstrates the close relationship between thought and expression, research and teaching. A true teacher is neither proud of his knowledge, nor interested on-

ly in impressing intellectual colleagues. Good teachers desire to impart reliable and essential knowledge about ultimate truth to everyone. They are not interested in scholar-
ship for its own sake. As Derek Kidner notes, they prefer to
move others to seek God.

> He is not the proud thinker who has no time for lesser
> minds: rather, he accepts the challenging ideal of perfect clari-
> ty. As verse 10 points out, it will take the skill and integrity, the
> charm and courage, of an artist and a scholar to do justice to
> the task. On the strength of that single verse, this man should
> be the patron saint of writers.[55]

The Seeker's words were profound and penetrating, but
their effect did not stop there. When blessed of God, they
had and continue to have a lasting—an eternal—effect.
Charles Bridges explains.

> Here was his wisdom—seeking to *find out acceptable words!*
> Think of the great moment belonging to them—of the great
> care *to seek and find them out*—like the pearls in the ocean. They
> were not men-pleasing words—not flattering words of vanity,
> but such that find an easy access to the heart—"pleasing our
> neighbor for his good unto edification." (Rom. 15:2.) The most
> considerate human wisdom can never make the humbling
> truth of God *acceptable* to the human heart. Yet crude and re-
> volting statements may add needlessly and hurtfully to the of-
> fence. Mr. Cecil wisely remarked—"It is a foolish project to
> avoid *giving offence.* But it is our duty to avoid giving *unneces-
> sary offence.* Good taste should be connected with good things;
> and the word is not *less faithfully spoken,* because it is *fitly* spo-
> ken" (Prov.15:23; 25:11). To *seek to be acceptable*—is by no means

---

[55] Derek Kidner, *A Time to Mourn and a Time to Dance, The Message
of Ecclesiastes* (Downers Grove: InterVarsity Press, 1976), 105.

inconsistent with faithfulness. Christian consideration directs us carefully to distribute unpalatable truth in all the sweetness of persuasion and sympathy.[56]

In verse 11, the author compares words to goads and nails:

> *The words of the wise are as goads, and as nails fastened by the masters of assemblies, which are given from one shepherd.*

The goad was a pointed stick that prodded the ox to move forward or faster. The nails were either those used in the temple or those used by shepherds to fasten their tents. Some words stimulate us to action and others fasten the teaching in our memories. The important point here is the source of these objects: these particular goads and nails were "given from one Shepherd." Commentators understand the shepherd to be either the king or God. I think it is better to understand him as God.

The "masters of the assemblies" may be many, but there is only one shepherd. Even the greatest of masters – the prophets and the apostles—did not make their own goads and nails. They received them all from the one shepherd. We desperately need both the goads and the nails: the goads because of our spiritual sluggishness, and the nails because we so easily forget. The person who is under the ministry of the shepherd's goads but remains unaffected, his skin not even pierced, is indeed a person most miserable. Likewise, when we do not obey truth, we quickly lose it, and when we have lost the truth, we have lost our greatest treasure.

---

[56] Charles Bridges, *Ecclesiastes, A Geneva Series Commentary* (1961. Reprint, Carlisle, PA: Banner of Truth, 1981), 303.

Someone has said, "When we cease to value truth, we are already in the atmosphere of error."

The Words of God—the Scriptures—have an awesome power. Meditation on even a single verse has delivered men and women from the depths of depression. Ray Steadman tells of his own experience.

> Scripture is also a "nail (an anchor) firmly fixed." You can hang onto it and hold fast by it in times of danger and temptation. Once in my own life when I was severely troubled of heart and deeply disturbed so that I could not even eat, one phrase from the lips of Jesus came into my mind again and again. It was the phrase in the fourteenth chapter of John, where Jesus said to his troubled disciples, "Let not your heart be troubled," (John 14:1a). I was especially gripped by those two words, "Let not." They said to me that a troubled heart in the believer is subject to the will of that believer. He can let his heart be troubled or he can let it not be troubled. The ground for letting it not be troubled is in the words that immediately follow: Jesus said, "You believe in God, believe also in me," (John 14:1b). Again and again he said, "Let not your heart be troubled, for I am with you." When the realization struck me that my living Lord was there, with wisdom and power to handle the situation, I felt the lifting of my heart's load. I was free to let not my heart be troubled. That is the power of Scripture.[57]

In verse 12, the Seeker implies that Scripture is the source of true wisdom.

> *And further, by these, my son, be admonished: of making many books there is no end; and much study is a weariness of the flesh.*

---

[57] Taken from a taped sermon by Ray Stedman, preached at Peninsula Bible Church, Palo Alto, CA, 1982.

The NIV translates verse 12 as warning against adding anything to the words given by the shepherd. *Be warned, my son, of anything in addition to them.* In the King James, the reader must infer this meaning from the text, and many readers have misunderstood the words *by these* to refer to what follows, rather than by what precedes the phrase. The words *by these* in verse 12 refer back to the idea stated in verse 11—the words of the shepherd. They do not refer to the "making of many books" and "study that wearies the flesh." Eaton has caught the truth of the text.

In the closing remarks, a warning is given comparable to those which close a number of biblical writings (*cf.* Rom 16:17–20; 2 Thess 3:14 ff.; 1 Tim 6:20 ff.; 1 Jn 5:21; Rev 22:18 ff.). *By these* refers back to the sayings "given by the one Shepherd," outside of which caution is required. The form of words used has a reflexive force: "take warning," "admonish yourself." It points to the private judgment and responsibility of the individual reader.

The *making of many books* began long before any conceivable date for Ecclesiastes. Writing was well established as a hallmark of civilization from about 3500 BC onwards. "Books" were written first on clay tablets, later on papyrus or leather. When an alphabetical script came into Syria-Israel in the second millennium BC, it brought the possibility of "no end" of books. A mass of cuneiform tablets and papyri exists to prove the point. Evidently, there was much in this body of literature that the wise man thought fit to warn against, since it did *not* come from one Shepherd. Israel shared much with the wisdom traditions of surrounding nations and doubtless had profited from its acquaintance with pagan literature (*cf.* Acts 7:22), as did the Apostle Paul at a later age (Acts 17:28; Tit.1:12). Yet the Old Testament warns that pagan wisdom stands under the ever-imminent judgment of God (*cf.*

Is.19:11ff.; Ezek.28:2ff.), as does the New Testament (1 Cor1:17ff.; 2:6). No doubt within Israel too there would be a "wisdom" that deserved rebuke rather than discipleship (*cf.* Jer.8:9).[58]

In this verse, the Seeker condemns neither books nor studying. The problem is the *kind* of books consulted and the result of that study. God wants us to think, but not to think independently of his truth. We are to think God's thoughts after him. We must avoid ever learning and never coming to a knowledge of the truth. At the same time, we must recognize that God calls us to use the intellectual capacities he has given us. We are to develop those abilities and use them to glorify him. We need goads to propel us out of the mental complacency produced by intellectual laziness and sloth.

It is indeed a weariness of both flesh and soul to try to find truth and reality outside of Scripture—in the wisdom of men. Attempting to gain a true knowledge of God in the words of anyone except the Shepherd is both futile and frustrating. That is the message of the book of Ecclesiastes. The Shepherd's words alone are the words of authority. They and they alone are the final answers.

The great tragedy of learning *under the sun* is that a person may become addicted to knowledge for its own sake. Learning becomes a drug that feeds an addiction that nothing can satisfy. If the thirst for gaining knowledge were satisfied, it would spoil everything for this type of person. C. S. Lewis has perfectly described that against which the

---

[58] Michael A. Eaton, *Ecclesiastes, An Introduction & Commentary* (Downers Grove, IL: IVP, 1983), 155.

Seeker warns. A life-long searcher, or pretending searcher after truth, is on the borders of heaven. Lewis records the following dialogue where the White Spirit is inviting the searcher after truth to come in.

"I can promise you ... no scope for your talents, only forgiveness for having perverted them. ... No atmosphere of inquiry, for I will bring you to a land not of questions but of answers, and **you shall see the face of God.**"

"Ah, but we must all interpret those beautiful words in our own way! For me there is no such thing as a final answer. The free wind of inquiry must *always* continue to blow through the mind, must it not? ..."

"Listen!" said the White Spirit. "Once you were a child. Once you knew what inquiry was for. There was a time when you asked questions because you wanted answers, and were glad when you had found them. Become that child again: even now."

"Ah, but when I became a man I put away childish things."

No argument, no appeal will avail against this infinite elasticity. The encounter, already fruitless, ends with the gentle sophist's remembering an appointment, making his apologies, and hurrying off to his discussion group in hell.[59]

In verse 13, we finally arrive at the Seeker's conclusion. So far, every path *under the sun* has taken us nowhere but to futility. At the end of every road, we came to a sign that said "vanity of vanity, all is vanity." In this verse, the Shepherd gives us the true goad and nail. Two simple and clear statements sum up the whole duty of humanity. People are to "fear God" and "keep his commandments." The Seeker ex-

---

[59] C.S. Lewis, *The Great Divorce* (UK: Geoffrey Bles, 1945), 40.

alts two things: (1) the greatness of God, and (2) the absolute
authority of his Word.

> *Let us hear the conclusion of the whole matter: Fear God, and keep*
> *his commandments: for this is the whole duty of man.*

Fearing God is not being afraid or terrified of God. Rather, it is having an awareness and appreciation of God's
sovereign power and justice. It is the attitude that will deliver us from both wickedness and self-righteousness and lead
us to hate sin. Proverbs 1:7 states that the fear of God is the
beginning of wisdom. There is a sense in which it is also the
end (or goal) of wisdom. True growth in grace must always
be accompanied by a growing biblical fear of God.

The word order that lists *fear* first and *obey* second is no
accident. Personal conduct does not grow out of a vacuum;
it is affected by our knowledge of truth. The Apostle Paul
repeatedly exhorts us to "grow in grace and the knowledge
of our Lord Jesus Christ." We can grow in knowledge without growing in grace, but we cannot grow in grace without
growing in knowledge. If all of our "reading of books" and
"searching for truth" does not lead us to genuine fellowship
with God, then we are like the person described by C. S.
Lewis. True knowledge of God leads to worship. It is not the
other way around. The more we know God, the more we
will worship him.

When we read, "keep his commandments," we must not
think only of ten commandments. Commandments refers to
the "whole duty of man," which encompasses everything
that we know that is God's will for us.

Verse 14 is the final goad and the last nail. The truth that
God sees and knows everything we do or think and will

bring it into judgment affects different people in different ways. I remember a story of a little girl coming home from Sunday school and her mother asking her what she had learned. The girl said, "We learned that God sees every single thing we do." The mother commented, "I bet that frightened you." The girl replied, "Oh, no, I'm glad God sees every sin I commit. If he didn't, then he could not lay that sin on Jesus." We must remember that our God is full of more than justice and truth; he is also full of love and grace. God's Word contains both promise and precept for his people, whether they live under the New or the Old Covenant.

John Bunyan said that the road to heaven has two big ditches on either side. The one ditch is called despair and the other is called presumption. God has planted a hedgerow of promises to keep us out of the ditch of despair and another hedgerow of precepts to keep us out of the ditch of presumption. Let saints rejoice in God's free grace, but let them also fear God.

Michael Eaton has an excellent postscript in his commentary on Ecclesiastes. It is a lengthy quotation but it is quite appropriate.

Postscript—by Michael Eaton

In this commentary, I have tried to resist the temptation of treating the Preacher as a twentieth-century thinker; and with the exception of the term 'secularism', for which I could find no precise ancient equivalent, I have avoided twentieth-century theological or philosophical terminology. Yet, when 'all has been heard,' the message of Ecclesiastes is strikingly relevant to this century. For it is twentieth-century man who is supremely troubled about being 'thrown into existence' and asks why is there something rather than nothing. Probably the twentieth-century, at least in the western world, is the most bored epoch the world has yet seen. 'Stop the world, I want to get off' is a popular cliché. Western intellectual tradition from Schopenhauer onwards has been preoccupied with 'life's ultimate certainty', the fact of death. Albert Camus wrote, "There is but one truly serious philosophical problem and that is suicide."

Modern man is also a striking confirmation that the universe sours when secularism grips his thinking. He loses his love of nature which becomes caught up in his weariness. "The sun shone, having no alternative on the nothing new" begins a twentieth-century novel, giving Ecclesiastes 1:3 a further turn. Similarly, history is no longer seen to have any purpose. The Judeo-Christian tradition with its linear view of history has been replaced either by some kind of determinism in which man, individually or collectively, plays no significant role and so has no meaning, or by a cyclical view in which all human achievements return inevitably to chaos and so is ultimately futile.

This purposelessness is no mere academic stance, but a hideous reality that permeates the consciousness of the whole of society and gnaws away mercilessly at the human soul. There is no exit. The universe is silent before all questions and mankind knows what Blaise Pascal meant in saying, "I am terror stricken before the silence of infinite space." He shuns talk about death as the Victorian shunned talk about sex. Meanwhile the "man in the street" spends his time shielded by the television screen or by the popular newspapers with ready-packed thinking and diverting entertainment.

To such a world, Ecclesiastes has something to say. He does not come as a formal philosopher; it is a word from God that he has to share, despite his low-key approach. He does not present half-a-dozen arguments for the existence of God. Instead, he picks up our own questions. Can you cope with life without having any idea where you are going? You don't have all the answers to life's enigmas, do you? Your neo-pagan view of life doesn't give you any hope of achieving very much, does it? Nature does not answer your questions, and you are bored by it anyway. You don't like to think about your death; yet it is the most certain fact about your existence.

What would it be like, asks the Preacher, if things were utterly different from what you thought? What if this world is not the ultimate one? What if God exists and is the rewarder of those who seek him? What if one of his supreme characteristics is his utter, incredible generosity, his willingness to give and give and give again, his utter acceptance of us just as we are? Could it be, asks this provocative and seemingly negative preacher, that the barrenness and hideous purposelessness of life stems only from the fact that you will not believe in such a God?

We leave the Preacher here. His message is not complete, for he lived before the full light of the gospel of Jesus Christ. He saw "afar off," and still leaves us with some questions. How *can* God accept us in such a way? What is the explanation for the hideous mess of this world? On what grounds can we feel confident that some future judgment will put it all right? Is there not a missing link in all of this? The missing link is Jesus Christ, the Son of God. It is in Christ, the Savior and the sin-bearer, that God says to us: "God is reconciled to you ...You be reconciled to God" (2 Cor 5:18 ff.). He has set a day when he will judge the world with justice by the man whom he has appointed. He has given proof of this to all men by raising him from the dead (Acts 17:31).

"Some ... sneered ... Others said, 'We want to hear you again.' ... A few ... believed."[60]

I pray dear reader that you are among the last group.

---

[60] Eaton, 157–159.

2119846

Made in the USA